HIGH STAKES: reading

David Alan Herzog

THOMSON

PETERSON'S

Australia • Canada • Mexico • Singapore • Spain • United Kingdom • United States

About The Thomson Corporation and Peterson's

With revenues of US$7.2 billion, The Thomson Corporation (www.thomson.com) is a leading global provider of integrated information solutions for business, education, and professional customers. Its Learning businesses and brands (www.thomsonlearning.com) serve the needs of individuals, learning institutions, and corporations with products and services for both traditional and distributed learning.

Peterson's, part of The Thomson Corporation, is one of the nation's most respected providers of lifelong learning online resources, software, reference guides, and books. The Education Supersite℠ at www.petersons.com—the Internet's most heavily traveled education resource—has searchable databases and interactive tools for contacting U.S.-accredited institutions and programs. In addition, Peterson's serves more than 105 million education consumers annually.

For more information, contact Peterson's, 2000 Lenox Drive, Lawrenceville, NJ 08648; 800-338-3282; or find us on the World Wide Web at www.petersons.com/about.

ISBN 0-7689-1071-4

Printed in the United States of America

10 9 8 7 6 5 4 3 2 1   05 04 03

CONTENTS

CONTENTS

PART III—EXERCISES

CONTENTS

BEFORE YOU GET STARTED

Directions: Choose from **(A)**, **(B)**, **(C)**, or **(D)** the words that make the completed sentence most accurate.

High Stakes tests are

(A) performed by supermarkets to ensure the highest quality beef for their customers.

(B) administered by vampire slayers to ensure the demise of their enemies.

(C) very tall poles.

(D) taken by students to determine whether they are ready to graduate from high school.

We're going to take a wild guess that you chose **(D)** as the correct answer.

All kidding aside, we refer to the exit-level proficiency exams as **"high stakes"** tests because your high school diploma is *at stake*. Your diploma is probably the most valuable piece of paper you'll ever have in your hands. Without it, you may be limited in the kind of work you can do as an adult, and you also won't earn as much money as people who have diplomas. So, unless you're the next Britney Spears or one of those lucky people who wins the million-dollar lottery, these tests *are* high stakes for you.

We're not going to lie to you. Most of the test questions on your exit-level exams will not be as easy to answer as the question above. We're sure you already know that. But we'd bet that you *don't* know what kind of questions will pop up on these exams. And this is one case where what you don't know *can* hurt you.

But not to worry. We have diligently studied the standards for **math, reading, writing,** and **science** skills set by the state educational professionals, as well as the test questions that appear on these exams. We're not only going to tell you what you will be tested *on* but also *how* you will be tested. So, whether your state is going to use multiple-choice questions, essays, or open-ended response, if you've got a *High Stakes* skill book in your hands, we've got you covered.

So that's the good news . . .

But here's even better news! Unlike the SAT, which tests "critical thinking," the state proficiency exams test only what you've learned in school. It's actually pretty hard to study for something as vague as *critical thinking,* which is why you'll find that most SAT test-prep books are full of tricks on how to squeeze out a couple of hundred more points on the test. But the exit-level proficiency exams test **real subject knowledge.** That's not vague, that's simple! And if you've bought this book, we're going to assume you're prepared for some review. So, the bottom line is that if you study the material we give you in this book (which is not that big, right?), you can do more than just pass these exams—you can score high!

Let's Get Organized

The organization of this book is really straightforward. The book is divided into three parts:

Part I provides a short guide to the state exit-level exams and a chapter on strategies and tips to help you plan your study and alleviate test anxiety.

Part II reviews all the topics that will be covered on your state exam.

Part III contains lots of practice questions to help you get comfortable answering the test questions on high stakes exams. We also give you answers and explanations to make sure you understand everything.

Now that you know you can rely on us to help you succeed, we hope we've reduced your stress level. So . . . sit down, take a deep breath, and . . . *relax.* We're going to take you step-by-step through everything you need to know for test day.

PART I

INTRODUCTION

CHAPTER 1

ALPHABET CITY

Have you checked out the shaded bands on the top of the pages in this book? You'll see some pretty odd combinations of letters, such as TAAS, BST, FCAT, OGT, CAHSEE, and MEAP.

> MEAP? What the heck is that? Sounds like Martian for
> salad or something.

More likely you've recognized some of the letters because they are *acronyms*, which means they are letters that stand for the name of your state exam. MEAP, by the way, stands for Michigan Educational Assessment Program. You have to admit that *Meap* rolls off the tongue a bit more easily.

In this chapter, we list all sixteen states that require exams for graduating high school. Each of the high-stakes states (can you say that 5 times fast?) sets its own rules for the exams, and you'll find some students may appear to have it easier than others. North Carolina tests its students in reading and math only, and the question types are multiple choice only. Students in Minnesota, however, are tested in reading, math, *and* writing, and the question types include multiple choice, short answer, *and* essays! But don't worry, beginning in 2005, students in North Carolina will be tested in reading, math, science, social studies, English, *and* grammar. Perhaps that's why the official state beverage of North Carolina is milk . . . those students will need their strength!

The point is that you should look carefully at the rules for your own state. For example, if you're one of those lucky North Carolinians taking the test in 2003 or 2004, you can skip any practice question that is not multiple choice. As we said earlier, it's our job to make sure we cover all the bases for everyone, but you only have to study what you're actually being tested on.

You may have to take other subject tests in high school, which are not required for graduation. Some tests are for advanced diplomas (such as the Regents Math B). Other tests are actually testing your teachers and your school system. We're here to help you graduate, and we focus only on the tests where the stakes are high for *you*.

> Log on to www.petersons.com/highstakes for your Graduation Checklist, which will highlight information you need to have on your state's scoring, test dates, required topics of study, and more!

The following list of states is in alphabetical order.

Alabama

Exit-Level Exam: Alabama High School Graduation Exam (**AHSGE**)

State Education Department Website: www.alsde.edu

Students take the AHSGE in eleventh grade. Beginning with the graduating class of 2003, students must pass all subject-area tests in order to graduate. Students have six opportunities to take these exams.

Test	# Questions	Time	Question Type
Reading	84	approx. 3 hrs.	multiple choice
Language	100	approx. 3 hrs.	multiple choice
Science	100	approx. 3 hrs.	multiple choice
Math	100	approx. 3 hrs.	multiple choice
Social Studies	100	approx. 3 hrs.	multiple choice

California

Exit-Level Exam: California High School Exit Exam (**CAHSEE**)

State Education Department Website: www.cde.ca.gov

Students take the CAHSEE in tenth grade. As of the 2003–04 school year, students are required to pass both parts of the CAHSEE. Students have multiple opportunities to retake one or both portions of the exam.

Test	# Questions	Time	Question Type
English-Language	82	untimed	multiple choice
English-Language	2	untimed	short essays (includes written response to text and prompt)
Math	80	untimed	multiple choice

Florida

Exit-Level Exam: Florida Comprehensive Assessment Test (**FCAT**)

State Education Department Website: www.firn.edu/doe/sas/fcat

Students take the FCAT in tenth grade and must pass the reading and math parts of the exam in order to graduate. Students have multiple opportunities to retake the exams.

Test	# Questions	Time	Question Type
Reading	105	untimed	multiple choice
Math	100	untimed	multiple choice

Georgia

Exit-Level Exam: Georgia High School Graduation Tests (**GHSGT**)

State Education Department Website: www.doe.k12.ga.us/sla/ret/ghsgt.asp

Students take the GHSGT in eleventh grade and must pass each of the 5 tests in order to graduate. Students have five opportunities to take each of the tests before the end of twelfth grade.

Test	# Questions	Time	Question Type
English/ Language Arts	50	3 hrs. max	multiple choice
Math	60	3 hrs. max.	multiple choice
Social Studies	80	3 hrs. max.	multiple choice
Science	70	3 hrs. max.	multiple choice
Writing	1	90 mins.	essay

Louisiana

Exit-Level Exam: Graduation Exit Examination for the 21st Century (**GEE 21**)

State Education Department Website: www.doe.state.la.us

Students take the GEE 21 in the tenth grade (English language arts *and* mathematics) and must pass them both to graduate. Students also take the GEE 21 in the eleventh grade (science *or* social studies) and must pass one of these to graduate. Students have multiple opportunities to retake each portion of the exam.

Test	# Questions	Time	Question Type
English / Language Arts	61	untimed	multiple choice and essay

Math	60	untimed	multiple choice and short answer
Science	44	untimed	multiple choice and short answer
Social Studies	64	untimed	multiple choice and short answer

Massachusetts

Exit-Level Exam: Massachusetts Comprehensive Assessment System (**MCAS**)

State Education Department Website: www.doe.mass.edu/mcas

Students take the MCAS in the tenth grade and must pass the English Language Arts and Math portions of the exam in order to graduate. Students have multiple opportunities to retake both portions of the test.

Test	# Questions	Time	Question Type
Math	51	untimed	multiple choice, short answer, and open response
English/ Language Arts	55	untimed	multiple choice and writing prompt

Michigan

Exit-Level Exam: Michigan Educational Assessment Program High School Tests (MEAP HST)

State Education Department Website: www.meritaward.state.mi.us/mma/meap.htm

Students take the MEAP HST in eleventh grade and must pass all parts of the exam in order to graduate. Students have the opportunity to retake portions of the exam in the twelfth grade.

CHAPTER 1

Test	# Questions	Time	Question Type
Math	43	100 min.	multiple choice and open response
Reading*	29	80 min.	multiple choice and open response
Science	50	90 min.	multiple choice and open response
Social Studies	42	80 min.	multiple choice and open response
Writing*	2	120 min.	open response

As of the 2003–04 school year, Reading and Writing will be combined into an English Language Arts test along with a Listening test.

Minnesota

Exit-Level Exam: Basic Skills Test (**BST**)

State Education Department Website: http://cflapp.state.mn.us/CLASS/stds/assessments/bst/index.jsp

Students take the math and reading portions of the BST in eighth grade and the writing portion in tenth grade and must pass all portions of the exam in order to graduate. Students have multiple opportunities to retake each section of the exam.

Test	# Questions	Time	Question Type
Reading	40	120–150 min.	multiple choice and short answer
Writing	several	90–120 min.	short essays
Math	68	120–150 min.	multiple choice and short answer

ALPHABET CITY

New Jersey

Exit-Level Exam: High School Proficiency Assessment (**HSPA**)

State Education Department Website: www.state.nj.us/education

Students take the HSPA in eleventh grade and must pass both sections in order to graduate. In 2004–05, a social studies assessment will be phased in, and in March 2005, science will be added. Students have two additional opportunities to retake each portion of the exam in their senior year.

Test	# Questions	Time	Question Type
Language Arts/ Literacy	55	4 hrs.	multiple choice and open ended
Mathematics	48	2 hrs.	multiple choice and open ended

New York

Exit-Level Exam: Regents Exams

State Education Department Website: www.emsc.nysed.gov/deputy/Documents/ alternassess.htm

Students take the Regents in tenth and eleventh grades and must pass the five Regents Examinations listed below to graduate. In general, students in the tenth grade are tested in science, math, and global history and geography. Students in the eleventh grade are tested in English language arts, and U.S. history and government. Students who fail portions of the exam twice are required to pass a component test for that portion in order to graduate.

Test	# Questions	Time	Question Type
English	29	3 hrs.	multiple choice and essay
Math	35	3 hrs.	multiple choice and open ended

PT/HSPA, FCAT, MEAP HST, MCAS, GEE21, Regents Exams, SOL, NCCT, AHSGE, GHSGT, BST
NCCT, AHSGE, GHSGT, BST, BSAP, WASL, CAHSEE, TAAS, OGT HSPT/HSPA, FCAT, MEAP H
GT, HSPT/HSPA, FCAT, MEAP HST, MCAS, GEE21, Regents Exams, SOL, NCCT, AHSGE, GHSG
T, GHSGT, BST, BSAP, WASL, CAHSEE, TAAS, OGT, HSPT/HSPA, FCAT, MEAP HST, MCAS, G

CHAPTER 1

Global History and Geography	60–62	3 hrs.	multiple choice and open ended
U.S. History and Government	60–62	3 hrs.	multiple choice and open ended
Science	62–94	3 hrs.	multiple choice and open ended

North Carolina

Exit-Level Exam: North Carolina Competency Tests (**NCCT**)

State Education Department Website: www.ncpublicschools.org/accountability/testing/policies/

Students take the NCCT in eighth grade. Students who do not pass may retake portions of the test three times each year in grades 9–11 and four times in twelfth grade in order to graduate. Passing scores in both portions of the exam are needed in order to graduate.

Test	# Questions	Time	Question Type
Reading	156	1 hr. 40 mins.	multiple choice
Math	165	1 hr. 40 mins.	multiple choice

Ohio

Exit-Level Exam: Ninth Grade Proficiency Tests and Ohio Graduation Tests (**OGT**)

State Education Department Website: www.ode.state.oh.us

Students take the Ninth Grade Proficiency Tests and must pass all of the portions to graduate. Beginning in the 2003–04 school year, students will take the exams (to be renamed OGT) in the tenth grade and are also required to pass all portions of the exam to graduate. Students have multiple opportunities to retake portions of both the Ninth Grade Proficiency Tests and the OGT.

Test	# Questions	Time	Question Type
Writing	2	2.5 hrs.	essay
Reading	49	2.5 hrs.	multiple choice and open response
Math	50	2.5 hrs.	multiple choice and open response
Science	50	2.5 hrs.	multiple choice and open response
Citizenship	52	2.5 hrs.	multiple choice and open response

South Carolina

Exit-Level Exam: Basic Skills Assessment Program (**BSAP**) and Palmetto Achievement Challenge Tests (**PACT**)

State Education Department Website: www.myscschools.com/offices/assessment

Students take the BSAP in tenth grade and must pass all portions to graduate. Students may retake portions of the test once in eleventh grade and twice in the twelfth grade. The PACT will be given to tenth graders in the spring of 2004 and will test in English language arts, mathematics, and social studies.

Test	# Questions	Time	Question Type
BSAP Reading	60	untimed	multiple choice
BSAP Math	50	untimed	multiple choice
BSAP Writing	1	untimed	essay

Texas

Exit-Level Exam: Texas Assessment of Academic Skills (**TAAS**)

State Education Department Website: www.tea.state.tx.us

Students take the TAAS in tenth grade and must pass all three portions to graduate. Students have multiple opportunities to retake each portion of the exam.

Note that students who will be in the eleventh grade in spring 2004 or later and plan to graduate in spring 2005 or later will take a new test: the Texas Assessment of Knowledge and Skills (TAKS). This will cover English language arts, mathematics, science, and social studies.

Test	# Questions	Time	Question Type
Reading	40	untimed	multiple choice/essay
Writing	48	untimed	multiple choice/essay
Mathematics	60	untimed	multiple choice

Virginia

Exit-Level Exam: Standards of Learning (SOL)

State Education Department Website: www.pen.k12.va.us

Students must pass two SOL end-of-course English tests and any other four SOL end-of-course tests to graduate. Students entering ninth grade in 2003–04 must pass two English tests, one math test, one history test, one science test, and one test of their choosing in order to graduate. Students have multiple opportunities to retake portions of the exam.

The SOL tests are different from other exit-level exams in that there is no specific test for each subject area. Instead, numerous tests are offered in the required disciplines (i.e., biology and physics are tests offered in the science discipline). Listed below are the discipline areas where passing test scores are required for graduation.

Discipline Area	Time	Question Type
English	untimed	multiple choice and short answer
Math	untimed	multiple choice and short answer
Science	untimed	multiple choice and short answer
History & Social Sciences	untimed	multiple choice and short answer
Fine or Practical Arts	untimed	multiple choice and short answer
Health & Physical Education		
Electives		
Student Selected Test		

Washington

Exit-Level Exam: Washington Assessment of Student Learning (**WASL-10**)

State Education Department Website: www.k12.wa.us/assessment

Students take the WASL-10 in the tenth grade and are required to pass all subject-area tests to graduate. Students have multiple opportunities to retake portions of the exam. As of the 2003–04 school year, science will also be a required test.

Test	# Questions	Time	Question Type
Reading	40	untimed	multiple choice, short answers, extended answers
Math	42	untimed	multiple choice, short answers, extended answers
Writing	2	untimed	essay
Communication	8	untimed	multiple choice, short answers, extended answers

CHAPTER 2

TEST-TAKING TIPS AND STRATEGIES

Before you decide to skip this chapter and jump right into the grammar and writing sections, it's important to think about the entire preparation process. You need to make a study plan and stick to it, so you don't burn out too soon, or worse, end up cramming the night before the exam. You also need a plan for taking the actual test. Once you've got that in place, all you have to do on exam day is follow your plan in a calm, unstressed way.

Make a Study Plan

Hey, it's another test; you've seen them before. Studying for this test will be simpler and much more efficient if you figure out your situation and make a plan before you start. It should take you only a few minutes to make a study plan, but it will take loads of stress off you, so let's do it now.

First, figure out how many days you have between today and your exam day. Then subtract from that total the days you won't be able to study because of holidays, family obligations, or regular school exams or events.

Finally, figure out how much time you'll have to put in each day. You are the only one who knows exactly how much time it usually takes you to study for a regular test in school. If you've allowed yourself a month to review for the exam, you probably won't have to do more than 45 minutes to an hour every day, even if you need work in all subject areas of the exam. If, however, you only need to brush up your skills in one particular area, say essay writing, you may be able to reduce your study time to just 30 minutes a day.

The most important step in the study plan process is actually following the plan. Don't get so relaxed (or paralyzed by panic) about the test that you don't study a little every day. And, don't fall into the trap of thinking that you can spend 4 hours on Sunday night working exercises instead of doing them every day. It's much more effective to study for shorter periods every day than to do long sessions every now and then. Believe us, we know about these things.

Make a Test Day Plan

You can be incredibly well prepared because you made and stuck to your study plan, but if you're not prepared for the actual events of test day, your efforts will be wasted. The more you do to prepare for test day, the less that can go wrong. And if you're prepared for everything, you won't be as stressed out by anything minor that does happen.

TEST-TAKING TIPS AND STRATEGIES

HIGH STAKES

Chance favors the prepared mind. The more you do to prepare for things going wrong, the less likely it will be that anything will happen.

Location, Location, Location

Most state writing tests are given in your high school during the regular school day. However, some states reserve the right to schedule the test at a central location. Find out in advance where the test will be held. Double-check this information with your English teacher the day before the test. If, for any reason, the test will not be given at your school, make a dry run to the testing site at least once before test day. Your parents will be happy to do this if you point out that making a dry run will help you get a higher score on the test.

Think about how it would feel to be driving around in the car with your mom desperately looking for an unknown test location while you're supposed to be sitting down to take the test. Awful. Now, think about how great it would feel to breeze on in to the test with plenty of time to collect yourself before it starts.

Time

If the test is going to be given during the regular school day, you don't have to worry about time, since your teacher will probably herd the whole class to the cafeteria or wherever the test will be administered at the appropriate hour.

If the test administration falls on a day or time that conflicts with your religious observance, let your teacher know about this as far in advance as possible. She or he will be able to help you find out how you can get an alternate testing time.

The Night Before

It's probably pretty obvious that you shouldn't go out partying the night before the exam and come home an hour before you have to leave for school. But we're saying it anyway. On the other hand, you shouldn't spend the night before the test frantically cramming to try to soak up one last bit of information. In fact,

T/HSPA, FCAT, MEAP HST, MCAS, GEE21, Regents Exams, SOL, NCCT, AHSGE, GHSGT, BST
NCCT, AHSGE, GHSGT, BST, BSAP, WASL, CAHSEE, TAAS, OGT, T/HSPA, FCAT, MEAP H
GT, HSPT/HSPA, FCAT, MEAP HST, MCAS, GEE21, Regents Exams, NCCT, AHSGE, GHSC
GHSGT, BST, BSAP, WASL, CAHSEE, TAAS, OGT, HSPT/HSPA, FCAT, MEAP HST, MCAS, C

CHAPTER
2

READING

cramming could actually hurt your performance on the test by causing anxiety and erasing some of the other stuff in your short-term memory (like what time the test starts).

A better use of your time the night before the test is to do something that relaxes you. Something that makes you laugh is even better. So rent a funny movie, watch it, and go to bed at a decent time. If you have trouble sleeping, try some of the relaxation techniques we mention in the Test Anxiety section below.

Know Your Enemy

Not all writing tests are the same. As soon as you can (but finish reading this page first!), you should find out exactly what the format of the writing test is in your state. On pages 3–12 of this book, we have provided a short guide to the state exams. Look under your state and you will find out the question types that you will encounter for each subject area. Check carefully to see whether you will have to deal with a multiple-choice section, a short-response section, and if you will need to write an essay.

Test Anxiety

> Test anxiety is like the sound of a buzzing mosquito in the middle of the dark. It can become so all-consuming that you forget what a tiny thing a mosquito bite really is.

Many students get positive results by using some relaxation techniques. One easy technique is called "observed breathing." Simply close your eyes and take note of your breaths in and out. Do not force the breath or change it in any way. Simply observe when you are taking air into your body and when you are expelling it. Stay quiet and observe your breathing for about 5 minutes. You should find that you'll start to feel a lot calmer.

TEST-TAKING TIPS AND STRATEGIES

In addition to relaxation techniques, there are more things you can do to control any anxiety you may have on test day.

Clothes

Dress in layers. You want to be able to put on clothes or strip down until you find the most comfortable temperature for you. You don't want your body to divert any of its thinking energy into shivering or sweating energy. And dress for comfort, not style. Sweats may not be your most flattering look, but sitting for a couple of hours in something tight or uncomfortable can have a negative effect on your performance.

Food and Drink

Eat breakfast the day of the test. A combination of protein and carbs will give you the energy you need to stay focused for several hours of testing. Eat eggs and oatmeal, bacon and toast, soba noodles with tofu, or whatever you like. Just stay away from lots of sugar, since you'll crash and burn right about the time you need to start writing.

Remember that if you drink a lot of liquids before the test, you need to get rid of them before you sit down to write. Make a pit stop before you go into the test room.

Your Mental State

Once you know you can write the essays and are physically comfortable during the test session, the only other factor to account for is your mental state. This is the trickiest aspect to have real control over, but it's also the one that can make all your preparation worthless if you don't manage it well. Try to keep your life in the week or so before the test as normal as possible. This way you won't have anything more pressing than the test to think about when you're actually taking the test. Intrigue about breaking up with your boyfriend or girlfriend or worrying about

PT/HSPA, FCAT, MEAP HST, MCAS, GEE21, Regents Exams, SOL, NCCT, AHSGE, GHSGT, BST
NCCT, AHSGE, GHSGT, BST, BSAP, WASL, CAHSEE, TAAS, OGT, HSPA, FCAT, MEAP
GT, HSPT/HSPA, FCAT, MEAP HST, MCAS, GEE21, Regents Exams, NCCT, AHSGE, GHS
GHSGT, BST, BSAP, WASL, CAHSEE, TAAS, OGT, HSPT/HSPA, FCAT, MEAP HST, MCAS,

CHAPTER
2

the friendship you just ended, your prom dress, or your summer vacation will do nothing but hurt your test score. So, try to keep everything as boring as possible so you can't help but focus on the test.

> The test itself is nothing but a few pieces of paper. Some of them have words written on them that you should read. The others are blank, and you have to write words on them.

If you've been doing relaxation exercises, take the time to do them on test day. If you find yourself freaking out right before or even during the test, put down your pencil, close your eyes, take a few deep breaths, and count or meditate. You'll lose a few minutes of your test time, but it's worth it to be calm and focused.

Ready for the fun to begin? Turn the page and start the grammar review.

PART

II

READING REVIEW

CHAPTER 3

WHAT YOU'LL ENCOUNTER

In this chapter, we will review each of the skills you'll need for each question type, and we'll provide examples, which we hope will help to increase your comfort level. Now, let's look at the types of questions you'll encounter.

Main Idea

You can always expect to encounter main idea questions about reading passages. A main idea question may present several phrases or potential titles for the selection that you have read and you will have to choose the one that best expresses the main idea of the passage. Main idea questions may also ask about the author's purpose or intent in writing the passage. Main ideas can often be found in a topic sentence, which usually appears in the first paragraph as part of an introduction to the subject. A topic sentence expresses the main idea—that is, the topic—hence the name "topic sentence." Sometimes, the topic sentence may also appear in the last sentence as a summary. Here's an example of a passage with a main idea question:

> The social standing of a wife in colonial days was determined by the standing of her husband, as well as by her own ability and resourcefulness. She married not only a husband, but also a career. Her position in the community was established in part by the quality of the bread she baked, by the food she preserved for the winter's use, by the whiteness of her washing on the line, by the way her children were clothed, and by her skill in nursing. Doctors were scarce. In case of the illness or death of a neighbor, a woman would put aside her own work to help, and she was honored for what she could do.

> The title that best expresses the main idea of this selection is
>
> **(A)** Care of Children in Colonial Times
>
> **(B)** Community Spirit
>
> **(C)** Medical Care in Pre-Revolutionary Times
>
> **(D)** The Colonial Housewife

The correct answer is (D). The reading passage describes the various homemaking duties a colonial woman was expected to perform. Choices (A), (B), and (C) each describes one such a duty, but choice (D) summarizes them all.

Supporting Details

Supporting details are the facts and ideas in a reading passage that explain and support the passage's main idea. Remember, a hammock would be a piece of cloth on the ground if it were not for the posts or tree trunks that support both its ends. The following is an instance of such a selection:

> There are many signs by which people predict the weather. Bunions are one of my personal favorites. Some of these have a true basis, but many have not. There is, for example, no evidence that it is more likely to storm during one phase of the moon than during another. If it happens to rain on Easter, there

is no reason to think that it will rain on the next seven Sundays. The groundhog may or may not see his or her shadow on Groundhog Day, but it probably won't affect the weather either way.

Which of the following is *not* listed as a predictive weather phenomenon?

(A) Rain on Easter

(B) The phases of the moon

(C) Pain in a person's joints

(D) The groundhog's shadow

The correct answer is (C). Each of the other choices was mentioned in the paragraph as being treated as predictive of weather, but joint pain is not mentioned. By the way, extrapolation of information in the selection above (another tested-for skill) tells us that Easter falls on Sunday.

Vocabulary, or Words, Words, Words

This type of question, often referred to as "words in context," asks you to choose a synonym (a word that means the same thing as another word) for one of the words in the reading passage. Look at the following passage.

The maritime and fishing industries find perhaps 250 applications for rope and cordage. There are hundreds of different sizes, construction, tensile strengths, and weights in rope and twine. Rope is sold by the pound but ordered by length, and is measured by circumference rather than by diameter.

In this context, the word *applications* means

(A) uses.

(B) descriptions.

(C) sizes.

(D) types.

The correct answer is (A), "uses." Cover the answer choices and find a synonym. Then, look to see which answer choice is like *your* word. The word "uses" makes sense in the context of the passage and keeps the meaning of the sentence intact.

Inference Is Not a Fluffy Animal

Contrary to popular opinion in some circles, an inference is not a small fluffy animal (in-*fur*-ence); yuck! An *inference* is a conclusion drawn from the details in a reading selection. The answer to an inferential question will never be directly stated in the passage, and it is therefore one of the most difficult types of comprehension question to answer. It is an answer that the reader (you!) must provide. You must read carefully and think logically in order to draw the appropriate conclusion from the information provided in the passage:

> The facts, as we see them, on drug use and the dangerous behaviors caused by drugs are that some people do get into trouble while using drugs, and some of those drug users are dangerous to others. Sometimes, a drug is a necessary element in order for a person to commit a crime, although it may not be the cause of his or her criminality. On the other hand, the use of a drug sometimes seems to be the only convenient explanation by means of which the observer can account for the undesirable behavior.

The author apparently feels that

- **(A)** the use of drugs always results in crime.
- **(B)** drugs and crime are only sometimes related.
- **(C)** the relationship of drug use to crime is purely coincidental.
- **(D)** drugs are usually an element in accidents.

The correct answer is choice (B). The author states that drugs are sometimes a necessary element in a crime, but at other times are just an excuse for criminal behavior. Well, isn't that essentially what choice (B) says?

A Closer Look at Analogies

Analogies test your ability to recognize the relationships between pairs of words. You'll be given a pair of words in capital letters (the stem pair) that have a particular relationship to one another. You'll then be given four or five additional pairs of words (depending on your particular state's exit-level test), labeled (A), (B), (C), (D), and (E) (the answer choices) or even (1), (2), (3), and (4). No matter how many choices you are given from which to choose, your job is to select that answer choice with a pair of words whose relationship is similar to the relationship between the words in the stem pair. There is no way to tell how many analogy questions (if any) will be on your examination, but it is a good idea to be prepared for them.

> There is no way to tell how many analogy questions (if any) will be on your examination, but it is a good idea to be prepared for them.

Question Format

Here is a sample analogy question that should help you to familiarize yourself with the format.

Directions: Each question below consists of a related pair of words or phrases, followed by five pairs of words or phrases labeled (A) through (E). Select the pair that best expresses a relationship similar to that expressed in the original pair.

CRUMB : BREAD ::

(A) ounce : unit

(B) splinter : wood

(C) water : bucket

(D) twine : rope

(E) cream : butter

The correct answer is (B). Can you see why? If you can't, read on—the answer's in the next section.

READING

Solving Analogies: Strategies that *Really* Work

BUILD A BRIDGE

A **bridge** is a short sentence that contains both words in the stem pair and shows how they are related. Let's call the two words in the stem pair "X" and "Y." A typical bridge would define X in terms of Y. So, for the sample question from the directions above, the bridge might say, "A CRUMB is a very small piece that falls off or breaks off a piece of BREAD." Notice how this sentence explains the relationship between the two words. It also defines CRUMB (tells what a crumb is) in terms of BREAD. What a lovely bridge!

Here are a couple of other examples. Suppose the stem pair was "OPERA : MUSIC." (By the way, you would read this aloud as, "opera is to music.") The bridge might say, "An OPERA is a long, elaborate, classical work of MUSIC." If the stem pair were "SURGEON : SCALPEL," the bridge might be, "A SURGEON is a professional who uses a SCALPEL." Get the idea? Building a bridge forces you to explain to yourself exactly how the two words logically fit together.

PLUG IN THE ANSWER CHOICES

After you've created a bridge, the next step is to turn to the answer choices. One by one, try to plug in the words from the answer choices into the same sentence.

> If your bridge is a strong one, only one pair of words will make sense.

Try this with the five answer choices for the previous sample question. Only the words in choice (B) fit comfortably into the bridge: "A SPLINTER is a very small piece that falls off or breaks off of a piece of WOOD." Try it with the others. Is an OUNCE a very small piece of a UNIT (choice (A))? No; an ounce is a kind of unit—a unit of weight. Is WATER a very small piece of a BUCKET (choice (C))? We don't think so; water might be carried in a bucket. The same with the other answers. So, choice (B) is correct. (By the way, you would read the stem pair and the correct answer this way: "CRUMB is to BREAD as SPLINTER is to WOOD.")

What if our stem pair is OPERA : MUSIC?

> Which of these five answer choices fits the bridge we thought of for "An OPERA is a long, elaborate, classical work of MUSIC?
>
> **(A)** novel : artistry
>
> **(B)** painting : landscape
>
> **(C)** oboe : instrument
>
> **(D)** epic : poetry
>
> **(E)** microphone : recording

The correct answer is (D), because only that word pair fits into the same bridge. "An EPIC is a long, elaborate, classical work of POETRY." Isn't this getting to be almost fun? Oh well, but hopefully, it is becoming a bit more clear.

GET NARROW AS NEEDED (NOT A DIET PLAN)

Sometimes, the differences among the answer choices will be subtle—so subtle that the first bridge you've built won't eliminate the wrong answers. When that's the case, two or more answer choices may fit the bridge. Here's an example:

> SURGEON : SCALPEL ::
>
> **(A)** judge : gavel
>
> **(B)** painter : canvas
>
> **(C)** executive : computer
>
> **(D)** farmer : fertilizer
>
> **(E)** carpenter : saw

If you build the bridge, "A SURGEON is a professional who uses a SCALPEL" and then tried plugging in each of the answer pairs (A) through (E), you'd be dismayed to find that all five answer pairs could fit the bridge! A JUDGE uses a GAVEL (it's the hammer a judge uses to pound on the bench), a PAINTER (often) uses a CANVAS, an EXECUTIVE (often) uses a COMPUTER, a FARMER uses FERTILIZER, and a CARPENTER uses a SAW. Based on this bridge, all five answer choices could be considered correct! Now what should you do?

READING

The solution is to narrow your bridge—that is, add details to the sentence to make it more specific. In this case, you might narrow the bridge like this: "A SURGEON is a professional who uses a SCALPEL as a tool for cutting." Now, plug in the answer choices. Only choice (E) fits the new, narrower bridge, so that must be the correct answer.

Of course, picking the correct answer depends on narrowing the bridge correctly. You could concoct a misleading bridge that included details that point to a different answer. For example, you could say, "A SURGEON is a professional who wears a protective smock while using a SCALPEL." With that bridge, choice (B) is arguably correct, since artists, like surgeons, often do wear protective smocks. (The robe a judge wears isn't "protective," so choice (A) doesn't work. And the people in the other choices don't wear smocks at all. Does this mean that choice (B) is just as good as choice (E)?

> Of course, picking the correct answer depends on narrowing the bridge correctly. You could concoct a misleading bridge that included details that point to a different answer.

No—in fact, if you think about it, you probably find choice (B), and the bridge we made up that points to it, a little silly. The smock that a surgeon (or an artist) wears isn't central to his or her work; and it certainly has little to do with the use of the scalpel. The first narrow bridge we created—the one that refers to the scalpel as a cutting tool—seems more sensible. It defines exactly what the scalpel does in the hands of the surgeon, which is similar to what the saw does in the hands of the carpenter.

The point is that it takes a bit of judgment to build the right bridge. You want to focus on the central, basic nature of the relationship between the two words—not on side issues that are irrelevant (like the surgeon's smock). It's a little subjective, but you'll get the hang of it.

> Nine times out of ten, devising the right bridge will strike you as a matter of "common sense."

In fact, in the example we've been looking at, you may have been able to "see" the similarity between SURGEON : SCALPEL and CARPENTER : SAW even without consciously building the new, narrow bridge. That's fine. But as you prepare for the test, practice your bridge-building technique. It'll give you crucial help on the handful of really tough analogies your test may contain.

Look for the Test Makers' Favorite Relationships

Pity the folks who write test questions by the hundred, week in and week out. Like anyone else, they eventually start to repeat themselves. (Ever notice how the third album by your favorite rock band sounds a lot like their first and second albums, only less interesting?) But this is a good thing for you, as the test taker. It means that analogies fall into repeated patterns that you can practice and learn. If you know and understand the test makers' favorite analogy relationships, you'll quickly pounce on them if they pop up on your exam. And, rest assured, they will!

Here are the top nine analogy relationships we've found on past and current standard tests. If any of the examples that follow contain words you're not sure about, you know what to do: Grab your dictionary!

> By the way, in case you didn't already know this, never prepare for a test on language without having a dictionary handy.

1. Part : Whole

In this kind of analogy, one word names something that is part of what's named by the other word. Here are a couple of examples:

> LID : POT :: roof : house
>
> MOVEMENT : SYMPHONY :: scene : play

Take care to note that in an analogy, order matters:

> LID : POT :: roof : house is correct.
>
> LID : POT :: house : roof is *NOT* correct. The *order* is wrong.

2. Opposites

Here, the two words in the pair are opposite or opposed in meaning.

> NAIVE : SOPHISTICATED :: untutored : educated
>
> WATER : DROUGHT :: food : famine

3. Actor : Action

This kind of analogy links a person or thing with what they commonly do.

> COUNTERFEITER : FAKE :: blackmailer : extort
>
> DETERGENT : CLEAN :: bleach : whiten

4. Actor : Acted Upon

The word pair includes a person or thing and another person or thing that is commonly acted upon or affected by the first.

> TEACHER : CLASS :: orator : audience
>
> NET : FISH :: trap : game

That should be pretty clear, don't you think?

5. Action : Acted Upon

Here, an action is paired with the person or thing that commonly receives or is affected by the action.

> ALPHABETIZE : FILES :: catalog : books

> RAZE : BUILDING :: fell : tree

That's to "chop down" (fell) a tree; not what the tree did after it was chopped down. Was "to fell" a part of your everyday vocabulary before the last analogy?

6. Action : Emotion

One of the words describes an action, the other an emotion commonly associated with it.

> LOSS : MOURN :: triumph : celebrate

> TREMBLE : FEAR :: shiver : cold

7. Thing : Description

This kind of word pair includes one word that names a person or thing, another that describes it.

> MISER : STINGY :: spendthrift : wasteful

> GLADE : SHADY :: clearing : open

Notice that the relationship is what matters within each pair. A glade is a shady place, since there are trees; a clearing is an open place.

8. Description : Quality

Here, an adjective that describes a particular quality is paired with a noun that names the quality.

> LIFELIKE : VIVIDNESS :: truthful : honesty

> ARROGANT : PRIDE :: modest : humility

9. Differing Connotations

In this kind of analogy, two words are linked that have similar meanings but different feelings, moods, or nuances—in other words, different connotations.

> CAR : JALOPY :: house : shanty

> HIGH : SHRILL :: bright : blinding

Now, not every analogy on your exam is going to fit into one of these nine categories, but three quarters of them will. Those that don't fit into one of these nine categories will have "miscellaneous" relationships of their own, like these examples:

> MUSICIAN : CONCERT :: poet : reading

Here, a type of artist is paired with an event at which he or she might perform.

> BOTANY : PLANT :: astronomy : star

A field of science is paired with a typical object that is studied in that field.

> GAUNTLET : HAND :: helmet : head

A gauntlet is an armored glove, worn, of course, on the hand; a helmet is an armored hat worn on the head.

Solving Analogies: The Best Tips

Use the Analogy Structure to Guess Words You Don't Know

On some analogies, you're going to come across words whose meaning you aren't sure of. Don't throw up your hands in despair. You can use the analogy structure to help you figure out the meaning of the unknown words. First, realize that all the word pairs contain words that are the same parts of speech. For example, if the stem pair contains a noun and a verb, like this:

> TYRANT : OPPRESS

then each of the other word pairs will also contain a noun and a verb, in that order. So, in any analogy with an unknown word, you can tell whether the unknown word is a noun, verb, adjective, or any other part of speech by looking at any of the other word pairs, which can be very helpful in guessing the meaning of the unknown word.

Next, try using what you know about analogy relationships and the words in the question that you *do* understand to make an informed guess about the meaning of the unknown word. Look at this example:

ETYMOLOGY : WORD ::

(A) etiology : disease

(B) history : event

(C) literature : author

(D) microscopy : microbe

(E) psychology : insanity

We deliberately included some difficult, specialized words in this section to illustrate a point; actually, a word like etiology is unlikely to be used in an analogy on the real test.

You may or may not know what ETYMOLOGY means in the stem pair, but you can tell by glancing at the other word pairs that it must be a noun, since the first word in every pair is a noun. And, you can probably guess from the way the word looks that it refers to a study or science of some kind.

Words that end in -ology, like **anthropology**, usually refer to science.

ETYMOLOGY is paired with WORD. From what you know about analogy relationships, you obviously know that ETYMOLOGY has something to do with a word or words. Given that fact, what's a possible meaning of ETYMOLOGY? Your first guess is likely to be that ETYMOLOGY is "the science or study of words." As it happens, that's not quite correct; but never mind. That guess is probably close enough to enable you to eliminate choices (B), (C), and (E) as clearly wrong, History can't be defined as "the science of events"; it's the study of the past, including events, people, forces, trends, and so on. Literature isn't "the science of authors"; it's the study of what authors produce, namely books and other writings. And psychology isn't "the science of insanity"; psychology studies the mind and human behavior. So, by sheer guesswork—and a bit of word-sense— you can narrow your choices to two, giving you great odds for guessing, even if you have little or no idea what *etiology* or *microscopy* mean.

The correct answer, by the way, is (A). ETYMOLOGY is actually the study of word origins—where words come from. Similarly, *etiology* is the study of the origins of disease—where particular illnesses come from. So the analogy is close. (Microscopy has nothing to do with the origin of microbes, in case you're wondering.)

Not every obscure word in an analogy may be placed quite so well for guessing. But, many will be. Don't let one or more unknown words in a question alarm you; work from what you *do* know to make reasonable guesses as to the meaning of the new words, and you don't be afraid to base your answer choice on these guesses.

> Don't let one or more unknown words in a question alarm you; work from what you do know to make reasonable guesses as to the meaning of the new words, and don't be afraid to base your answer choice on these guesses.

Don't Fear the Flip-Flop

The logical relationship in the stem pair will "run" in a certain direction; the relationships in the answer choices will run the same way. We mentioned order counting before, but let's take a closer look. Suppose you face the following stem pair:

PROLIFIC : CREATOR

The relationship here is "Description : Thing," and it might be the bridge, "A PROLIFIC CREATOR is one that produces a lot (of offspring, ideas, artwork, or whatever)." Your job would be to find the answer choice with the same "Description : Thing" relationship, preferably using words that fit nicely into the same bridge. Choosing the right answer, as you've already seen, may at times be subtle, even tricky. But one kind of trick you *usually don't* have to worry about is the "flip-flop." The test makers *usually* do *not* try to trick you by giving you a correct word pair in reverse order, like this:

SOURCE : ABUNDANT

As we said before, you'll find that all the answer choices *usually* match the stem pair in their parts of speech. Similarly, you'll find that relationship reversals are *usually* not used to try to trick you. So don't worry too much about flip-flops, because the odds are that they won't turn up on the test.

When All Else Fails

Sometimes, you won't be able to find the one best answer for an analogy question. Remember, the questions may get harder as you move through them. So, in a group of thirteen analogies, you're likely to find the last three or four to be quite hard. And, you may encounter words whose meaning you don't know, and can't guess, even using the clues provided by the analogy structure. When this happens, work by elimination. Build the best bridge you can and plug in the answer choices. Eliminate any answer pairs that don't seem to fit, and guess from among the remaining answers.

On occasion, you may find that you've eliminated all the answers you understand, leaving only an answer choice that contains words you don't know. Don't be afraid—choose it! It's a safe bet that you're not going to get the answer right if you leave it blank.

CHAPTER
3

Solving Analogies: The Most Important Warnings

IGNORE THE TOPICS OF THE WORD PAIRS

This is very good advice, so pay close attention. It's easy to go wrong by focusing on the surface meanings of the words in the word pairs rather than on their underlying relationship. Consider this example:

WING : FEATHER ::

(A) turtle : shell

(B) eagle : talon

(C) fish : fin

(D) roof : shingle

(E) bird : flight

The words in the stem pair refer to parts of a bird, of course. A hasty glance at the answer choices shows that four of them also refer to animals of one kind or another, and two choices, (B) and (E), refer specifically to birds. Don't fall prey to the temptation to pick one of these answers, misled by the surface similarity.

The correct answer, however, is (D). A well-thought-out bridge will tell you why. The relationship between the words in the stem pair might be described this way: "The WING of a bird is covered by many small, overlapping segments, each called a FEATHER." Only choice (D) fits the same bridge: "The ROOF of a house is [or may be] covered by many small, overlapping segments, each called a SHINGLE." Can you picture the similarity? No such similarity exists when you picture the turtle and its shell, the eagle and its talon (or claw), or any of the other items named in the other choices. Now wasn't that easy?

Summary: What You Need To Know about Analogies

- ☞ Analogies test your ability to find relationships between paired words.
- ☞ When you don't know the capitalized words, work backward.

WHAT YOU'LL ENCOUNTER

BE PREPARED TO JUMP FROM THE CONCRETE TO THE ABSTRACT

The test makers sometimes like to make you connect a pair of **concrete** words (related to the physical world) with a pair of **abstract** words (related to the world of ideas). Practice recognizing those kinds of analogies. Here are a couple of examples:

SPARK : FIRE :: inspiration : invention

SPARK and FIRE are concrete, physical things; a SPARK is a small thing that helps to create a larger, more powerful force, a FIRE. *Inspiration* and *invention* are abstract ideas that have much the same relationship.

RETRACE : PATH :: reiterate : argument

When you RETRACE a PATH, you are walking over the same steps you took before, in a physical sense. When you *reiterate* an *argument,* you are repeating the same ideas you stated before, in an abstract sense. Think about it.

Sentence Completions Strategies

Let's take a look at yet another type of question. Sentence completion questions test your vocabulary as well as your ability to understand what you read. In this kind of question, you are given a sentence that has one or more blanks, and you're asked to choose the best word or pair of words to "fill-in" those blanks. This section will help you to become familiar with the format of sentence completion questions, and to learn the most effective strategies for finding the right answers to this type of question.

A CLOSER LOOK AT SENTENCE COMPLETIONS

Are you drawing a blank? Get used to it, because you'll see a lot of them in the sentence completion questions on your exam (that was a joke). In this kind of question, you are given a sentence that contains one or more blanks. A number of words or pairs of words are suggested to fill in the blank spaces. It's up to you to select the word or pair of words that will best complete the meaning of the sentence. In a typical sentence completion question, several of the choices could be inserted into the blank spaces. However, only one answer choice will make sense and carry out the full meaning of the sentence.

SENTENCE COMPLETION QUESTIONS AND FORMAT

Your exit-level exam may have groups of sentence completion questions. Each group of questions will be preceded by a set of directions and an example for your reference, like the example listed below. Don't forget that you're being tested on your ability to find the best answer. Though more than one answer may seem to work, only one is correct, so be sure to make your choice very carefully.

> **Directions:** Each of the sentences below contains one or two blanks. Each blank indicates that a word (or words) has (or have) been omitted. Following the sentence are five lettered words or phrases labeled (A) through (E). Choose the word or phrase that best fits the meaning of the sentence as a whole.

> Medieval kingdoms did not become constitutional republics overnight; on the contrary, the change was _____.
>
> **(A)** unpopular
>
> **(B)** unexpected
>
> **(C)** advantageous
>
> **(D)** sufficient
>
> **(E)** gradual

The correct answer is (E). The clue here is the word "overnight," which indicates that the blank should be filled by a word dealing with a period of time. As a result, "gradual" should have been your choice.

THE SIX-STEP METHOD

Are you ready to start filling in some of those blanks? Following these six steps will help you to better answer sentence completion questions:

1. Read the sentence carefully.

2. Think of a word or words that will fit the blank appropriately.

3. Look through the answer choices for the word(s) you thought of in step 2. If you don't see it, move on to step 4.

4. Examine the sentence for clues to the missing word.

5. Eliminate any answer choices that are ruled out by the clues.

6. Try the ones that are left and pick whichever is best.

Now that you've seen how to approach these questions most effectively, try a few sample sentence completion questions:

> Those who feel that war is ridiculous and unnecessary think that to be wounded on the battlefield is _____.
>
> (A) courageous
>
> (B) pretentious
>
> (C) useless
>
> (D) illegal
>
> (E) heroic

Now, follow the steps to find the correct answer:

1. Read the sentence.

2. Think of your own word to fill in the blank. You're looking for a word that completes the logic of the sentence. You might come up with something like "dumb."

3. Look for "dumb" in the answer choices. It's not there, but "useless" is. That's pretty close, so mark it and go on. Hey, wasn't that cool?

4. If you couldn't guess the word, take your clue from the words *ridiculous* and *unnecessary* in the sentence. They sure do point toward some negative-sounding word.

5. The clues immediately eliminate choice (A), *courageous*, and choice (E), *heroic*, which are both positive words.

6. Try the remaining choices in the sentence, and you'll see that *useless* fits best. See? There's more than one way to get to the best answer.

Since this is usually a timed test, don't let sentence completion questions hold you up for an excessive period of time. Try to spend no more than 45-50 seconds on any single sentence completion, so that you'll have time to get through the rest of the test. Thinking up your own answer will help you kill two birds with one stone, so to speak. You will save precious time, because you will not need to read the sentence through five separate times to check five separate answer choices; you already will have formed a reasonable expectation of what belongs in the blank. Thinking up your own answer will also help you avoid answer choices that merely "sound good," but have no logical or grammatical reason to be the right answer.

> Try to spend no more than 45-50 seconds on any single sentence completion, so that you'll have time to get through the rest of the test. Thinking up your own answer will help you kill two birds with one stone, so to speak.

The Best Strategies for Sentence Completion Questions

The six-step method for solving sentence completion questions is a tried-and-true approach to solving this type of question. But, because you want to move through these questions as quickly as you can (while choosing the right answers, of course), you also need to arm yourself with some basic strategies for tackling even the most difficult sentence completion questions. The following sections offer some very simple—and effective—strategies for quickly and accurately answering sentence completion questions.

Thinking up Your Own Answer Is the Way to Start

If you've thought up the best answer before you even look at the choices, you've started solving the problem in advance and you've saved time. To test this theory, look at this typical sentence completion question:

Robert was extremely _____ when he received a B on the exam, for he was almost certain he had gotten an A.

(A) elated

(B) dissatisfied

(C) fulfilled

(D) harmful

(E) victorious

In this example, it is obvious that Robert would be "dissatisfied" with the grade he received. You may have come up with a different word, such as "upset" or "frustrated," but you can quickly figure out that choice (B) is the correct answer by the relationship of the answer choice to the word you guessed.

Use the Words in the Surrounding Sentence

The words in the surrounding sentence offer clues to the missing word. Often, in sentence completion questions, the word that does *not* appear is the key to the meaning of the sentence. But, by thinking about the words that *do* appear, we can see the connection between the two parts of the sentence. Most sentences contain not only a collection of words but also a number of *ideas* that are connected to one another in various ways. When you understand how these ideas are connected, you can say that you really understand the sentence.

Some Blanks Go with the Flow

In sentence completion questions, the missing word may be one that supports another thought in the sentence, so you need to look for an answer that "goes with the flow." Check this out:

The service at the restaurant was so slow that by the time the salad had arrived we were_____.

(A) ravenous

(B) disappointed

(C) incredible

(D) forlorn

(E) victorious

CHAPTER 3

READING

Where is this sentence going? The restaurant service is very slow. That means you have to wait a long time for your food, and the longer you wait, the hungrier you'll get. So, the word in the blank should be something that completes this train of thought. Choice (A), "ravenous," which means very hungry, is the best answer. It works because it "goes with the flow."

Here's another example:

> As a teenager, Rebecca was withdrawn, preferring the company of books to that of people; consequently, as a adult, Rebecca was socially _____.
>
> (A) successful
>
> (B) uninhibited
>
> (C) intoxicating
>
> (D) inept
>
> (E) tranquil

The word *consequently* signals that the second idea is an outcome of the first, so again, you are looking for a word that completes the train of thought. What might happen if you spent so much time with your nose stuck in a book (except for this one, of course) and hardly interacted with others? Most likely, you would be more comfortable with books than with people. Choice (D), "inept," meaning awkward, is a good description of someone who lacks social graces, making this the right answer.

Here's yet another example:

> A decision that is made before all of the relevant data are collected can only be called _____.
>
> (A) calculated
>
> (B) insincere
>
> (C) laudable
>
> (D) unbiased
>
> (E) premature

The word "called" tells you that the blank is the word that the rest of the sentence describes. A decision that is made before all the facts are collected can only be described as premature, choice (E).

SOME BLANKS SHIFT GEARS

Sometimes in sentence completion questions, the missing word may be one that reverses a thought in the sentence, so you need to stay on the lookout for an answer that "shifts gears." Try this technique in the following example:

> The advance of science has demonstrated that a fact that appears to contradict a certain theory may actually be _____ a more advanced formulation of that theory.
>
> (A) incompatible with
>
> (B) in opposition to
>
> (C) consistent with
>
> (D) eliminated by
>
> (E) foreclosed by

The correct answer is (C). Look at the logical structure of the sentence. The sentence has set up a contrast between what appears to be and what is actually true. This indicates that the correct answer will "shift gears" and be the opposite of the word "contradict." The choice "consistent with" provides this meaning. The other choices do not.

Here's another example:

> Although she knew that the artist's work was considered by some critics to be _____, the curator of the museum was anxious to acquire several of the artist's paintings for the museum's collection.
>
> (A) insignificant
>
> (B) important
>
> (C) desirable
>
> (D) successful
>
> (E) retroactive

The correct answer is (A). The very first word of the sentence, "although," signals that the sentence is setting up a contrast between the critics and the curator. The critics had one opinion, but the curator had a different one. Since the curator liked the artwork well enough to acquire it, you can anticipate that the critics disliked the artwork. So the blank requires a word with negative connotations, and choice (A), "insignificant," is the only one that works.

Here's one last example of this type of contrast in a sentence completion question:

> After witnessing several violent interactions between the animals, the anthropologist was forced to revise her earlier opinion that the monkeys were _____.
>
> **(A)** peaceable
>
> **(B)** quarrelsome
>
> **(C)** insensitive
>
> **(D)** prosperous
>
> **(E)** unfriendly

Where do you begin? The words "forced to revise" clearly signal a shift in the anthropologist's ideas. Her discovery that the monkeys were violent made her abandon an earlier contrasting opinion. Among the answer choices, the only contrast to "violent" is choice (A), "peaceable." Now what kind of monkey-business was that?

The Right Answer Must Be Both Logical and Grammatically Correct

When you're answering sentence completion questions, you can always simply toss out any answer choices that do not make sense in the sentence or that would not be grammatically correct. Try this technique in the following example:

> An advocate of consumer rights, Nader has spent much of his professional career attempting to _____ the fraudulent claims of American business.
>
> **(A)** expose
>
> **(B)** immortalize
>
> **(C)** approve
>
> **(D)** construe
>
> **(E)** import

What would you do with a fraudulent claim? Immortalize it? Approve it? Import it? Not likely. These choices are not logical. The only logical answer is choice (A). You would expose a fraudulent claim.

Two-Blank Questions Give You Two Ways to Get it Right

Many sentence completion questions—the number will vary—have two blanks rather than one. This provides another way of working by elimination. Sometimes you can guess the meaning of one blank, but not the other. Good! Scan the answer choices, looking only for the word you've guessed. Eliminate the answers that *don't* include it (or a near-synonym). Cross them out with your pencil if you like (this saves time if you look back at the question later). Then, guess from what remains.

Difficult Questions Generally Have Difficult Answers

As with the analogy questions, easier sentence completions typically have easier answers and harder sentence completions typically have harder answers. This does not mean that you should always guess the hardest words on the hardest questions.

Summary: What You Need to Know about Sentence Completions

☞ The sentence completion questions are usually arranged in order from easiest to most difficult.

☞ Sentence completion questions test your vocabulary and your reading comprehension skills by presenting sentences with one or two blanks and asking you to choose the best words to fill the blanks.

☞ In general, you follow these six steps to answer sentence completion questions:

1. Read the sentence carefully.

2. Think of a word or words that will fit the blank appropriately.

3. Look through the five answer choices for the word(s) you thought of in step 2. If you don't see it, move on to step 4.

4. Examine the sentence for clues to the missing word.

5. Eliminate any answer choices that are ruled out by the clues.

6. Try the ones that are left and pick whichever is best.

T/HSPA, FCAT, MEAP HST, MCAS, GEE21, Regents Exams, SOL, NCCT, AHSGE, GHSGT, BS
NCCT, AHSGE, GHSGT, BST, BSAP, WASL, CAHSEE, TAAS, OGT HSPT/HSPA, FCAT, MEAP
GT, HSPT/HSPA, FCAT, MEAP HST, MCAS, GEE21, Regents Exams NCCT, AHSGE, GHS
GHSGT, BST, BSAP, WASL, CAHSEE, TAAS, OGT, HSPT/HSPA, FCAT, MEAP HST, MCAS

CHAPTER
3

Eliminate choices that are illogical or grammatically incorrect. Use both words within a two-word choice to "test" for the best response.

Try to spend no more than 45–50 seconds on any one sentence completion question.

Above all, don't stick your gum to the bottom of your desk or chair.

Pop Quiz

Directions: Questions 1–6 are based on the following poem by William Shakespeare.

> Tired with all these, for restful death I cry,
> As, to behold desert a beggar born,
> And needy nothing trimm'd in jollity,
> And purest faith unhappily forsworn,
> And gilded honour shamefully misplac'd,
> And maiden virtue rudely strumpeted,
> And right perfection wrongfully disgrac'd,
> And strength by limping sway disabled,
> And art made tongue-tied by authority,
> And folly, doctor-like, controlling skill,
> And simple truth miscall'd simplicity,
> And captive good attending captain ill:
>
> Tir'd with all these, from these would I be gone,
>   Save that, to die, I leave my love alone.

1. Which of the following best describes the mood of this poem?
   (A) cheery
   (B) thankful
   (C) dark
   (D) light

2. Which of the following states a reason for which the author does not desire to die?

   (F) art

   (G) truth

   (H) virtue

   (J) love

3. The line, "And art made tongue-tied by authority," most likely means what?

   (A) The author does not like art.

   (B) The author is frustrated because no one will buy his art.

   (C) The author believes that expression through art is limited by bureaucracy.

   (D) The author was deaf.

4. Which of the following best describes the main idea of the poem?

   (F) The author is complaining about life.

   (G) The author is reminiscing about his life.

   (H) The author is dreaming of a future life.

   (J) The author is wishing for a better life.

5. Which of the following best characterizes the symbolism of the line, "And captive good attending captain ill?"

   (A) "Captive good" describes doctors and "captain ill" describes sick people.

   (B) "Captive good" represents the idea that universal good is enslaved and "captain ill" represents the evil which has enslaved it.

   (C) "Captain ill" represents the captain of a ship.

   (D) "Captive good" represents the common man.

6. Which of the following would be the best title for this poem?

   (F) Wishing For A Better Life

   (G) How I Mourn For My Lost Love

   (H) Without These Things, Life Would Be Without Meaning

   (J) Tired With All These, For Restful Death I Cry

/HSPA, FCAT, MEAP HST, MCAS, GEE21, Regents Exams, SOL, NCCT, AHSGE, GHSGT, BST
NCCT, AHSGE, GHSGT, BST, BSAP, WASL, CAHSEE, TAAS, OGT HSPA, FCAT, MEAP H
T, HSPT/HSPA, FCAT, MEAP HST, MCAS, GEE21, Regents Exams NCCT, AHSGE, GHS(
GHSGT, BST, BSAP, WASL, CAHSEE, TAAS, OGT, HSPT/HSPA, FCAT, MEAP HST, MCAS, (

CHAPTER
3

Directions: Choose from among the four choices the word that is related to the third word in the same way that the second word is related to the first.

7. GASOLINE : PETROLEUM :: sugar :

   (A) sweet

   (B) oil

   (C) plant

   (D) cane

8. PUNGENT : ODOR :: shrill :

   (F) whisper

   (G) sound

   (H) piercing

   (J) shriek

9. DIZZINESS : VERTIGO :: fate :

   (A) adversity

   (B) order

   (C) destiny

   (D) pride

Directions: Fill in the blank with the two words that logically complete the sentence.

10. Unruly people may well become _____ if they are treated with _____ by those around them.

    (F) angry..kindness

    (G) calm..respect

    (H) peaceful..abuse

    (J) interested..medicine

Answer Explanations

1. **The correct answer is (C).** This poem has a very dark and sad mood, especially since the theme revolves around death and dying.

2. **The correct answer is (J).** The author states that the only reason that he does not want to die is for his love. His love, therefore, is the only factor that motivates the author.

3. **The correct answer is (C).** The author uses this language to say that the government limits his ability to express himself freely.

4. **The correct answer is (F).** The author is complaining about all the problems with life.

5. **The correct answer is (B).** The author uses this symbolic language to say that even the good in life has been tainted because good often is overpowered by and motivated by evil.

6. **The correct answer is (J).** It is common for the title of a poem to also be the poem's first line. Regardless of the fact that the first line is also the title, choice (J) best summarizes the rest of the poem.

7. **The correct answer is (D).** The relationship is that of the product to its source. Gasoline comes from petroleum; sugar comes from cane.

8. **The correct answer is (G).** The relationship is that of adjective to the noun it modifies. An odor may be described as pungent, though there are many other adjectives that may be also used. A sound may be described as shrill, though certainly not all sounds are shrill. *Shriek* is not the best answer because a shriek is always shrill.

9. **The correct answer is (C).** The relationship is one of synonyms. *Vertigo* is dizziness; *destiny* is fate.

10. **The correct answer is (G).** Now, here are your steps for finding the right answer:

- Read the sentence. This time there are two blanks, and the missing words need to have some logical connection.

- Think of your own words to fill in the blanks. You might guess that the unruly people will become "well-behaved" if they are treated with "consideration."

- Now look for your guesses in the answer choices. They're not there, but there are some possibilities.

- Go back to the sentence and look for clues. *"Become"* signals that the unruly people will change their behavior. How that behavior changes will depend on how they are treated.

- You can eliminate choice (F) because a negative behavior change (*angry*) doesn't logically follow a positive treatment (*kindness* and *love*). Likewise, you can eliminate choice (H), because *peaceful* behavior change is not likely to follow from *abuse*. Finally, you can eliminate choice (J) because *interested* and *medicine* have no logical connection.

- The only remaining choice is (G), which fits the sentence and so must be the correct answer.

CHAPTER 4

REVIEWING CRITICAL READING

In this section, you'll have a chance to work with critical reading questions. You'll also learn about the format of the questions and the best strategies for answering these questions quickly and accurately. And, you'll get a chance to practice what you've learned. Wow! Don't worry, we'll walk you through what you need to know.

An Up Close and Personal Look at Critical Reading

Critical reading questions test your ability to quickly read a given passage and understand its content. These questions don't test your ability to memorize details or become an expert in the topics discussed in the passages. And, you don't have to

be an expert in the areas of fiction, humanities, social studies, or science—the four subject areas from which the passages are mostly drawn.

Reading passages can be anywhere from a 250 word group of paragraphs to several pages long. Some may begin with a short introduction that gives you some idea of where the passages came from and often, when they were written. Each passage contains all of the information you need to answer the questions about it. Sometimes, you will see a pair of passages on subjects that relate to one another. These paired passages will be followed by a single set of questions that refer to each passage individually or to the two passages together.

> Reading passages can be anywhere from a 250 word group of paragraphs to several pages long. Each one begins with a short introduction that gives you some idea of where the passage came from and often when it was written.

Please note that the critical reading questions are not arranged in order of difficulty. The questions for each passage are usually arranged in the order in which the information is presented in the passage. In other words, the first questions deal with the early parts of the passage, and latter questions deal with the latter parts of the passage.

Question Format

Most critical reading passages and question sets start with directions that look like this:

> **Directions:** Each passage below is followed by a set of questions. Read each passage and then answer the accompanying questions, basing your answers on what is stated or implied in the passage and in any introductory material provided. Mark the letter of your choice on your answer sheet.

or

> **Directions:** The two passages given below deal with a related topic. Following the passages are questions about the content of each passage or about the relationship between the two passages. Answer the questions based upon what is stated or implied in the passages and in any introductory material provided. Mark the letter of your choice on your answer sheet.

The questions that follow each passage are in the standard multiple-choice format with four or five answer choices each. They are presented in the order in which information appears in the passage. Most often, these questions ask you to do one of the following:

- Identify the main idea or the author's purpose
- Define a word based on its meaning in the passage
- Choose a phrase that best restates an idea in the passage
- Draw inferences from ideas in the passage
- Draw conclusions based on information in the passage
- Identify the author's tone or mood
- Separate fact from opinion in a practical passage
- Identify implications of a practical passage

For some exams, you may get one or two open-ended questions for each passage. These questions will determine how well you can discuss in writing things that are implied in the passage. For these questions, you will need to read "between the lines." More on that later.

How to Ace Critical Reading Questions

As you read these passages, notice special things about the words or the information. For instance, keep an eye out for an unfamiliar word that is defined right there in the sentence; you'll probably encounter a question about it. Also, be alert for similes and metaphors, which often have questions about them, too. And, notice the line numbers along the left-hand side of the passage. Use them! They'll help you find answers more quickly.

To answer multiple-choice critical reading questions, follow these steps:

1. Read the introduction, if one is provided.

2. Read the passage.

3. Read the questions and their answer choices.

4. Go back to the passage to find answers.

5. For any question you're not sure of, eliminate obviously wrong answers and take your best guess.

Now, let's take a look at this process in more detail.

1. You don't want to blow past the introductory paragraph, because it can be very helpful to you. It might provide some important background information about the passage or it might "set the stage" so you know what you're reading about.

2. Now, read the passage pretty quickly. Try to pick up main ideas, but don't get bogged down in the factual trivia. Remember, you won't even be asked about most of the material in the passage you've read!

3. Read the questions with their answer choices, and answer every question you can. Remember, all the answers are somewhere in the passage, so go back and reread any sections that will help you!

4. Here's the process of elimination again. If you're still not sure of an answer, toss the ones that are obviously wrong and take your best guess from the choices that are left.

Note that the critical reading questions are not arranged in order of difficulty. The questions for each passage are arranged in the order in which the information is presented in the passage.

Remember: *Never* skip the introduction, tempting as that may be. The introduction is likely to contain some important information about both the passage and the types of questions that accompany it. The introduction will identify the type of passage being presented, the source or author of the passage, the era in which the passage was written, or the event that the passage describes. All of this information will help you focus your reading and find the correct answers to the questions. Now that you're familiar with how to approach critical reasoning passages and questions, let's try a few.

Sample Critical Reading Passage

The following is an excerpt from a short story, "Miss Tempy's Watchers," by Sarah Orne Jewett, a novelist and short story writer who lived from 1849–1909. In the story, two women watch over their deceased friend on the evening before her funeral and share their memories of her.

Line The time of year was April; the place was a small farming town in New Hampshire, remote from any railroad. One by one the lights had been blown out in the scattered houses near Miss Tempy Dent's, but as her neighbors took a last look out of doors, their eyes turned with instinc-
5 tive curiosity toward the old house where a lamp burned steadily. They gave a little sigh. "Poor Miss Tempy!" said more than one bereft acquaintance; for the good woman lay dead in her north chamber, and the lamp was a watcher's light. The funeral was set for the next day at one o'clock.

PT/HSPA, FCAT, MEAP HST, MCAS, GEE21, Regents Exams, SOL NCCT, AHSGE, GHSGT, BS
NCCT, AHSGE, GHSGT, BST, BSAP, WASL, CAHSEE, TAAS, OGT HST/HSPA, FCAT, MEAP
GT, HSPT/HSPA, FCAT, MEAP HST, MCAS, GEE21, Regents Exams, NCCT, AHSGE, GHS
GHSGT, BST, BSAP, WASL, CAHSEE, TAAS, OGT HST/HSPA, FCAT, MEAP HST, MCAS

CHAPTER
4

READING

10 The watchers were two of her oldest friends. Mrs. Crowe and Sarah
Ann Binson. They were sitting in the kitchen because it seemed less
awesome than the unused best room, and they beguiled the long hours
by steady conversation. One would think that neither topics nor opinions would hold out, at that rate, all through the long spring night, but
15 there was a certain degree of excitement just then, and the two women
had risen to an unusual level of expressiveness and confidence. Each
had already told the other more than one fact that she had determined
to keep secret; they were again and again tempted into statements that
either would have found impossible by daylight. Mrs. Crowe was knit-
20 ting a blue yarn stocking for her husband; the foot was already so long
that it seemed as if she must have forgotten to narrow it at the proper
time. Mrs. Crowe knew exactly what she was about, however; she was
of a much cooler disposition than Sister Binson, who made futile attempts at some sewing, only to drop her work into her lap whenever the
25 talk was most engaging.

Their faces were interesting—of the dry, shrewd, quick-witted New
England type, and thin hair twisted neatly back out of the way. Mrs.
Crowe could look vague and benignant, and Miss Binson was, to quote
her neighbors, a little too sharp-set, but the world knew that she had
30 need to be, with the load she must carry supporting an inefficient wid-
owed sister and six unpromising and unwilling nieces and nephews.

The eldest boy was at last placed with a good man to learn the mason's
trade. Sarah Ann Binson, for all her sharp, anxious aspect never de-
fended herself, when her sister whined and fretted. She was told every
35 week of her life that the poor children would never have had to lift a
finger if their father had lived, and yet she had kept her steadfast way
with the little farm, and patiently taught the young people many useful
things for which, as everybody said, they would live to thank her. However pleasureless her life appeared to outward view, it was brimful of
40 pleasure to herself.

Mrs. Crowe, on the contrary, was well-to-do, her husband being a rich
farmer and an easy-going man. She was a stingy woman, but for all of
that she looked kindly; and when she gave away anything, or lifted a

finger to help anybody, it was thought a great piece of beneficence, and
45 a compliment, indeed, which the recipient accepted with twice as much
gratitude as double the gift that came from a poorer and more generous
acquaintance. Everybody liked to be on good terms with Mrs. Crowe.
Socially, she stood much higher than Sarah Ann Binson.

1. The word "bereft" (line 6) means

   (A) without hope

   (B) greedy

   (C) anxious

   (D) sad

   (E) lonesome

The introduction and the rest of the sentence talk about the death of a well-liked person. Sadness would probably be the first thing you'd feel after someone died, so the best answer is choice (D).

2. The author implies that the two women have divulged secrets to each other because

   (A) they are lonely

   (B) it is nighttime

   (C) it is a sad occasion

   (D) they trust each other

   (E) it is the only time they talk to each other

We already know that folks are sad, but the author doesn't say anything about the women being trusting or lonely or only talking because of the situation. The author does makes a specific reference to the time of day. Reread that sentence and you'll see why the best answer is choice (B).

3. If Mrs. Crowe were confronted with an emergency in the future, you would expect her to
   (A) remain calm
   (B) ask Miss Binson for help
   (C) become distracted
   (D) panic
   (E) run away

The passage has clues to Mrs. Crowe's character, talking about her knowing "exactly what she was about" (line 22) and her "cooler disposition" (line 23). Now you can see that choice (A) is clearly the best answer.

4. The phrase "a little too sharp-set" (line 29) means
   (A) thin
   (B) stem and anxious-looking
   (C) strong-featured
   (D) angular
   (E) well-defined

The description of Miss Binson's everyday life with her nieces and nephews illustrates that she runs a tight ship and keeps them all in line. So, choice (B) is the best answer.

5. Sarah Ann Binson seems to be a woman who is
   (A) terribly unhappy
   (B) jealous of Mrs. Crowe
   (C) disloyal
   (D) quite wealthy
   (E) self-contented

To all outward appearances, Miss Binson seemed to have an especially hard life. However, the author ends that sentence saying that "it was brimful of pleasure to herself." Since Miss Binson was pretty happy with her life, choice (E) is the best answer.

Sample Paired Critical Reading Passages

Among the great loves in history are those of the composer Robert Schumann for his wife, Clara, and of Napoleon Bonaparte for his wife, Josephine. Their love is public knowledge due to the hundreds of love letters they left behind. The excerpts that follow are from letters. The first one is from Schumann to his then-fiancée, and the second is from Napoleon on the battlefield to his wife at home.

Passage 1—Robert Schumann to Clara Wieck (1838)

Line I have a hundred things to write to you, great and small, if only I could do it neatly, but my writing grows more and more indistinct, a sign, I fear, of heart weakness. There are terrible hours when your image forsakes me, when I wonder anxiously whether I have ordered my life as
5 wisely as I might, whether I had any right to bind you to me, my angel, or can really make you as happy as I should wish. These doubts all arise, I am inclined to think, from your father's attitude towards me. It is so easy to accept other people's estimate of oneself. Your father's behaviour makes me ask myself if I am really so bad—of such humble standing—
10 as to invite such treatment from anyone. Accustomed to easy victory over difficulties, to the smiles of fortune, and to affection, I have been spoiled by having things made too easy for me, and now I have to face refusal, insult, and calumny. I have read of many such things in novels, but I thought too highly of myself to imagine I could ever be the hero
15 of a family tragedy of the Kotzebue sort myself. If I had ever done your father an injury, he might well hate me; but I cannot see why he should despise me and, as you say, hate me without any reason. But my turn will come, and I will then show him how I love you and himself; for I will tell you, as a secret, that I really love and respect your father for his
20 many great and fine qualities, as no one but yourself can do. I have a natural inborn devotion and reverence for him, as for all strong characters, and it makes his antipathy for me doubly painful. Well, he may some time declare peace, and say to us, "Take each other, then." You cannot think how your letter has raised and strengthened me ... You are
25 splendid, and I have much more reason to be proud of you than of me. I have made up my mind, though, to read all your wishes in your face. Then you will think, even though you don't say it, that your Robert is a really good sort, that he is entirely yours, and loves you more than words can say. You shall indeed have cause to think so in the happy future. I

30   still see you as you looked in your little cap that last evening. I still hear you call me *du*. Clara, I heard nothing of what you said but that *du*. Don't you remember?

Passage 2—Napoleon Bonaparte to Josephine Bonaparte (1796)

Line   I have not spent a day without loving you; I have not spent a night without embracing you; I have not so much as drunk a single cup of tea without cursing the pride and ambition which force me to remain separated from the moving spirit of my life. In the midst of my duties,
5   whether I am at the head of my army or inspecting the camps, my beloved Josephine stands alone in my heart, occupies my mind, fills my thoughts. If I am moving away from you with the speed of the Rhóne torrent, it is only that I may see you again more quickly. If I rise to work in the middle of the night, it is because this may hasten by a matter of
10   days the arrival of my sweet love. Yet in your letter of the 23rd and 26th Ventóse, you call me vows. Vous yourself! Ah! wretch, how could you have written this letter? How cold it is! And then there are those four days between the 23rd and the 26th; what were you doing that you failed to write to your husband? ... Ah, my love, that vous, those four
15   days make me long for my former indifference. Woe to the person responsible! May he, as punishment and penalty, experience what my convictions and the evidence (which is in your friend's favour) would make me experience! Hell has no torments great enough! Vous! Vous! Ah! How will things stand in two weeks? ... My spirit is heavy; my heart
20   is fettered and I am terrified by my fantasies... You love me less; but you will get over the loss. One day you will love me no longer; at least tell me; then I shall know how I have come to deserve this misfortune...

1. In Passage 1, the word "calumny" (line 13) means

   (A)   remorse

   (B)   chance

   (C)   victory

   (D)   kindness

   (E)   slander

Here's a prime example of context to the rescue. Take a look at the sentence, and then test each choice in place of calumny. Basically, Schumann is talking about the hard time he is having with Clara's father, so you would not choose a positive word; eliminate choices (C) and (D). Out goes choice (B), because it makes no sense in the sentence. Choice (A) technically makes sense, but it is not a roadblock to success like insults and refusals are. Therefore, the remaining answer is the best one—choice (E).

2. To what does Napoleon refer in Passage 2 when he writes of "the moving spirit of my life" (line 4)?

   (A) France

   (B) ambition

   (C) the army

   (D) his wife

   (E) the Rhóne River

Now, you have to do some interpretation using the information in the passage. To do this, you must know the author's intent. After you find the phrase, read the sentences around it. They all deal with Napoleon's love for Josephine. Since he curses his pride and ambition, choice (B) is out. He is with his army in France, so you can toss out choices (A) and (C). Choice (E) doesn't make sense, so the only choice is (D), his beloved wife.

3. How do the authors feel about being separated from their lovers?

   (A) Separation raises doubts and fears.

   (B) Separation is due to parental disapproval.

   (C) Separations never last long.

   (D) Separations improve a relationship.

   (E) Separations between lovers are inevitable.

This is where the comparison comes into play. The question asks about both authors, so you have to think about both passages and find the similarities. Let's start eliminating choices. The first to go are choices (D) and (E), since neither author mentions these at all. Choice (C) goes out because the authors don't tell us anything about the length of their separations. We know that while Robert Schumann has a big problem with Clara's dad, Napoleon doesn't seem to have a parental problem; so choice (B) is gone. Why is choice (A) the best answer? Take a look

PT/HSPA, FCAT, MEAP HST, MCAS, GEE21, Regents Exams, SOL, NCCT, AHSGE, GHSGT, BS
NCCT, AHSGE, GHSGT, BST, BSAP, WASL, CAHSEE, TAAS, OGT HST/HSPA, FCAT, MEAP
OGT, HSPT/HSPA, FCAT, MEAP HST, MCAS, GEE21, Regents Exams NCCT, AHSGE, GHS
GHSGT, BST, BSAP, WASL, CAHSEE, TAAS, OGT, HSPT/HSPA, FCAT, MEAP HST, MCAS

CHAPTER
4

back at both passages. Schumann mentions his doubts, and Napoleon tells Josephine that he is "terrified." Choice (A) is the only answer that fits both authors' thoughts.

4. Why do the writers refer to the words *du* and *vous*?

(A) To remind their readers of their rank

(B) To refer to their lovers' intimacy or formality

(C) To ask their lovers to be faithful

(D) To demonstrate their knowledge of languages

(E) To address their unborn children

This is the kind of question that can send you into a panic. Calm down—you don't really have to know what the two words mean, you just have to figure out why the authors use them. Reread the sentences in which the authors mention these special words. Are both authors happy about hearing the words? Are they both upset? Do they feel differently about hearing their sweethearts use these words? Aha! That's the key; Schumann is pleased that Clara used the word *du* (which is an informal word in German), but Napoleon is insulted and worried because Josephine used *vous* (a formal French word). Only choice (B) indicates that the authors might feel differently; the other choices aren't supported at all by a rereading of the information.

CRITICAL READING USING PRACTICAL TEXT

Reading is an essential part of everyday life. Some reading exams include passages you encounter practically every day. These passages are usually directions, forms, applications, schedules, rules and other documents that you use to get information and to get things done. You should handle these just as you would any other critical reading passage. Here's a sample of a label from an over-the-counter pain reliever.

The questions below refer to the following label.

IBUPROFEN TABLETS
24 COATED 100 mg each

For the temporary relief of headache, muscular aches, toothache, minor aches and pains associated with the common cold, and for reduction of fever.

Adults: Take 1 tablet every 4 to 6 hours while symptoms persist. If pain or fever does not respond to 1 tablet, 2 tablets may be used, but not exceed 6 tablets in 24 hours, unless directed by a doctor. The smallest effective dose should be used. Take with food or milk if occasional and mild heartburn or stomach pain occurs.

Children: Do not give this product to children under 12 except under the advice and supervision of a doctor.

WARNINGS: Allergy Alert: ibuprofen may cause a severe allergic reaction which may include:

- hives
- facial swelling
- asthma (wheezing)
- shock

STOP USE AND ASK A DOCTOR if an allergic reaction occurs. Seek medical help right away.

1. The maximum dosage for adults in any 24-hour period of time is
   (A) 2 tablets
   (B) 4 tablets
   (C) 6 tablets
   (D) 12 tablets
   (E) 24 tablets

This may look like a math question, but it really isn't. Although the label gives you information about how many tablets an adult take a one time, it clearly states that no more than 6 tablets should be taken within 24 hours. The correct answer is obviously choice (C).

2. A 10-year-old child could be given ibuprofen if she
   (A) has a severe cold
   (B) has no allergies
   (C) takes it with milk
   (D) is under a doctor's care
   (E) weighs as much as an adult

Although you may think that the dosage of ibuprofen has more to do with the body's weight than age, any information you need to answer the question is in the passage. According to the label, no one under twelve should take the ibuprofen unless the doctor says it's ok. The correct answer has to be (D).

Learn the Most Important Critical Reading Tips

Critical reading questions can eat up a lot of your time. But you can use some specific strategies and techniques to move through this portion of the test efficiently. Check out these tips for smarter solutions to help you with solving critical reading questions quickly and accurately.

DO THE CRITICAL READING QUESTIONS LAST

In addition to the critical reading questions, your test may also contain analogies and sentence completions. Because the critical reasoning questions require the most time to complete, you should, if directions permit, save these questions for last. You've already learned time-saving tips for the analogies and sentence completions (in Chapter 3), so do those questions first. That way, you'll save extra time for critical reading.

FINISH UP WITH ONE PASSAGE BEFORE MOVING ON TO THE NEXT

There won't be time to go back to the passages at the end of this section, so you'll want to answer every question that you can about each passage before moving on. Guess if you have to, but finish all the questions that you can before you move on to the next passage.

> If you skip a question and try to come back to it later, you might have to reread the whole passage to find the answer—and you'll be out of time.

ORDER IN THE COURT!

The questions are like a map to the passage; in other words, the order of the questions follows the order of the information in the passage. The first questions refer to the early part of the passage, and later questions refer to later parts of the passage. If there are two passages, the first questions are for Passage 1, the next are for Passage 2, and the end questions refer to both. This helps you locate the information quickly.

Do Paired Readings One Passage at a Time

Since the questions are arranged like a map, take advantage! Read Passage 1 then answer the questions that relate to Passage 1. Then read Passage 2 and answer the questions that relate to Passage 2. Finally, answer the comparative questions. In this way, you won't have to read too much at once and you won't confuse the message of Passage 1 with that of Passage 2.

Don't Be Afraid of Strangers

The passages are supposed to be unfamiliar to you. In their attempt to be fair, the test makers sometimes purposely choose passages from the darkest recesses of the library. This helps make sure that no test taker has ever seen them before. Remember, you're not being tested on your knowledge of the topic, but on how well you:

- Figure out the meaning of an unfamiliar word from its context
- Determine what an author means by noting certain words and phrases
- Understand the author's assumptions, point of view, and main idea
- Analyze the logical structure of a piece of writing

Remember, If You Need To Know It, It's Right in Front of You

The introductory paragraph and the passage have all the information you'll need to answer the questions. Even if the passage is about the price of beans in Bulgaria or the genetic makeup of a wombat, don't worry. The answers you need are all right there on the page.

Start with the Interesting Stuff

The passages that interest you are easier to work on. If there's a choice, it's best to start with the passage that's more interesting to you, whether it's fiction, a science article, or whatever. If the style appeals to you, you will probably work through the passage more quickly and find the questions easier to deal with.

A Word of Caution

Don't choose answers that only work for one of a pair of passages. When you're working with paired passages, some questions ask you to identify a common idea. When that happens, you can immediately reject any answer choice that only applies to one of the passages.

Highlight the Highlights

It pays to be an active reader. When you read, use your pencil actively to highlight important names, dates, and facts. Though you aren't required to memorize specific details, the questions are likely to reference the more important information in the passage. If you've highlighted those pieces of information, you'll be able to find them easily when you need them to answer the questions.

Don't Get Bogged Down in the Details

Remember, you don't have to understand every bit of information. You just have to find the information you need to answer the questions. Don't waste your time trying to analyze or memorize technical details or information that the questions don't ask for.

Don't Confuse a "True" Answer with a "Correct" Answer

The fact that an answer choice is true doesn't mean it's right. What does that mean? It means that a certain answer choice may be perfectly true—in fact all of the answer choices may be true. But the right answer must be the correct answer to the question that's being asked. Only one of the answer choices will be correct and, therefore, the right choice. Read carefully—and don't be fooled!

STRATEGIES FOR ANSWERING SPECIFIC QUESTION TYPES

As you learned earlier in this chapter, critical reading questions ask you to do one of these things:

- ☑ Identify the main idea or the author's purpose
- ☑ Define a word based on its meaning in the passage
- ☑ Choose a phrase that best restates an idea in the passage
- ☑ Draw inferences from ideas in the passage
- ☑ Draw conclusions based on information in the passage
- ☑ Separate facts from opinions in a practical passage
- ☑ Identify implications of a practical passage
- ☑ Identify the author's tone or mood

We will now present real strategies for dealing with the specific categories of critical reading questions. Before you move to the strategies, however, read the introductory paragraph and the two passages below; the tips and questions that follow relate to these passages.

John Dewey, an American educator and philosopher of education, was a prolific writer on the subject. He was particularly interested in the place of education in a democratic republic.

Line The place of public education within a democratic society has been
widely discussed and debated through the years. Perhaps no one has
written more widely on the subject in the United States than John Dewey,
sometimes called "the father of public education," whose theories of
5 education have a large social component, that is, an emphasis on education as a social act and the classroom or learning environment as a rep-
lica of society. Dewey defined various aspects or characteristics of education.

First, it was a necessity of life inasmuch as living beings needed to main-
10 tain themselves through a process of renewal. Therefore, just as humans
needed sleep, food, water, and shelter for physiological renewal, they

also needed education to renew their minds, assuring that their socialization kept pace with physiological growth.

A second aspect of education was its social component, which was to be
15 accomplished by providing the young with an environment that would provide a nurturing atmosphere to encourage the growth of their as yet undeveloped social customs.

A third aspect of public education was the provision of direction to youngsters, who might otherwise be left in uncontrolled situations with-
20 out the steadying and organizing influences of school. Direction was not to be of an overt nature, but rather indirect through the selection of the school situations in which the youngster participated. Finally, Dewey saw public education as a catalyst for growth. Since the young came to school capable of growth, it was the role of education to provide oppor-
25 tunities for that growth to occur. The successful school environment is one in which a desire for continued growth is created—a desire that extends throughout one's life beyond the end of formal education. In Dewey's model, the role of education in a democratic society is not seen as a preparation for some later stage in life such as adulthood. Rather,
30 education is seen as a process of growth that never ends, with human beings continuously expanding their capacity for growth. Neither did Dewey's model see education as a means by which the past was recapitulated. Instead, education was a continuous reconstruction of experiences, grounded very much in the present environment.

35 Since Dewey's model places a heavy emphasis on the social component, the nature of the larger society that supports the educational system is of paramount importance. The ideal larger society, according to Dewey, is one in which the interests of a group are all shared by all of its members and in which interactions with other groups are free and full. Ac-
40 cording to Dewey, education in such a society should provide members of the group a stake or interest in social relationships and the ability to negotiate change without compromising the order and stability of the society.

Remember: The Answer to a Main Idea Question Is Neither Too General Nor Too Specific

While we've talked about main idea questions earlier, it can't hurt to mention them again. For a question about the main idea or the author's purpose, look for an answer choice that states it. Don't be too general or too specific.

1. The main idea of this passage can best be stated as which of the following?

   (A) The role of education is extremely complex.

   (B) Dewey's notion of education contains a significant social component.

   (C) Dewey's model of education is not relevant today.

   (D) Direction provided in education must not be overt.

   (E) Public education should be a catalyst for growth.

Choices (A) and (C) are very general; you'd be hard-pressed to find any supporting information in the passage for those main ideas. Choices (D) and (E) seem as if they were single sentences plucked right out of the passage; too specific! Choice (B)—the correct answer—gives an overall statement, and you could find supporting details for it as a main idea.

Check Introductory and Concluding Paragraphs for the Main Idea

We've mentioned this before, too. Hopefully that will convince you that *it's important* to look in the first or last (or both) paragraphs of the passage for answers to main idea/author's purpose questions. Choice (B) above is stated in the last sentence of the first paragraph and restated in the last paragraph. Remember to mark stuff like this as you read. Though the main idea may occur elsewhere in the passage, most often you'll find it in the first or last paragraph.

Plug in Choices To Solve Vocabulary-in-Context Questions

For vocabulary-in-context questions, plug the choices into the original sentence and don't be fooled by the obvious synonym.

2. The word "nurturing" (line 16) means

   (A) nourishing

   (B) educational

   (C) critical

   (D) supportive

   (E) motivational

The correct answer is (E). Take a look at the sentence in the passage (line 16), " ... nurturing atmosphere to encourage the growth..." and then try each of the answer choices. You might be tempted to just pick choice (A), "nourishing," but choice (D), "motivational," makes sense and supports the idea of the sentence.

> **Remember:** Don't expect the answer to a vocabulary-in-context question to rely upon the most common meaning of a word. More often, you can count on the question revolving around an unusual or uncommon usage of the word.

FIND THE RIGHT RESTATEMENT ... BY FIRST RESTATING AN AUTHOR'S PHRASE IN YOUR OWN WORDS

3. The phrase "a continuous reconstruction of experiences" (lines 33–34) used in reference to education means that education is

   (A) based in life experiences

   (B) a neverending process

   (C) a meaning-based endeavor

   (D) an individual pursuit

   (E) something unattainable

Not to put words into your mouth, but if you had stated this phrase in your own words you might have used "ongoing" as a substitute for "continuous". If you take it one more step, you come to choice (B), "a neverending process."

READ BETWEEN THE LINES TO DRAW INFERENCES AND MAKE CONCLUSIONS

When a critical reading question asks for something the author has suggested, implied, or not stated directly, you have to use the information in the passage and draw your own conclusions.

4. While not directly stated, the passage suggests that
   (A) true education fosters the desire for lifelong learning
   (B) a truly educated person has an understanding of physics
   (C) Dewey was a radical philosopher
   (D) education must cease at some point
   (E) Dewey's model has been embraced by all

> Read between the lines to see if the author has given any hints that would lead you to the correct answer.

In this question, the correct answer is (A), because the author's stated positions logically lead to this statement. Choice (B) is a pretty far-fetched conclusion to make, and choices (C), (D), and (E) are not logical extensions of the information in the passage.

LOOK FOR DESCRIPTIVE WORDS TO CLUE YOU IN TO THE TONE OR MOOD

5. The tone of this passage can best be described as
   (A) humorous
   (B) serious
   (C) dramatic
   (D) informal
   (E) frivolous

This passage probably did not make you even chuckle, so choice (A) can be eliminated right off the bat. The topic is not frivolous, and the language was quite formal, so you can drop choices (E) and (D). There were no episodes or scenes that could be considered dramatic, choice (C), so the best answer is, of course, choice (B). Take a minute to go back and scan the passage, look at the kind of language you find, and see how it sets the tone.

The Short Answer Is . . .

While multiple choice questions form the bulk of most of the high stakes exit exams, they are not the only types of question that are used. Many states use what are known as short constructed responses, or open-ended questions. They differ from the kind we've been discussing in that your choice of answer is not restricted to four or five choices. It is, in fact, unlimited. It therefore becomes up to you to figure out what response is being looked for. Check out the following passage:

Line   A vast stretch of land lies untouched by civilization in the back country of the eastern portion of the African continent. With the occasional exception of a big-game hunter, foreigners never penetrate this area. Aside from the Wandorobo tribe, even the neighbors shun its confines

5   because it harbors the deadly tsetse fly. The Wandorobo nomads depend on the forests for their lives, eating its roots and fruits and making their homes wherever they find themselves at the end of the day.

  One of the staples of their primitive diet, and their only sweet, is honey. They obtain it through an ancient and symbiotic relationship with a

10   bird known as the Indicator. The scientific community finally confirmed the report, at first discredited, that this bird purposefully led the natives to trees containing the honeycombs of wild bees. Other species of honey guides are also known to take advantage of the foraging efforts of some animals in much the same way that the Indicator uses men.

15   This amazing bird settles in a tree near a Wandorobo encampment and chatters incessantly until the men answer with whistles. It then begins its leading flight.

Chattering, it hops from tree to tree, while the men continue their musical answering call. When the bird reaches the tree, its chatter becomes shriller
20 and its followers examine the tree carefully. The Indicator usually perches just over the honeycomb, and the men hear the humming of the bees in the hollow trunk. Using torches, they smoke most of the bees out of the tree, but those that escape the nullifying effects of the smoke sting the men viciously. Undaunted, the Wandorobos free the nest, gather the honey, and
25 leave a small offering for their bird guide.

1. What is the meaning of the word symbiotic?

2. According to the passage, where is the Wandorobos permanent home?

3. Why don't the Wandorobos fear the tsetse fly?

4. What would be a good title for the passage?

FIGURING OUT THE OPEN-ENDED ANSWERS

1. Determining the meaning of words in context is common to multiple-choice and open-ended questions. The main difference is that this time you have to go figure it out without a menu of answers to choose from. Go back to line 9 of the passage, where the word *symbiotic* is used. That symbiotic relationship is what the rest of the passage explains—the relationship between the bird and the natives. It is a relationship that both benefit from. The bird leads the men to honey; the men gather the honey and leave some for the bird. Isn't that sort of like a partnership? Well, then that is the meaning: Symbiotic means partnership, or mutually beneficial relationship.

Fun, eh?

2. Look at lines 5 through 7. Even if you don't know what the word nomads means, it tells you that the Wandorobos make their homes wherever they find themselves at the end of the day. They are wanderers, and have no permanent home. Once again, it's all in the passage; you just have to find it.

3. The passage tells us nothing about the relationship between the Wandorobo and the tsetse fly—only that they live in the same area. The Wandorobo may be deathly afraid of the tsetse fly, have no knowledge of the tsetse fly, or be immune to the insect's bite. Maybe they taste bad, so the tsetse fly is afraid to bite them. The bottom line is that there is not enough information to answer this question, and so, "Not Enough Information" is the answer.

4. This is the most interesting, and challenging question of the four. A good title should tell what the passage is about. What is it about? The Wandorobo? East Africa? The tsetse fly? Finding honey? Well it's about all of these things and none of them. The main idea of the story is that this African tribe, the Wandorobo, and this Indicator Bird work together to get honey. That means that that idea should be conveyed by the title. "A Bird and a People Working Together", or "A Partnership Between a People and a Bird," or, capriciously, "A Honey of a Partnership."

On second thought, you'd better not use that last title. Test prep people have no sense of humor!

Now, try an open-ended question based on the passage about John Dewey that began on page 72.

After you reread the passage, try this open-response question.

6. Provide a concluding paragraph to the following passage.

We've already discussed that the concluding paragraph may provide you with the main idea of the passage. Here's your chance to restate and elaborate on the main idea. A good concluding paragraph could be:

" Therefore, Dewey's basic concept of education in a democratic society is based on the idea that education has a large social component that is designed to provide direction and to make sure that children develop through their participation in the group to which they belong."

SEPARATING FACT FROM OPINION AND IDENTIFYING IMPLICATIONS

When you read practical or informational text, you should always read critically to separate the author's opinion from facts. In most cases, information text contains a combination of facts and opinion. A fact is something that can be proved beyond the point of reasonable argument. For example, "Bill Clinton was elected President of the United States in 1992" is a fact that you can prove. On the other hand, "Bill Clinton was a great president" is an opinion. Ask yourself if there are words or phrases that might suggest the author is relaying an opinion. *For example:*

☑ *I believe...*

☑ *It's obvious...*

☑ *They should...*

Can what the author writes be proved or be demonstrated to be true?

On your exam, you'll more than likely encounter an advertisement or a brochure with a question about distinguishing fact from opinion. Here's an excerpt from a washing machine warranty.

DRUCKER'S APPLIANCES

All warranty service is provided by our Factory Service Centers or an authorized Customer Care technician. For service and/or repairs, call 1-800-555-1234.

We know that you will be satisfied with your purchase. If necessary, we will replace within one year:

Any part of the washer which fails due to defect in materials or workmanship. During this full one-year warranty, we will also provide, free of charge, all labor and in-home service to replace the defective part.

We will replace within two years:

Any part of the washer which fails due to a defect in materials or workmanship. During this additional one-year limited warranty, you will be responsible for any labor or in-home service costs.

All warranty periods are calculated from the date of the original purchase of the washing machine.

This warranty is extended to the original purchaser and any succeeding owner for products purchased for home use within the USA. In Alaska, the warranty excludes the cost of shipping or service calls to your home.

1. Which is an opinion?

   (A) We will provide, free of charge, all labor and in-home service to replace the defective part.

   (B) For service, call 1-800-555-1234.

   (C) This warranty is extended to the original purchaser.

   (D) We know that you will be satisfied with your purchase.

   (E) In Alaska, the warranty excludes the cost of shipping or service calls to your home.

Your first clue to the answer should be the words, "We know." The manufacturer hopes that you'll be satisfied with your purchase, but can't possibly "know" that you'll be satisfied. Isn't that why the repair telephone number is included? The correct answer is (D). Choices (A), (B), (C), and (E) are stated facts.

2. Your neighbor sold her house and moved away, and you bought her washing machine that she had purchased three years earlier from Drucker's Appliances. Something goes wrong with the machine. Under the terms of this warranty, you

   (A) would have to pay for any repairs to the machine.

   (B) would not have to pay for the parts to repair the transmission.

   (C) would not have to pay for parts or labor to replace the washer basket.

   (D) could only claim the warranty rights if you live in Alaska.

   (E) can sue your neighbor for selling you a defective machine.

The machine is more than two years old now. According to the warranty, it's too late for you to get it repaired without costs. The correct answer is choice (A). It makes no difference where you live.

Summary: What You Need to Know About Critical Reading

☑ All of the information you need is right in the passage.

☑ Read the introduction, if one is provided.

☑ Read the passage without getting bogged down in details.

☑ Read the questions and their answer choices. Go back into the passage to find answers.

☑ Critical reading questions usually follow the order of information in the passage. Unlike other verbal questions, they are not usually arranged in order of difficulty.

☑ Answer every question for a passage before starting the next passage.

☑ For any question you're not sure of, eliminate obviously wrong answers and take your best guess.

☑ For short constructed-responses, or open-ended, questions craft your responses carefully. This is another opportunity to demonstrate what you know.

T/HSPA, FCAT, MEAP HST, MCAS, GEE21, Regents Exams, SOL, NCCT, AHSGE, GHSGT, BST
NCCT, AHSGE, GHSGT, BST, BSAP, WASL, CAHSEE, TAAS, OGT HSPT/HSPA, FCAT, MEAP
GT, HSPT/HSPA, FCAT, MEAP HST, MCAS, GEE21, Regents Exams NCCT, AHSGE, GHS
GHSGT, BST, BSAP, WASL, CAHSEE, TAAS, OGT HSPT/HSPA, FCAT, MEAP HST, MCAS

CHAPTER
4

Pop Quiz

Directions: Items 1–6 are based on the following passage.

Line   The traveling art exhibition "Italian Renaissance Masters" recently made a stop at the local university and gave local art enthusiasts an opportunity to witness some of the masterpieces of the Italian Renaissance without having to travel abroad. While many of the works of art took my

5   breath away, the one work that stood out was the "David" by Michelangelo. The polished marble hero stood glistening in the lights of the museum hall as passersby stopped in awe. The colossal athletic figure spoke to all who stared in amazement. The gentle slopes and curves of his body, the incredible detail on his hands and feet and the

10   perfectly proportioned torso told a story of a craftsman who toiled for countless hours in search of perfection. The master had created a work of art that looked like it might step down from the pedestal at any moment. The figure looked like a Roman god. Every detail had been artfully considered. The hero's hair, cloak and facial features all looked

15   lightly delicate though they were made of solid marble. As I examined every detail of the masterpiece, I couldn't help but think that a higher being must have created this perfect figure. I enjoyed all of the art and highly recommend the exhibit to everyone. However, I must suggest that you save the "David" for last as all other works of art simply pale in

20   comparison.

1. Which of the following lines from the passage exemplifies the use of personification?

  (A) "...the works of art took my breath away..."

  (B) "The colossal athletic figure spoke to all..."

  (C) "...other works of art simply pale in comparison..."

  (D) "The polished marble hero stood glistening..."

2. The passage is most likely which of the following?

  (F) an excerpt from a play

  (G) a commentary

  (H) an inter-office memo

  (J) a persuasive essay

REVIEWING CRITICAL READING

3. The figure referred to in the passage is most likely which of the following?

   (A) a figure in a painting

   (B) a model

   (C) a character in a movie

   (D) a sculpture

4. In line 13, "The figure looked like a Roman god" is an example of which of the following?

   (F) alliteration

   (G) simile

   (H) metaphor

   (J) personification

5. The overall mood or tone of the passage could best be described as which of the following?

   (A) apprehensive

   (B) reserved and stoic

   (C) negative and condescending

   (D) positive and laudatory

6. Which of the following best describes the author's feelings about what he saw at the exhibition?

   (F) The author was amazed at what he saw.

   (G) The author liked what he saw but was not too impressed.

   (H) The author would not recommend the exhibit to anyone else.

   (J) The author did not like any one thing more than another at the exhibit.

Directions: Questions 7–10 are based on the following passage, an excerpt from *Journey to the Interior of the Earth* by Jules Verne.

Line On the 24th of May, 1863, my uncle, Professor Liedenbrock, rushed into his little house, No. 19 Konigstrasse, one of the oldest streets in the oldest portion of the city of Hamburg.

Martha must have concluded that she was very much behindhand, for
5 the dinner had only just been put into the oven.
"Well, now," said I to myself, "if that most impatient of men is hungry, what a disturbance he will make!"

"M. Liedenbrock so soon!" cried poor Martha in great alarm, half opening the dining-room door.

10 "Yes, Martha; but very likely the dinner is not half cooked, for it is not two yet. Saint Michael's clock has only just struck half-past one."

"Then why has the master come home so soon?"

"Perhaps he will tell us that himself."

"Here he is, Monsieur Axel; I will run and hide myself while you argue
15 with him."

And Martha retreated in safety into her own dominions.

I was left alone. But how was it possible for a man of my undecided turn of mind to argue successfully with so irascible a person as the Professor? With this persuasion I was hurrying away to my own little re-
20 treat upstairs, when the street door creaked upon its hinges; heavy feet made the whole flight of stairs to shake; and the master of the house, passing rapidly through the dining-room, threw himself in haste into his own sanctum.

25 But on his rapid way he had found time to fling his hazel stick into a corner, his rough broadbrim upon the table, and these few emphatic words at his nephew: "Axel, follow me!"

I had scarcely had time to move when the Professor was again shouting after me: "What! not come yet?" And I rushed into my redoubtable master's study.

30 Otto Liedenbrock had no mischief in him, I willingly allow that; but unless he very considerably changes as he grows older, at the end he will be a most original character.

He was professor at the Johannaeum, and was delivering a series of lectures on mineralogy, in the course of every one of which he broke
35 into a passion once or twice at least. Not at all that he was over-anxious about the improvement of his class, or about the degree of attention with which they listened to him, or the success which might eventually crown his labours. Such little matters of detail never troubled him much. His teaching was as the German philosophy calls it, 'subjective'; it was
40 to benefit himself, not others. He was a learned egotist. He was a well of science, and the pulleys worked uneasily when you wanted to draw anything out of it. In a word, he was a learned miser.

7. Which of the following is the setting of this passage?
   (A) Twentieth-century Germany
   (B) Nineteenth-century Germany
   (C) Eighteenth-century Germany
   (D) At the center of the earth in the nineteenth century

8. In lines 4–5, "Martha must have concluded that she was very much behindhand, for the dinner had only just been put into the oven," which of the following is the best meaning for *behindhand*?
   (F) without a hand
   (G) in need of a hand

(H) running behind schedule

(J) hurting in her hands

9. Which of the following is the best interpretation of line 16 "And Martha retreated in safety into her own dominions?"

(A) Martha locked herself in her room

(B) Martha ran away

(C) Martha moved to another country

(D) Martha went back into the kitchen where she was most comfortable

10. Which of the following best describes the professor?

(F) high strung and demanding

(G) laid back and relaxed

(H) dimwitted and confused

(J) harsh and bitter

Answer Explanations

1. **The correct answer is (B).** By saying that the figure, a sculpture, spoke to all, the author is using a literary technique called personification. In other words, the author gave human qualities to an inanimate object.

2. **The correct answer is (G).** The passage is a commentary or critique of an art exhibition and of a specific work of art in the exhibition.

3. **The correct answer is (D).** The figure described by the author is a very famous sculpture by the Renaissance artist Michelangelo called "David."

4. **The correct answer is (G).** By saying the figure "looked like" a Roman god, the author is using a literary tool called a simile. A simile makes a comparison using *like* or *as*.

5. **The correct answer is (D).** The author uses language that gives much praise throughout the passage.

6. **The correct answer is (F).** The author expresses his wonder and amazement, especially about the statue, "David."

7. **The correct answer is (B).** The setting is Germany, 1863. You can deduce this from the date, the German names, the mention of Hamburg and the mention of German philosophy.

8. **The correct answer is (H).** Martha was running behind schedule because she had just put dinner in the oven but the professor was ready to eat.

9. **The correct answer is (D).** Martha went back into the kitchen, her dominion, where she was in control and felt the most comfortable.

10. **The correct answer is (F).** The professor is portrayed as very high strung and very demanding of the people around him.

CHAPTER 5

SUCCESS STRATEGY—FIXING COMMON ERRORS

Skim to My Lou

Does "skim to my Lou" sound like the refrain of a song from elementary school? It is, sort of. The actual phrase is "*skip* to my Lou," but we're talking about skimming. As in most other parts of this test, you'll be given a passage to read. *Skim the passage before reading.* Just a few seconds of skimming will help you better focus your reading. After you've skimmed, read the entire passage. Now, let's get down to it.

... Ah, That Is the Question!

You've read the selection, so you turn your attention to the first question, which refers you to an underlined section (granted, not every question in your English or reading exit-level test uses underlined phrases, but we'll talk about strategies for the other question types later in this chapter). Before attempting to answer the question, be sure to read the *whole sentence* for that question, *not* just the words that are underlined. This can be tricky, because while the mistake itself (if there is one) will be in the underlined section, the reason *why* it's a mistake often lies elsewhere in the sentence. If a pronoun is wrong, you need to know the word to which it refers. If a verb's number is wrong, you need to know the number of the subject. If a verb's tense is wrong, you need to know the tense of the rest of the sentence. Get the picture? By the way, about a quarter of the passages you encounter will have *no error*, so don't go out of your way to find one. That's why the choice "NO CHANGE" or something similar is given with many questions.

THIS DESERVES A HEARING

While you read the whole sentence, *listen for the mistake*. Most of us make fewer grammar mistakes when we speak everyday English than when we stop and make conscious decisions about each word to use. Do you know why? Because, we learn to talk before we learn to write, so speech is our primary form of communication. Throughout the day—in class, on radio, and on TV—we hear standard English.

> In some way, we know most of the rules of grammar even if we cannot explain them.

On your test, you don't have to explain a mistake. You merely have to "hear" when a mistake is being made, which is relatively easy, because it will be in the underlined part. Then, from the available choices, you have to "hear" the best alternative. That's another reason why reading the whole sentence is necessary. You need to be able to put the mistake within the context of the entire sentence, so that you can both hear if the underlined section sounds "funny" or "weird" and can find the right replacement. Listening can reveal a wide range of problems, from those involving subject-verb agreement to those that contain incorrect usage of idioms (expressions that are always said a certain way "just because" they are). Hearing or listening for mistakes does not mean you have to read the sentence aloud. Doing so would be guaranteed to get you ejected from the examination room! Read the sentence so that you hear it inside your head. That should be enough to allow you to listen for the mistake. Use this technique with all the grammar-type questions in this book, so that you'll have the technique fully developed by actual test time.

Correct It First

When you find a mistake, *correct the mistake on your own first.* After you've "heard" the mistake, even if you can't explain what it is, try to correct it in your head before looking at the answer choices. Only after you have "your" correction in mind, look over the answers.

Why correct the mistake first when the correction is there to be found? There are two reasons. (1) If your exact correction is among the choices, your answer is probably right. (2) On the other hand, if two of the remaining choices are very close to the wording of your correction, you can at least eliminate those choices that did not appear to correct the mistake. So, either way, you save time. It might be nice to save money too, but hey, for the purpose of doing well on the test, time is money. Now, where have you heard that before?

So Much in Common

Look for common mistakes. Although there are many possible grammatical mistakes, the ones most commonly made fall into just a few categories. If you can't "hear" the mistake in the underlined section, look instead to see if it contains one of the following common types of errors:

- Sentence fragments
- Mistakes in subject-verb agreement
- Problems with verb tense or verb form
- Incorrect referents
- Dangling or misplaced modifiers
- Lack of parallel construction
- Incorrect usage of idioms

PT/HSPA, FCAT, MEAP HST, MCAS, GEE21, Regents Exams, SOL, RITE, AHSGE, GHSGT, BS
NCCT, AHSGE, GHSGT, BST, BSAP, WASL, CAHSEE, TAAS, OGT, HSPA, FCAT, MEAP
GT, HSPT/HSPA, FCAT, MEAP HST, MCAS, GEE21, Regents Exams NCCT, AHSGE, GHS
T, GHSGT, BST, BSAP, WASL, CAHSEE, TAAS, OGT, HSPT/HSPA, FCAT, MEAP HST, MCAS, C

CHAPTER
5

> If you are not sure of the rules for any of the things on this list,
> first check Chapter 6, where many of those rules are reviewed.
> If you still can't find it, try Peterson's Get Wise! Mastering
> Grammar Skills.

When to Look for What

Some of the errors in the previous list frequently show up in the same way on the test. Here are some tips on "when to look for what:"

☑ *Sentence fragments* are often present when an underlined section includes a period. For example:

> In the park Saturday, I threw a Frisbee to the dog in the <u>red collar. Because</u> I wanted to meet its owner.

"Because I wanted to meet its owner" is not a sentence. You would correct this by changing the period to a comma and lowercase the B " ... collar, because I ..."

☑ Mistakes in *subject-verb agreement* are often present when an underlined verb is relatively far away from the subject. Look at the following example:

> The woman, persuaded by dozens of encouraging phone calls from her children, grandchildren, and great-grand-children and even by multiple letters from strangers who had seen the newspaper articles, <u>are traveling</u> round the world.

Here you would correct by substituting *is* traveling: The subject of this sentence—the woman—is singular and therefore requires a singular verb.

Incorrect idiom usage is often present when the underlined portion and all the choices are prepositions. Here's an example with answer choices:

It's not surprising that caffeine and coffee are viewed <u>like</u> being synonymous.

(A) NO CHANGE

(B) as like

(C) for

(D) as

The correct answer is (D). "Like" means "similar to." Certainly, that is not the intention of the writer of the sentence.

Listening Help Wanted

Do you need help "listening" for mistakes and corrections? Then, try this. Pick someone whose grammar is nearly flawless and whose voice is so distinctive you can readily hear it in your mind: a parent, a teacher, a friend, a newscaster, James Earl Jones. Then, when you're trying to hear a mistake, imagine this person saying the sentence. Try to imagine what the person would naturally say instead. If you don't have a clue, check the answer choices and decide which one of those would sound most natural—the sentence as it is or the sentence with one of the test choices? Chances are good the sentence that sounds most natural coming from your "authority" is the right choice.

If you don't have a clue, check the answer choices and decide which one of those would sound most natural—the sentence as it is or the sentence with one of the test choices?

Shorter Is Better

Remember, *shorter is usually better.* On occasion, you'll find that eliminating all the answers that contain errors does not narrow your options to a single choice. You might find that two (or rarely, three) answer choices all appear completely correct and equally clear, graceful, and unambiguous. When this happens, choose whichever answer is shortest. Generally speaking, a concise, tightly worded sentence is more effective stylistically than a wordy, loosely structured one. Therefore, when all other factors appear equal, the shortest sentence is the one that the test makers are most likely to consider correct.

Be Careful Not to Add a New Mistake

When there are two closely worded choices or two possible ways to correct the error—be careful. Often, one of the choices creates a new error. Read each choice as part of the whole sentence and "listen" for any new mistakes. Try this one:

Although my brother was a talented painter, he gave up his dream of a life as an <u>artist. Making instead</u> a living as an electrical engineer and painting on weekends.

- **(A)** NO CHANGE
- **(B)** artist, instead making
- **(C)** artist. Instead, he makes
- **(D)** artist. Rather, making

The correct answer is (B). Choice (C) corrects the error of a sentence fragment (your tip-off: The underlined portion includes a period). However, if you now read the new version of the sentence using "Instead, he makes" as its opening words, you see that a new problem crops up. The phrase at the end, "and painting on weekends," doesn't grammatically match "he makes." (If it read "and paints on weekends," it would be correct). Choice (B) solves the problem without creating a new one. This is what we mean when we say, " by using parallel grammatical constructions." Use "making" with "painting," because both are gerunds, or use "he makes" and "he paints." Both pairs of constructions are correct, but should not be mixed in the same sentence.

STAKES

HIGH

To Find the Right Sequence, Find the First Item

Questions on mechanics and usage test grammar and punctuation. You're not likely to see too many, but every so often you'll encounter one. Questions on rhetorical skills deal with larger issues of organization, choice of content, and style.

One such item you'll certainly encounter is an overall structure question, which is often a question about the sequence of ideas. You might be asked to select the best sequence of sentences within a paragraph or the best sequence of paragraphs for the passage as a whole.

Here's an example:

> [1] The immigration laws led, ultimately, to a quota system based on the number of individuals of each national origin reported in the 1890 census. [2] The United States, which was founded mainly by people from northern Europe, had an essentially open-door immigration policy for the first 100 years of its existence. [3] But starting in the 1880s and continuing through the 1920s, Congress passed a series of restrictive immigration laws. [4] The door to freedom hadn't been slammed shut, exactly, but it was now open only to the "right" sort of people.
>
> Which of the following sequences of sentences will make this paragraph most logical?
>
> (A) 4, 3, 1, 2
>
> (B) 2, 3, 1, 4
>
> (C) 1, 3, 2, 4
>
> (D) 2, 3, 4, 1

The easiest way to find the right sequence is to find the opening element—the first sentence or the first paragraph. The opening element will often introduce the overall topic about which the rest of the material talks. After you've found the opening element, the others should quickly fall into place. You'll usually note some clear time sequence or progression of action that will make the correct order apparent. Once you've figured out that sentence #2 goes first, the rest is pretty easy. The correct answer, by the way, is (B).

> Notice the bracketed numbers that precede each sentence. When you see bracketed numbers or numbers in parentheses, that's pretty much a tip-off that the test makers will be asking you a question about the sequence of sentences.

One Idea to a Paragraph, Please

Another type of question you may encounter focuses on the clear and logical development of the ideas in the passage. You may be asked to do one of the following:

- ☑ Choose a sentence that would make a logical addition to the passage

- ☑ Decide whether it would be a good idea to delete a particular sentence from the selection

- ☑ Decide where in the passage a certain idea would fit best

Here's a sample of what this kind of question might look like:

> Many owners of professional baseball teams are concerned about sagging attendance figures. Various gimmicks have been tried to boost attendance, from ballpark giveaways to special "nights" honoring various ethnic groups. Teams have changed the colors of their uniforms, played rock music between innings, and set off fireworks after the game.
>
> **Question:** The writer wishes to add another relevant example to this paragraph without straying from the purpose of illustrating gimmicks used by baseball in an effort to improve attendance. Which of the following sentences does that best?
>
> **(A)** It's hard to see what playing Goo Goo Dolls over the centerfield loudspeakers adds to the experience of a ballgame.

(B) For many sports fans, baseball is just too-slow paced; they prefer the quick, constant action of basketball.

(C) They've even tinkered with the rules of the game, introducing the so-called designated hitter.

(D) Some teams claim they are losing millions of dollars each year due to poor attendance.

The most important principle to apply to a question like this is that every paragraph should be unified around a single idea. No sentence should appear in a paragraph that doesn't clearly relate to that idea, either by explaining it, illustrating it, defending it, elaborating on it, or otherwise supporting it. In this case, only choice (C) extends the paragraph's idea, which is "gimmicks have been tried to boost attendance."

Avoid the Repetition of Ideas

Another rhetorical skill type question focuses on wordiness or verbosity. One way to test for this type of mistake is to look for redundancy—the needless repetition of ideas—within the sentence containing the underlined phrase. When the same concept is stated twice or more in a given sentence, the test makers are sending you a broad hint that this is an ineffective sentence that needs to be simplified. Always be on the lookout for a member of the Department of Redundancies Department!

Here's another example:

> The remarkable growth in increased attendance currently being enjoyed by such formally moribund sports franchises as baseball's Cleveland Indians shows that building a new stadium can have a powerful effect on the popularity of a team.

(A) NO CHANGE

(B) The growth in attendance remarkably being enjoyed currently

(C) The remarkable growth in increased attendance currently enjoyed

(D) The remarkable attendance boom currently enjoyed

The correct answer is (D). The original phrasing here contains not just one, but two examples of redundancy. The words "growth" and "increased" both convey the same idea: getting bigger. The word "being" tells you that this thing is happening now—the same idea that the word "currently" expresses. Only choice (D) eliminates both redundancies without changing the meaning of the sentence.

Success Strategy Roundup: A List of DOs and DON'Ts

Here's the "short version" of the preceding advice, along with a few other miscellaneous tips, arranged in a handy list of DOs and DON'Ts. After you understand each point and the reasoning behind it, you'll need only remember the boldface sentence to jog your memory—whether you're working on the exercises that come later in the book, or working on the actual test itself.

Do

☞ **Skim the passage before reading it.** This will give you an idea of the overall structure, meaning, and purpose of the passage, which is especially important for questions dealing with rhetorical skills. Look for the general theme, style, tone, and basic sequence of ideas.

☞ **Find the grammatical error before looking at the choices.** If you need to, reread any sentence that contains an underlined segment. Try to find the error before considering the choices. Mentally correct the error, and then look for the answer choice that matches your mental correction. If you aren't able to correct the error, scan only that part of the choice in which the original error appeared. Then, eliminate any answer that does not correct the error. You can quickly eliminate at least one or two choices this way.

☞ **Check the underlined part for the most common types of errors.** If the error isn't apparent, ask yourself the following questions:

✓ Is the sentence a complete sentence?

✓ Do the subject and the verb agree?

SUCCESS STRATEGY—FIXING COMMON ERRORS

✓ Is the tense correct?

✓ Is the verb form right?

✓ Does the pronoun refer to the correct word and agree with it in person and number?

✓ Are similar ideas expressed in parallel construction? Are modifiers attached to what they're meant to modify?

Trust your ear. If you can't identify the error, silently listen for what "sounds wrong." Even when you can't identify an error by its grammatical name, you can often hear when something sounds wrong—and also when it sounds right. Remember that you can silently listen and increase the odds of your guessing the correct answer.

When adding a sentence, stay with the central idea. If you're asked to choose the next sentence in the paragraph, choose one that in some way further explains the main idea. Don't bring in unrelated topics.

For a sequence question, begin by finding the first sentence or the first paragraph. Look for the sentence or the paragraph that introduces the overall topic. After you have it, the order of the other sentences or other paragraphs will be more apparent.

For style, choose the shortest. When all the choices on a rhetorical skill type question say the same thing and all are grammatically correct, choose the shortest one. It's usually the best, most concise expression of the idea.

Don't

Don't try to "correct" every sentence. "NO CHANGE", "As it is", or "No change is necessary" is the correct answer to about 25 percent of the questions.

Don't be distracted by wordiness. The structural complexity of a sentence might have nothing to do with the question. Ignore anything that is not related to the question and focus only on what's being asked.

- **Don't choose an answer that contains a new error.** Some choices correct the original error but add a different one. Be careful when new words are added to the underlined part.

- **Don't worry about what's not there.** Don't look for mistakes in spelling, capitalization, and hyphenation unless all else fails. Those types of errors rarely appear on the test. Also, don't look for mistakes such as split infinitives and dangling prepositions. As these forms are increasingly used in daily language, the rules "against" them are weakening.

- **Don't try to change what isn't underlined.** If a choice includes any part of the passage that isn't underlined, eliminate it. That's not what's being questioned.

- **Don't separate basic sentence parts.** Subjects and verbs, verbs and objects, verbs and complements—in natural speech and in clear writing, these elements occur close to each other. So if a sentence separates, for example, the subject from the verb with a long complicated clause, look for a choice that positions subject and verb more closely together.

- **Don't be fooled by fragment length.** A sentence *must* have a subject and a verb in the main clause to be complete. No matter how long a fragment is, if it doesn't have a subject and a verb, it's not a sentence.

- **Don't confuse it's with its.** This is a very common mistake. "Its" is the possessive of the pronoun "it." "It's" is the contraction of the words "it is." Because nouns form their possessive with an apostrophe, the contraction *it's* is often mistakenly used in place of *its*. **Reminder:** its is a possessive pronoun. No possessive pronoun uses an apostrophe: *his, hers, yours, theirs, mine, ours,* and *its*.

SUCCESS STRATEGY—FIXING COMMON ERRORS

Pop Quiz

Directions: Read the following essay. Then, answer the questions that follow.

Edwidge Danticat, A Born Writer

Those who live in countries where a large proportion of the population is illiterate share their stories orally. In Haiti, <u>it being a small country</u>,
1

when someone has a tale to tell he or she will call out Krik? <u>Neighbors:</u>
2

friends and relatives will then gather around with an answering call of *Krak!*, signaling <u>there</u> willingness to listen.
3

The Haitian-born writer, Edwidge Danticat, was only twenty-six when she took these two words and made them the title for her collection of stories. The nine stories in *Krik? Krak!* focus on the hardships of living <u>alongside a</u> dictatorship and the struggles encountered by families who
4

flee Haiti and seek new <u>lives, in</u> the United States. The book received
5

<u>much</u> critical acclaim and even became a finalist for the National Book
6
Award.

Born in Port-au-Prince in 1969, Danticat moved to New York City when she was twelve. She spoke little as a new immigrant, because when she did speak, <u>you may find this hard to believe</u>, other children made
7
fun of her heavily-accented English. Her thesis in graduate school later became the novel *Breath, Eyes, Memory*. That novel, which was subsequently chosen by Oprah Winfrey for her book club, featured a heroine who, like the author, moved from Haiti to New York City at the age of twelve. Danticat's third book, *The Farming of Bones*, is also set <u>in a small</u>
8
<u>Caribbean country called Haiti.</u>

This young <u>authors</u> chosen subject matter, as well as the Creole-
9
accented language she uses to tell her stories, show that while she
has left Haiti for her adopted country of America, she has forgotten
<u>both the land of her birth and its</u> brave people.
10

1. (A) NO CHANGE
   (B) as one of the world's smaller countries
   (C) it being a small country
   (D) OMIT the underlined portion.

2. (F) NO CHANGE
   (G) Neighbors;
   (H) Neighbors
   (J) Neighbors,

3. (A) NO CHANGE
   (B) they're
   (C) their
   (D) they are

4. (F) NO CHANGE
   (G) under a
   (H) without a
   (J) in spite of a

5. (A) NO CHANGE
   (B) lives' in
   (C) lives in
   (D) life in

6. (F) NO CHANGE

   (G) many

   (H) too much

   (J) negative

7. (A) NO CHANGE

   (B) you may find this hard to believe

   (C) as hard to believe as you may find this

   (D) OMIT the underlined portion.

8. (F) NO CHANGE

   (G) in the country of the author's birth, which is called Haiti.

   (H) in Haiti, which shares a border with the Dominican Republic.

   (J) in Haiti.

9. (A) NO CHANGE

   (B) authors'

   (C) author's

   (D) author

10. (F) NO CHANGE

   (G) the land of her birth, its people

   (H) neither the land of her birth nor its

   (J) neither the land of her birth and its

11. Write a sentence to open the essay that will set the theme and tone of the essay.

12. The original title of this passage is "Edwidge Danticat, A Born Writer." If you were to give this essay a different title, what would it be?

READING

Answer Explanations

1. **The correct answer is (D).** The size of the country is irrelevant here.

2. **The correct answer is (J).** The word neighbors is part of a list and should be separated from the next item by a comma.

3. **The correct answer is (C).** The willingness refers to that of the neighbors, friends, and relatives and so the possessive pronoun is called for here.

4. **The correct answer is (G).** To live under a dictatorship is the idiomatic phrase.

5. **The correct answer is (C).** No punctuation is needed before the prepositional phrase that begins with the word *in*.

6. **The correct answer is (F).** The modifier indicates a quantity of critical acclaim, and acclaim is a singular noun. Too much would give the sentence an unwanted negative connotation.

7. **The correct answer is (D).** The underlined portion is irrelevant and deviates from the tone of the essay.

8. **The correct answer is (J).** This option avoids unnecessary words and irrelevant facts.

9. **The correct answer is (C).** Only one author is being referred to and the possessive form is used to indicate that the subject matter belongs to the author.

10. **The correct answer is (H).** This option is the most logical because of the author's subject matter. The negative construction requires the conjunctions neither, nor.

11. Here's an example of a sample sentence: "Whether or not they can read, people all over the world love stories."

12. Here's an example of a sample title: "A New Voice in Literature"

CHAPTER 6

REVIEWING ENGLISH AND LANGUAGE ARTS

To try to review twelve years of elementary, middle, and high school grammar in a single chapter of this book would be a task too exhausting for you to study in such a brief time. So, in this chapter, we'll simply focus on the rules of grammar that are most likely to be tested on your high-stakes examination. If you can master the rules in this chapter, you should be able to master your English or Language Arts exit exam.

This review covers the following areas:

English Grammar Errors

- ☑ Rules for verbs
- ☑ Modifying phrases
- ☑ Adjectives and adverbs
- ☑ Pronouns
- ☑ Connecting clauses
- ☑ Punctuation
- ☑ Points of grammar and logic
- ☑ Idioms
- ☑ Commonly confused words
- ☑ Avoidance of wordiness

Language Arts Review

- ☑ Diction, Tone, and Figurative Language
- ☑ Alliteration
- ☑ Personification, Symbolism, and Imagery

How Word Parts Work

- ☑ How words are built
- ☑ Prefixes
- ☑ Suffixes
- ☑ Roots

Trust us—this is going to help, so let's get started.

> If you can master the rules in this chapter, you should be able to master your English or Language Arts exit exam.

The Verbiage on Verbs

A *verb* is a word that shows action or a state of being. It tells what someone or something *is* or *does*. Every sentence has at least one verb. Grammatically speaking, if a group of words has no verb in the main clause, it is not a sentence. The "doer" of the action—the "someone" or "something" that "does" or "is" the verb—is called the *subject* of the verb. Let's take a look at a simple sentence:

> A chef prepared President Bush's dinner.

In this sentence, *prepared* is the verb—the word that shows action.

Chef is the subject of the sentence—the doer of the action. Let's take a look at the next example:

> Karen is a landscape architect.

In this sentence, *is* is the verb—the word that shows a state of being, and *Karen* is the subject of the sentence—the doer of the verb.

In the sections that follow, you'll learn the key rules regarding verbs likely to appear on your exit-level English or Language Arts exam.

A Verb Must Agree with Its Subject in Number

In a grammatically correct sentence, the verb and subject must agree in number. *Number,* here, refers to whether the verb and its subject are *singular* or *plural*. This is pretty straightforward. A singular subject and verb refer to one person or thing; a plural subject and verb refer to more than one person or thing. The number of the subject must match the number of the verb: If the subject is singular, the verb must be singular. If the subject is plural, the verb must be plural.

Use your ear to "listen" for errors in number.

You can often "hear" an error in number. Look at the following example:

> William are a railroad engineer.

This sentence should sound funny to you. It's incorrect because it combines a singular subject with a plural verb. *Is* would be the correct form of the verb. It would be just as incorrect to write the following sentence:

> People was very pleased by the stunning light show.

This sentence should also sound strange to you, because it combines a plural subject with a singular verb. The correct form of the verb is *were*.

In the examples we've just shown you, the errors in subject-verb agreement were easy to spot (or hear, as the case may be). In some sentences, however, it's not as easy. Let's take a look at a more difficult sentence:

Among those who played a crucial role in the allied victory in Europe were David Dwight Eisenhower (commonly known as Dwight David), an American general from Texas who later enjoyed a distinguished career as a university president and politician.

The verb in the main clause of the sentence (in this example, the clause that appears first) is *were*. The simplest way to find the subject is to ask, "Who or what *were*?" The answer is *David Dwight Eisenhower*. Now, ask yourself whether the subject is singular or plural. The subject in this sentence is obviously singular, since David Dwight Eisenhower was one person. Therefore, a singular verb is needed—*were* needs to be changed to *was*.

There are some special situations in subject-verb agreement. The following list reviews some of those special situations:

- **Collective nouns take a singular verb.** A *collective* noun is a noun that names a group of people or things, for example:

Team	Collection
Group	Bunch
Club	Platoon
Class	Organization
Family	

  Even names of institutions like *Harvard University, IBM,* and the *U.S. Senate* may be considered collective nouns, because each refers to a large number of individuals. The U.S. Senate *is* in recess.

- **Pronouns ending in** *-one, -body,* **and** *-thing* **take a singular verb.** These are called indefinite pronouns. There are twelve of them:

Someone	Nobody
Anyone	Everybody
No one	Something
Everyone	Nothing
Somebody	Anything
Anybody	Everything

  Although *everybody* and *everyone* refer to all people within a group, the words refer to each person of the group individually, so everybody *is* happy. Aren't you?

▱ **The SANAM pronouns—Some, Any, None, All, and Most—may be either singular or plural, depending on the sentence.** In determining agreement, you usually ignore prepositional phrases that appear between the subject and the verb. A group of pronouns known by their initials (SANAM) is the exception. These pronouns may be either singular or plural, depending on how they are used in the sentence. Often, the way to determine their use is to see if a prepositional phrase follows the pronoun. Look at the following example:

> If most of the reporters *are* here, we'll begin the press conference.

In this sentence, the SANAM pronoun *most* is followed by the prepositional phrase *of the reporters.* To decide whether *most* is singular or plural, you have to look at the object of the preposition *of.* Because that object is the plural noun *reporters,* the pronoun *most* is plural and the plural verb *are* is used. In contrast to this, look at the next sentence:

> If most of the cake *is* gone, I'll throw it out.

In this case, the object of the preposition *of* is the singular word *cake.* Therefore, the pronoun *most* is singular, and the singular verb *is* is used.

If the acronym SANAM doesn't stick to the roof of your mouth, make up a sentence that you'll remember: How about "Sarah Ate Nathan's Apple Monday"? If you don't like that one, make up one of your own.

Verbs Need To Get Tense—You Don't

The tense of the verb shows the time of one event or the sequence of several events. There are six main tenses in the English language. Look at the list of tenses below; we've used the verb *to study* to give you examples of each tense:

- Past tense (*studied*)

- Present tense (*study*)

- Future tense (*will study*)

- Past perfect tense (*had studied*)

- Present perfect tense (*have studied*)

- Future perfect tense (*will have studied*)

The perfect tenses describe events occurring *before* other events. For example, an event described in the **past perfect** tense is one that happened *before* an event in the past tense happened. For example:

> Before Ali took the high-stakes English test, she *had studied* for six weeks.

An event described in the **present perfect** tense is one that both happened *before* in the past and *continues* to happen up to the present. Look at the next example:

> Geoffrey *has studied* high-stakes math problems every day for an hour.

Though rarely used, there is also the future perfect tense. An event in the **future perfect** is one that will happen *before* another future event:

> I will take the high-stakes test next weekend; *by then, I will have studied* a total of 47 hours.

On test questions about tense, a sentence or paragraph will describe two or more events occurring in a particular, (hopefully) unmistakable order. For example:

> Lincoln announced his controversial Emancipation Proclamation, which declared all slaves held in rebel territory free, only after the North had won a significant military victory.

There are two events in this sentence: Lincoln's announcement of the Emancipation Proclamation and the North's winning a significant military victory. What is the time sequence of these two events? The sentence makes it obvious: Lincoln announced the Proclamation in the past, and the North's victory occurred *before* that. Therefore, the announcement is in the past tense (Lincoln *announced*) and the victory is correctly in the past perfect tense (only after the North *had won*).

There! Now that's what you'd have to call *perfect*.

THE PAST PARTICIPLE IS WHAT TO HAVE WITH THE HELPING VERB "TO HAVE"

In the preceding examples, you might have noticed that the past perfect, present perfect, and future perfect tenses all contain forms of the verb *to have*. When used to create tenses of other verbs, the verb *to have* is formally called an *auxiliary verb*. If you'd prefer not to wear the formal tuxedo or gown, you may more casually call it a *helping verb*.

It's essential to remember that when you are using *to have* as a helping verb, you must be careful to use the proper form of the basic verb. The proper form to use with *to have* is called the *past participle*. This is one of the three principal parts of any verb. The other two parts are the *infinitive* and the *past*. The infinitive is the "to" form of the verb—to *laugh, to type, to work,* etc. The past is the same as the simple past tense. The past participle is the part of the verb used with a form of *to have* to create the perfect tenses. I know it sounds like we're repeating ourselves, but we can't afford to leave room for doubt here.

> The past participle is the part of the verb used with a form of "to have" to create the perfect tenses.

Do you know how that past participle is created? That's where complications—and your exit-level exam English questions—come in.

For most English verbs, both the past and the past participle are formed the same way: by adding *–d* or *–ed* to the infinitive. Because the past and the past participle are the same, these verbs are called *regular* verbs. As an example, the following table gives the parts of three regular verbs.

Examples of Regular Verbs

Part	Example	Example	Example
Infinitive	to laugh	to squeeze	to consider
Past	laughed	squeezed	considered
Past Participle	laughed	squeezed	considered

Wouldn't it be dandy if all verbs were regular? Well, don't hold your breath. Many verbs form their past tense differently from the regular ones. What's more, many of these verbs change again for the past participle. Because there is such irregularity between the three parts, these verbs are called (can you guess what?) *irregular verbs*. The following table shows examples of the parts of three irregular verbs.

Examples of Irregular Verbs

Part	Example	Example	Example
Infinitive	to fly	to go	to eat
Past	flew	went	ate
Past Participle	flown	gone	eaten

A common error with irregular verbs—and one that you don't want to make—is to confuse the past and past participle forms, thus using the past tense where the past participle is needed. Look at the following example:

> By the time Lindbergh's little plane landed on an airfield outside Paris, the exhausted pilot had flew single-handedly for more than 30 hours without a break.

The past perfect tense is being used here. (Did you notice that one thing in the sentence happened before the other?) That means the past participle should have been used. The verb should be *had flown* rather than *had flew*.

Mastering Modifying Phrases

A *modifying phrase* is a group of words that works as a unit to modify (describe or give more information about) something else in the sentence. Both *adjectives* and *adverbs* are considered modifiers; both modify other words in the sentence. Please be clear that modifying phrases are groups of words that act as if they were adjectives or adverbs. Some modifying phrases work as adjectives and modify nouns or pronouns. Others work as adverbs and modify verbs, adjectives, or adverbs.

> A group of words that acts like an adjective or an adverb is a modifying phrase.

Now, look at an example sentence using a modifying phrase:

> After six o'clock, buses stop here once a hour.

The phrase *After six o'clock* acts as an adverb, modifying the verb *stop* by telling *when* the buses stop. Any word telling when is an adverb.

To really ace your exit-level exam, read through and familiarize yourself with the rules regarding modifying phrases, as discussed in the sections that follow.

Modifying Phrase Gets 20-Year Sentence

Actually, the word or phrase being modified (the person or thing being described) must be in the same sentence as the modifying phrase. If no such word or phrase appears in the same sentence, the modifying phrase is called a *dangling modifier*. Look at the following sentence and see if you can spot the problem:

> Dismayed by the news that a top executive had suddenly accepted a job with a competitor, the price of the company's stock fell sharply the next day.

In this example, *Dismayed by the news that a top executive had suddenly accepted a job with a competitor,* is a modifying phrase, intended to describe or give more information—but information about whom or what? Who or what, exactly, was "dismayed by the news"? Although we may understand that it was Wall Street that was dismayed or stockholders who were dismayed, neither appears in the sentence itself. In fact, as written, the sentence states that the *prices* were dismayed. Dismayed means disappointed and shocked. People can be shocked, prices can't. The modifying phrase "dangles"; there is no word or phrase to which it actually refers. To be correct, the sentence would have to be rewritten to name the person or people who were dismayed. Here's one possible way to rewrite the sentence:

> Dismayed by the news that a top executive had suddenly accepted a job with a competitor, stockholders sold off huge chunks of holdings and drove the stock's price down sharply.

Now, the modifying phrase has a clear reference, naming the people it modifies. Take care with this kind of error. On the high-stakes examination, modifying phrases often appear at the start of sentences. In an attempt to distract students with details that have little to do with the question being asked, modifying phrases at the start of sentences can also be very long, such as this one. When a sentence begins with a phrase—short or long—look closely to make sure that the person, thing, or idea being modified appears somewhere in the same sentence.

> On the high-stakes examination, modifying phrases often appear at the start of sentences.

Don't Misplace Your Next Door Neighbor

A *dangling* modifier lacks something clear to modify. A *misplaced* modifier has something in the sentence to modify, but the two are separated in such a way that the modifier ends up describing the wrong person or thing. Let's look at the following sentence:

> A fabled center of monastic life during the Middle Ages, each summer thousands of visitors travel to the island of Iona near the coast of Ireland.

A fabled center of monastic life during the Middle Ages is supposed to modify the island of Iona, because that's what it describes. However, the modifying phrase is misplaced. Rather than being next to what it modifies, the modifying phrase precedes the words *each summer* and *thousands of visitors*, almost as if either of these were the "fabled center..." One possible way to rewrite the sentence would be as follows:

> A fabled center of monastic life during the Middle Ages, the island of Iona near the coast of Ireland is visited by thousands of travelers each summer.

Know Your Adjectives from Your Adverbs

Adjectives modify (describe or give more information about) nouns or pronouns. Adjectives answer such questions as *what kind? how many?* or *which one?* The following are a few examples of adjectives (the adjectives appear in italics):

- ☑ *Blue* dress
- ☑ *Moving* object
- ☑ *Few* days

Adverbs modify verbs, adjectives, or other adverbs. Adverbs answer such questions as *how?, when?, where?, in what way?,* or *how often?* The following are examples of adverbs (the adverbs appear in italics):

- ☑ He ran *quickly.*
- ☑ She *quietly* closed the door.

T/HSPA, FCAT, MEAP HST, MCAS, GEE21, Regents Exams, SOL, N... AHSGE, GHSGT, BST
NCCT, AHSGE, GHSGT, BST, BSAP, WASL, CAHSEE, TAAS, OGT... I/HSPA, FCAT, MEAP
GT, HSPT/HSPA, FCAT, MEAP HST, MCAS, GEE21, Regents Exams... NCCT, AHSGE, GHSC
GHSGT, BST, BSAP, WASL, CAHSEE, TAAS, OGT, HSPT/HSPA, FCAT, MEAP HST, MCAS, G

CHAPTER
6

READING

☑ The phone rang *repeatedly.*

In the following sections, we will look at the basic rules for using adjectives and adverbs—information that will help you do your best on your exit-level exam. Make sure that you understand each of them.

Accept No Substitute

A common mistake when using adjectives and adverbs is to use an adjective where an adverb is needed, or vice versa. Let's take a look at one such sentence:

In the 90s, albums by Pearl Jam appeared consistent on the charts even without the exposure of music videos.

The word *consistent* is an adjective; it could be used to modify a noun (*a consistent success*) or a pronoun (*she is consistent in her habits*). However, in this sentence, an adverb is called for, because the word modified is the verb *to appear.* The author wants to answer the question *how often did Pearl Jam albums appear on the charts?* To answer this question, an adverb is needed. As in many cases, the adverb here is formed by adding *-ly* to the adjective. The sentence can then easily be corrected by changing *consistent* to *consistently.*

Comparative Adjectives and Adverbs vs. Superlative Adjectives and Adverbs

To compare *two* things, the "comparative" form of an adjective is used. The usual way to create the comparative form is to add *-er* to the adjective. To compare *more than two things*, the "superlative" form of the adjective is used. The usual way to create the superlative is to add *-est* to the adjective. Let's look at some examples:

☑ I am *tall.* (adjective)

☑ I am *taller* than my sister. (comparative adjective)

☑ But my brother Jason is the *tallest* in the family. (superlative adjective)

When an adjective has three or more syllables, adding yet another syllable makes it awkward. If that is the case, the comparative is created by adding the word *more* in front of the adjective, and the superlative by adding the word *most*. For example:

> Kira is *beautiful*. Rocio is *more beautiful*. Hailee Rhea Fosterr is the *most beautiful* woman in the galaxy.

Often, a writer may become confused about whether to use the comparative or superlative form of the adjective. Just a few differences in words can change which form is called for. For example, the following two sentences say the same thing, yet each correctly uses a different form of the adjective:

> Of the many strange creatures that inhabit the continent of Australia, the wallaby is more unusual than any other.

> Of the many strange creatures that inhabit the continent of Australia, the wallaby is the most unusual.

In the first example, the comparative form is correct because the sentence is literally comparing the wallaby to every other creature, one at a time. Thus, at any one time, only two animals are being compared.

In the second example, the superlative form is correct because the wallaby is being compared to all other creatures at once.

Comparative and superlative forms of adverbs are used in much the same way. The comparative form (made with the word *more*) is used when two things are being compared; the superlative form (made with the word *most*) is used when three or more things are being compared. Look at the next example:

> Jimmy swims *quickly*. Melissa swims *more quickly* than Jimmy. But Ian swims *most quickly* of anyone on the swim team.

> The -ly tip-off can tell you whether a word is an adverb or an adjective.

The surest way to know if a word is an adverb or an adjective is to use the *-ly tip-off* to determine the word's function in the sentence:

> Is it modifying a noun or pronoun (making it an adjective)?
>
> or
>
> is it modifying a verb, adjective, or other adverb (making it an adverb)?

To make a quick decision, look for the *-ly*. If the word ends in *-ly*, you can safely say it's an adverb. Although not every adverb ends in *-ly* (for example, often, tomorrow, very), words that end in *–ly* are almost always adverbs.

> Although not every adverb ends in -ly (for example, often, tomorrow, very), words that end in –ly are almost always adverbs.

Well, That's All Well and Good... and Well ...

Don't confuse the adjective *good*, the adverb *well*, and the adjective *well*. This trio of words can be confusing, and because they are used quite often it's important to get the differences straight. *Good* is an adjective with a broadly positive meaning. *Well* is the adverb form of good, it means, in effect, "in a good way." But *well* can also be an adjective meaning healthy or "the opposite of ill." Here is an example of each:

> The singing in this high school production sounds as good [adjective] as if performed by professionals.

> Ali, the understudy, sings especially *well* [adverb, that is, she *sings, in a good way*].

> She will have the opportunity to play the lead if Irene does not feel *well* tonight [adjective that equals healthy].

Pronouns

A *noun* names a person, place, or thing. A *pronoun* refers to and takes the place of a noun. If pronouns didn't exist, you would say things like:

> Melissa said that Melissa was planning to go with Melissa's friends to Times Square on New Year's Eve.

How could you make the preceding sentence better? Well, you'd want to use the pronouns *she* and *her* rather than repeating the word *Melissa* so often, and the resulting sentence would look like this:

> Melissa said that she was planning to go with her friends to Times Square on New Year's Eve.

The noun that the pronoun refers to is called its *antecedent*. In our example, above, the noun *Melissa* is the antecedent of the pronouns *she* and *her*. Notice that antecedent has an "e" following the "t." It is not *anti-* anything. The sections below outline the "rules" of pronouns and antecedents that you'll need to have a handle on for the high-stakes English exam.

A PRONOUN MUST HAVE A CLEAR AND LOGICAL ANTECEDENT

A common problem comes about when a reader can't easily tell who or what the antecedent is supposed to be. For example:

> Although the hospital administrators interviewed many staff members about the repeated cases of staph infections, they had no explanation for the puzzling pattern of outbreaks.

The second half of this sentence starts with the pronoun *they*. It's impossible to tell from the context who *they* are. From a strictly grammatical point of view, the antecedent should be *staff members*, since that's the noun closest to the pronoun; however, logically, the antecedent should be *hospital administrators*. If that was what was meant, the sentence should be rewritten. One possible revision is:

> Although they interviewed many staff members about the repeated cases of staph infections, the hospital administrators had no explanation for the puzzling pattern of outbreaks.

Now, it is unmistakable who is doing what.

Pronoun-Antecedent Agreement In Number

A pronoun and its antecedent must agree in number just like a subject and a verb must agree in number. If the antecedent is singular, the pronoun must also be singular; if the antecedent is plural, the pronoun must also be plural.

This is an example of a common mistake in pronoun-antecedent agreement:

> A member of the tour group should have their tickets by the end of this week.

Who or what does the pronoun *their* refer to in the sentence above? That is, what is the pronoun's antecedent? *Member* is the antecedent, yet *member* is singular while *their* is plural. The pronoun does not agree with the noun in number, and is therefore incorrect. To correct the sentence, the pronoun *their* must be changed to a singular pronoun *his* or *her*:

> A member of the tour group should have his or her tickets by the end of this week.

The sentence could also be corrected by changing the noun to a plural form; for example:

> Members of the tour group should have **their** tickets by the end of the week.

Who's the Third Person (Let Alone the Second One)?

Grammar allows for three "persons" (which helps avoid overcrowding). The three "persons" have singular and plural forms.

Singular

- First person (I, me)
- Second person (you)
- Third person (he, she, one, it)

Plural

☑ First person (we, us)

☑ Second person (you, *not youse!*)

☑ Third person (they, them)

A common mistake is to mix the "persons" and use them inconsistently, and this occurs most often in sentences that have an indefinite person. An *indefinite person* would be an implied *someone* or *anyone* as opposed to a definite person, like *Alan* or *the girl*. Look at the following sentence in which the "person" shifts:

> If one lives in the northern hemisphere, on most clear winter nights you can easily see the three stars in a row that mark the belt of the hunter in the constellation Orion.

The sentence describes how an indefinite person, meaning someone or anyone, can see Orion's belt in the winter sky. The sentence starts by using the indefinite third-person pronoun *one*. (Other such words that could have been used include the pronouns *someone* and *anyone* and expressions like *a person* or *an observer*.) However, the sentence shifts midstream to the second person: *you* can easily see...

To correct the mistake, the sentence should maintain the third person throughout. Or it might use the second person, as long as that, too, is used throughout the entire sentence. You dig? So, you would have a sentence that looks like this if you stuck with third person:

> If *one* lives in the northern hemisphere, on most clear winter nights *one* can easily see the three stars in a row that mark the belt of the hunter in the constellation Orion.

Or, a sentence that looks like this if you stuck with second person:

> If *you* live in the northern hemisphere, on most clear winter nights *you* can easily see the three stars in a row that mark the belt of the hunter in the constellation Orion.

The English (Not French) Connection

A clause is a group of words that contains both a subject and a verb. A clause is called a *main* or *independent* clause if it can stand alone as a complete sentence—that is, if it expresses a complete thought. If an independent clause had no other clause preceding it and had a period after it, it would be a sentence. A clause is called a *subordinate*, or dependent, clause if it cannot stand alone as a complete sentence—that is, if it does not express a complete thought.

> A clause is called a main or independent clause if it can stand alone as a complete sentence.

Conjunctions are connecting words: they connect words, phrases, or clauses. *Coordinating conjunctions* connect words, phrases, or clauses that are equal in grammatical importance—that is, they connect two independent clauses. *Subordinating conjunctions* are used mainly to connect clauses. The clause introduced by a subordinating conjunction is a *dependent* clause. It is less important than a clause without such a conjunction and its meaning is dependent on the other clause. Therefore, a dependent clause can't stand alone as a sentence.

> A dependent clause can't stand alone as a sentence.

The coordinating conjunctions are:

And	*Nor*
Or	*But*
For	*Yet*

The subordinating conjunctions are:

Because	*Until*
Although	*Before*
After	*As soon as*
If	*Unless*
When	*Though*
While	

Here are a few examples of dependent clauses introduced by subordinating conjunctions:

☑ …*although* it had begun to rain…

☑ …*when* the plumber arrived…

☑ …*because* the bicycle was broken…

None of the dependent clauses in the previous list is a complete thought; none could stand alone. Each needs to be connected to something else to complete the thought. Grammatically, the "something else" is an independent clause. The independent clause can come either before or after the dependent clause. Here are the same dependent clauses connected to independent clauses:

☑ They stayed on the beach *although it had begun to rain.*

☑ She locked the dog in the cellar *when the plumber arrived.*

☑ *Because the bicycle was broken,* he walked to school.

Now, let's look at the rules about connecting clauses that you may need to know for your exit-level Reading or English–Language Arts exam.

Petticoat Conjunction (Never Mind; It Was Before Your Time)

Each conjunction, of course, has its own meaning and cannot be used interchangeably with other conjunctions. A test question might ask whether you recognize the proper, logical conjunction to connect two particular clauses. The answer will depend on the meaning of the conjunction and whether it fits the context or not. Let's look at an example:

The city had fallen into ruins, and fortune-seekers from the country-side continued to pour in.

Here, two independent clauses have been joined by the coordinating conjunction *and*. Should they be connected by *and*, though? This is kind of tricky. Actually, the two clauses are opposed to each other in meaning rather than complementary: *"despite the fact* that the city was in ruins, fortune-seekers from the countryside continued to pour in." Given this near-contradiction, the conjunction *and* is not the best choice. Instead, the conjunctions that show opposition, *but* or *yet*, should be used. These more logically fit the opposition in meaning between the two clauses.

A Semicolon May Connect Two Independent Clauses

There is an alternative to using conjunctions. Instead of using a conjunction, independent clauses may also be connected using a semicolon (;). The next sentence is one such example:

I have never needed to study more in my life; I have never been more tired.

Both clauses are independent and both express a complete thought—therefore, a semicolon may be used. But if the sentence looked like the one below, the use of a semicolon would be wrong:

I have never needed to study more in my life; because tomorrows test affects my whole future.

The second part of the sentence is a dependent clause introduced by the subordinating conjunction *because*. The semicolon should be omitted.

Run-Off Is Unavoidable; Run-On Is Not!

A run-on sentence isn't necessarily a particularly long sentence. It might also be a sentence in which two (or more) independent clauses are incorrectly connected by being put in the same sentence without either a semicolon or a coordinating conjunction to join them properly.

Remember, the length of a sentence is never an issue in its being complete. A complete sentence can be a single word, like "Halt!" A fragment can be quite long. It all depends on whether the clauses are independent or dependent, and this in turn depends on the grammatical structure. Look at this sentence:

> In addition to being a writer and lecturer, Mark Twain fancied himself an entrepreneur, he made and lost several fortunes backing various business ventures.

If this sentence were divided into two sentences by placing a period after the word *entrepreneur*, each half could stand alone as a sentence. Therefore, it's a run-on sentence. The two possible corrections are to break it into two sentences or change the comma into a semicolon. Pretty clever, eh?

PT/HSPA, FCAT, MEAP HST, MCAS, GEE21, Regents Exams, SOL, NEST, AHSGE, GHSGT, BS
NCCT, AHSGE, GHSGT, BST, BSAP, WASL, CAHSEE, TAAS, OGT /HSPA, FCAT, MEAP
GT, HSPT/HSPA, FCAT, MEAP HST, MCAS, GEE21, Regents Exams NCCT, AHSGE, GHS
GHSGT, BST, BSAP, WASL, CAHSEE, TAAS, OGT, HSPT/HSPA, FCAT, MEAP HST, MCAS

CHAPTER
6

READING

Punctuation Does Not Mean Being on Time

Punctuation is the collection of marks that helps turn a string of written words into meaningful thoughts.

Although there are dozens of ways that punctuation can be used and misused, you are most likely to be tested on the rules covered in the following sections.

THE COLON

As already explained in a previous section, the semicolon (;) is used primarily to separate two independent clauses. The colon (:) can not be used as an alternative to the semicolon. Instead, the colon should be used to introduce a list or a restatement.

> For my term paper, I decided to write about the following hidden meanings in Nirvana's album *Nevermind:* references to Cobain's life, references to his wife, and references to major influences in his career.

The colon is used correctly here. It alerts you to the fact that a list is about to be presented. However, if a list is the object of a verb or a preposition, don't use a colon before the list.

> For my term paper, I decided to write about hidden meanings in Nirvana's album *Nevermind,* including references to Cobain's life, references to his wife, and references to major influences in his career.

A colon can also be used for a restatement. Here's an example such a use:

> Barbara was named valedictorian for one reason: her exceptional academic achievement.

What follows the colon "restates" what precedes it; the words "her exceptional academic achievement" name the "one reason" mentioned before the colon.

Commas

Commas in a Word Series (not the World Series)

When three or more words, phrases, or clauses are presented in sequence, they should be separated by commas. Let's first look at this example of sequential words:

> The Galapagos Islands boast some of the world's most unusual plants, birds, mammals, reptiles, and fish.

Here is an example of sequential phrases:

> We looked for the missing gloves under the sofa, in the closet, and behind the dresser, but we never found them.

Finally, here is an example of sequential clauses:

> I studied my high-stakes English, I studied my high-stakes math, I studied my high-stakes science reasoning, and I took acetaminophen for my headache.

You might have noticed in other pieces of writing that the last comma (the comma before *and*) is not always used. Once forbidden, then later required, the last comma has become optional and will not be tested on a high-stakes English question. The other commas, however, are not optional; they *must* be used.

Commas and the Parenthetical Phrase

A *parenthetical phrase* is an "interrupter"—it breaks into the flow of the main idea of the sentence, adding one or a few descriptive words in a convenient spot and then returning to the main idea. Although parenthetical phrases may literally be set off by parentheses (as this one is), they may also be set off from the rest of the sentence by a pair of commas. If the parenthetical phrase appears at the beginning or end of the sentence, only one comma is needed. Some parenthetical phrases are frequently used, such as *for example, as you see, that is, as I said before,* and so on. Whenever a phrase like this is used, it should be separated from the rest of the sentence by commas.

Not all men like cars; my uncle, for example, never learned to drive and can't tell a Porsche from a Volkswagen.

In the preceding sentence, *for example* is the parenthetical phrase, and it is set off from the rest of the sentence with commas.

Another type of parenthetical phrase is an *appositive*, which names or describes a noun. Look at the sentence below, which uses an appositive:

Sandy Koufax, the great left-handed Dodger pitcher, was Jack's idol during his teenage years.

In this sentence, "the great left-handed Dodger pitcher" is the appositive, it describes the noun "Sandy Koufax."

Don't Let Commas Break up Your Relationships

Commas should not separate parts of the sentence that are naturally joined, like subject and verb, verb and object, verb and complement, and preposition and object. Let's take a look:

The nineteenth-century explorers Lewis and Clark may be, two of America's most-admired historical figures.

In this sentence, the comma after the word *be* is incorrect; it separates the verb and complement.

Another common mistake of this kind is the use of a comma to set off the beginning of a parenthetical phrase but omitting the second comma to "close off" the phrase. Look at the following sentence for an example of this:

I was surprised to find out that Margo, my girlfriend from freshman year had moved back to town.

In this sentence, there is a comma correctly placed after *Margo,* but the second comma (after *year*) has been omitted. Thus, the use of only one comma ends up separating the subject *Margo* from the verb *had moved*.

Don't Let Apostrophes Cause Catastrophes

The apostrophe (') has two purposes in the English language, and both are frequently tested on your exit-level exam. There are two uses for the apostrophe, so let's take a look at each of them.

1. An apostrophe is used to show possession, ownership, or some other close connection between a noun or pronoun and what follows it. For example:

   Susan's car

   The **company's** employees

   The possessive is formed in different ways, depending on the noun. Here's how you form the possessive:

   - For a singular noun, simple add 's (the *dog's* collar)
   - For a plural noun that ends in s, add an apostrophe (the *Jones'* apartment)
   - For a plural noun that does not end in s, add 's (the *children's* teacher)
   - For possessive pronouns, add nothing (*his, hers, ours, its* etc.)

2. The apostrophe is also used to form a *contraction*. A contraction is formed when two words are combined into one word with an apostrophe inserted in place of the letters omitted. If in doubt, mentally "expand" the contraction to determine which letters have been left out; this is often a useful guide to where the apostrophe belongs. Here are some examples of contractions:

   - we have → we've
   - I would → I'd
   - will not → won't
   - it is → it's
   - you are → you're

Proper use of the apostrophe in a contraction is basically a matter of correct spelling. If you've had problems with this, get into the habit of noticing how contractions are spelled in good writing. It will greatly help your own writing, and it will definitely help you on tests.

Grammar Is Logical

Although the rules of grammar might sometimes seem arbitrary, they actually follow strict patterns of logic. It's like trying to compare apples and oranges. It really can't be done. One function of grammar is to establish rules so that oranges are compared to oranges and apples are compared to apples. This is logical, consistent thinking. Let's look at the rules regarding grammar and logic that may show up on your test.

PARALLELISM

In geometry, parallel lines run in the same direction. In grammar, the rule of parallelism requires that every word, phrase, or clause in a list be constructed in the same way. Look at the sentence below:

> Representatives to the student senate were asked to pursue often contradictory goals: boosting student acceptance of more homework, developing explanations for adding two hours to the length of each school day, and the reduction of rampant poor morale.

The sentence you just read is not parallel. The sentence lists three goals of the student senate representatives. The first two are written in parallel form—that is, in phrases that begin with *gerunds* (that's the fancy name given to *-ing* verbs that become nouns). However, the third goal is written in a different grammatical form. Instead of a beginning with a gerund, the phrase begins with a noun. To correct the sentence, the third item should be revised to match the other two by starting with a gerund: "...and reducing the rampant poor morale."

Using Parallelogram-mar

Like items in a list, items that are being compared to one another in a sentence also need to be grammatically parallel. Let's look at a sentence that uses a comparison:

> Because of advertising costs, to run for Congress today costs more than running for governor twenty years ago.

The costs of two kinds of political campaigns are being compared, a race for Congress today and a race for governor twenty years ago. As written, the sentence uses two different grammatical constructions to describe the races:

> *to run* for Congress today (infinitive)
>
> *running* for governor twenty years ago (gerund)

Either choice is correct, but using both in the same sentence is inconsistent. Correct the problem by using an infinitive in both phrases ("*to run* for Congress today costs more than *to run* for governor") or by using a gerund in both phrases ("*running* for Congress today costs more than *running* for governor").

Do You Take Me for an Idiom?

After so much emphasis on logic and consistency, it seems totally illogical that idioms play such a large part in the proper use of English. An idiom, after all, is a phrase that's peculiar to a particular language and that often has no logic or rule behind its use. "That's just the way you say it" is what we tell nonnative speakers. Yet despite this lack of logic, the improper use of an idiom is considered a grammatical mistake.

Because there may be no rule attached to the use of particular idioms listen for the way you *expect* the idiom to be used, the way you have heard it used in countless conversations and lectures.

The following are some of the rules governing idioms that may be covered in your exit-level exam.

When Idioms Come in Pairs, Always Complete the Pair

Certain idiomatic pairs of phrases must always be used together. When they aren't, the resulting sentence "sounds wrong," as if something is missing. For example:

> She claims her poor performance on the stage was caused as much by poor direction than by her own stage fright.

This sentence sounds incorrect because the idiom demands that the phrase *as much by X* always be followed by *as by Y*. It's incorrect to use the word *than* where the second *as* should be. So, with correct idiom usage, the sentence would look like this:

> She claims her poor performance on the stage was caused as much by poor direction as by her own stage fright.

Another idiomatic pair that must always be used together is *the more X... the more Y*. For example, here's a sentence you've probably heard a million times:

> The more things change, the more they stay the same.

More and *more* are often replaced by other comparatives:

> *The bigger* they are, *the harder* they fall.

> *The deeper* the pocket, *the tighter* the purse strings.

> *The stronger* the brew, *the better* the coffee.

Idiomatic Prepositions Matter

A variation on paired idiomatic phrases is paired idiomatic words; that is, one word is always followed by another. This happens most frequently (and most confusingly, it seems) with prepositions. Certain words always take a certain preposition. For example, one may *look at, look in, look through*, etc. However, one always disagrees *with* rather than disagrees against, or has scorn *for* rather than scorn at. Can you spot the mistake in the following sentence?

> The quarterback assured the waterboy that he had no intention to encroach on the latter's interest in the captain of the cheerleaders.

According to idiomatic usage, the word intention should be followed by the preposition *of*, so the preposition must be changed to the correct one. Because the preposition *of*, like all prepositions, must have an object, and the object must be a noun or pronoun, the verb *encroach* must also be changed to a noun form—the *gerund* (the -*ing* construction) *encroaching*. The fully corrected sentence then reads:

> The quarterback assured the waterboy that he had no intention of encroaching on the latter's interest in the captain of the cheerleaders.

Encroach *on* rather than encroach *against*—yet another idiom. The list goes on and on.

> Even native speakers can find these idiom constructions difficult; nonnative speakers must think that all idioms were invented at a drunken New Year's Eve party; that's how much sense they make.

The only proven advice is to "listen" carefully as you read test questions. If a preposition on the test sounds "funny," scan the answer choices to see whether the answers include a change in the preposition. If you spot another preposition that sounds better, choose it.

Learn To Distinguish between Easily Confused Words

So many people confuse two different words in casual speech that the "incorrect" one can be mistaken for the grammatically correct one, even in more formal writing. So, it's important to be sure to know the meanings of commonly confused words. Look over these examples and be sure to choose the right word on the test:

EXAMPLES OF EASILY CONFUSED WORDS

Word	Definition or Distinguishing Function
likely	*definition*: probably destined to happen
liable	*definition*: legally responsible
like	*function*: a preposition that must take an object; cannot be used as a conjunction, as in *He fixed it like he said he would*—incorrect
as	*function*: a subordinating conjunction, as in *He fixed it as he said he would*—correct

SPT/HSPA, FCAT, MEAP HST, MCAS, GEE21, Regents Exams, SOL, NCCT, AHSGE, GHSGT, B
, NCCT, AHSGE, GHSGT, BST, BSAP, WASL, CAHSEE, TAAS, OGT, /HSPA, FCAT, MEAF
GT, HSPT/HSPA, FCAT, MEAP HST, MCAS, GEE21, Regents Exams, NCCT, AHSGE, GH

CHAPTER 6

much	*definition*: a large quantity that can't be counted, as in *so much blood, so much sand, so much dissatisfaction*
many	*definition*: a large quantity that can be counted, as in *so many pints of blood, so many grains of sand, so many demonstrations of dissatisfaction*
less	*definition*: a decrease that can't be counted, as in *less busy than yesterday*
fewer	*definition*: a decrease that can be counted, as in *interrupted fewer times than yesterday*
affect	when used as a verb, meaning to influence or to move emotionally
affect	when used as a noun, meaning a feeling or an emotion
effect	when used as a verb, meaning to bring about
effect	when used as a noun, meaning result or consequence
if	indicates a condition or uncertainty
whether	indicates a choice
last	the final item in a series; indicates position
latest	the most recent; indicates time

WORLDLINESS IS OKAY; WORDINESS IS NOT!

The best writing is usually the most concise writing. This is especially true in nonfiction when style and embellishment take second place to the clear presentation of information. Wordiness can occur in several ways, you'll want to be on the lookout for each one. The following sections discuss the things you'll need to know about eliminating wordiness when you take your high-stakes test.

Blah, Blah, Blah

Verbosity is the use of too many words. The construction of the sentence might be grammatically correct, but there are simply too many words. Verbosity on the high-stakes test will be fairly obvious, even exaggerated. Here's an example:

As I previously mentioned to you when explaining at last week's meeting the incredible and undisputed advantages of combining our two clubs, *The Poetry Society* and *Poets Out of the Closet,* I have written up here for your further study my thoughts on the matter, detailing the many benefits that will accrue to both organizations.

There's nothing "mechanically" wrong with this sentence. It's a complete sentence and not a fragment, the subjects and verbs within the clauses agree with one another, and the punctuation is correct. However, it would be more concise to write:

At last week's meeting, I said there were benefits to combining our two clubs. Here's a note repeating why.

Be Careful Not To Change Meaning When Editing

Every long sentence is not necessarily verbose. When editing, be sure not to butcher the original style of the writing. Even more important, editing should not result in a shorter piece of writing that is confusing or that even changes the meaning of the original. Compare the three versions of a sentence below:

1. Spielberg's *Amistad* is the filmmaker's second attempt to show that someone who is an unexcelled creator of funny, fast-paced action movies can also be a producer of films that try to deal in a serious fashion with weighty historical and moral themes. (42 words)

2. Spielberg's *Amistad* is the filmmaker's second attempt at dealing in a serious fashion with weighty historical and moral themes. (19 words)

3. Spielberg's *Amistad* is the filmmaker's second attempt to show that an unexcelled creator of funny, fast-paced action movies can also produce films dealing seriously with weighty historical and moral themes. (30 words)

Although the second version is less than half the length of the original, it loses the original meaning: the contrast between the two types of movies that Spielberg makes. The third version, being only 29 percent shorter, retains the meaning while expressing it more economically.

An effective way to edit wordiness is to look for "empty" clauses. The empty clause in "Jack is a man who is good to all" can be dropped entirely: "Jack is good to all."

Avoid Redundantly Repeating Redundancies

Needless repetition is called *redundancy*. Just in case you didn't notice, the title of this section is redundant. Repetition in writing sometimes serves a purpose; it might be intended style, or it might be deliberate emphasis.

> Needless repetition is called redundancy.

Here's an example of a redundant sentence:

> He is taller in height than I am.

Is there a way to be taller other than height? No, so the words *in height* can be deleted. Look at another example of redundancy:

> As much as 125 years ago, the science fiction writer Jules Verne wrote predictions that foretold the future existence of such modern mechanical devices as the airplane, the submarine, and even the fax machine.

We're told that Jules Verne wrote "predictions that foretold the future existence" of many things. Because the words *foretold* and *future existence* are both contained within the meaning of *predictions*, both can be deleted.

Active Is Good, Passive Is Bad

Don't be a couch potato in writing or in life. When the subject of the verb is the doer of the action, a sentence is said to be in the *active voice*. Here's a sentence in the active voice:

> Sharon built the birdhouse.

When the subject of the verb receives the action, a sentence is said to be in the *passive* voice. Here's a sentence in the passive voice:

> The birdhouse was built by Sharon.

Although it is sometimes appropriate to use the passive voice, like when the "doer" isn't known:

> Our house was vandalized while we were away.

We don't know who specifically vandalized the house, so we use the passive voice.

However, the active voice is preferable in most cases because it is not only shorter but more concise and vigorous. Look at the following example of a sentence in passive voice:

> When the basic elements of the theory of natural selection were conceived by Darwin, it was unknown to him that most of the same ideas had already been developed by a rival naturalist, Charles Russel Wallace. (36 words)

Here's how the improved sentence reads when the active voice is used instead:

> When Darwin conceived the basic elements of the theory of natural selection he didn't know that rival naturalist Charles Russel Wallace had already developed most of the same ideas. (29 words)

Unless there is a good reason to use the passive voice in a particular sentence, choose the active instead.

Hopefully, this chapter was useful to you. Refer back to the points discussed here if necessary.

Pop Quiz A

Directions: For each question, choose the answer that would result in the most effective writing. Some sentences may be correct as written.

(1) Painting a room can be a time consuming task that can take a long time. (2) First, all the pictures must be removed from the walls then the nail holes must be patched and sanded. (3) After all this is done the furniture must be covered so paint doesn't splash on it and ruin it. (4) The trim takes a long time, it has to be done carefully. (5) Finally, the walls can be painted. (6) When the job looks done it really isn't. (7) Cleaning up, and re-hanging the pictures can take a long time.

1. **Sentence 1:** Painting a room can be a time consuming <u>task that can take a long time</u>.

   Which is the best way to write the underlined portion of this sentence?

   (A) task that can take a long time

   (B) task, that can take a long time

   (C) task.

   (D) task; that can take a long time

2. **Sentence 2:** First, all the pictures must be removed from the <u>walls then</u> the nail holes must be patched and sanded.

   Which of the following is the best way to write the underlined portion of this sentence?

   (F) walls then

   (G) walls, then

   (H) walls; then

   (J) walls. Then

3. **Sentence 3:** After all this is done the furniture must be covered so paint doesn't splash on it and ruin it.

   What correction should be made to this sentence?
   (A) Add a comma after done
   (B) Add a comma after covered
   (C) Add a comma after it
   (D) Add a semicolon after covered

4. **Sentence 4:** The trim takes a long <u>time, it</u> has to be done carefully.

   Which of the following is the best way to write the underlined portion of this sentence?
   (F) time, it
   (G) time; it
   (H) time. It
   (J) time, and

5. **Sentence 6:** When the job looks done it really isn't.

   What correction should be made to this sentence?
   (A) add a semicolon after done
   (B) add a comma after when
   (C) add a comma after looks
   (D) add a comma after done

6. **Sentence 7:** Cleaning up, and re-hanging the pictures can take a long time.

   What correction should be made to this sentence?
   (F) remove the comma
   (G) replace the comma with a semicolon
   (H) add a comma after pictures
   (J) no correction is necessary

PT/HSPA, FCAT, MEAP HST, MCAS, GEE21, Regents Exams, SOL, AHSGE, GHSGT, BS
NCCT, AHSGE, GHSGT, BST, BSAP, WASL, CAHSEE, TAAS, OGT, HSPA, FCAT, MEAP
GT, HSPT/HSPA, FCAT, MEAP HST, MCAS, GEE21, Regents Exams, NCCT, AHSGE, GHS
GHSGT, BST, BSAP, WASL, CAHSEE, TAAS, OGT, HSPA, FCAT, MEAP HST, MCAS,

CHAPTER
6

Solutions for Pop Quiz A

1. **The correct answer is (C).** *Time consuming task* and *can take a long time* mean the same thing. Including both is redundant.

2. **The correct answer is (H).** Although it would be possible to place a period after *walls* and begin a new sentence, the sentences would be short and choppy. A semicolon separates the independent clauses but keeps the ideas together in one sentence.

3. **The correct answer is (F).** *After all this is done* is a dependent clause, which must be separated from the independent clause by a comma.

4. **The correct answer is (B).** A semicolon after *time* is appropriate for joining the two short independent clauses.

5. **The correct answer is (J).** *When the job looks done* is a dependent clause introducing the dependent clause.

6. **The correct answer is (A).** No comma is necessary in this sentence.

Diction, Tone, and Figurative Language

The term **diction** refers to word choice. Just as you change your spoken words to make them appropriate for different situations, writers change their words to clarify and strengthen their idea. Diction can be casual, formal, informal, conversational, or even full of slang. As writers make decisions about their diction, they are developing the tone of their writing. **Tone** is the attitude, or feeling, that a passage conveys. The tone of a passage can be funny, scary, impersonal, or passionate—anything the writer wants it to be. The following two sentences show how different word choices can change the tone of a passage:

Sentence 1: Demetrius listened with quite surprise to his mother's words; then he put down the phone and walked into the hall.

Sentence 2: Demetrius listened with astonishment to his mother's lecture; then he slammed down the phone and stormed into the hall.

Another tone that you will find in the reading passages is **irony**. Irony in literature—and in life—happens when there is a startling difference between what you expect to happen and what actually happens.

Diction and, especially, tone go a long way toward conveying the author's main idea because they hint at the narrator's feelings toward the characters in the story. An ironic tone, for example, may indicate that the narrator disapproves of the characters' actions. Understanding diction and tone can, therefore, help you grasp the underlying meaning g of a passage.

Recognizing Figurative Language

Sometimes writers use **figurative language** to create a humorous, vivid image or mental picture. When you read figurative language, remember that the words aren't supposed to be taken literally. They're meant to capture your imagination and help you see new relationships between things. Compare these types of figurative language:

Sentence 1: Juanita's sparkling eyes are like gemstones. (simile)

Sentence 2: Juanita's smile is blinding! (metaphor)

A **simile** is a comparison. You can always recognize a simile because it contains the words *like* or *as*. A **metaphor** takes the comparison one step further: two things are described as if they are one and the same. The words *like* or *as* do not appear.

For example, to make a stronger point about Juanita's powerful smile, the writer of sentence 2 says her smile actually is blinding.

Recognizing Alliteration

"Who is the bravest, boldest, and best leader that our beloved country has ever seen?"

This question contains four words that begin with *b*. Read it out loud and notice how the words beginning with *b* catch your attention. Think, too, about how the sound links the "leader" with the "country". Poets often place words that start with the same letter near each other to create this kind of effect. This technique is called **alliteration**.

Personification, Symbolism, and Imagery

Like other writers, poets sometimes depend on figurative language to communicate ideas and observations. Figurative language is not meant to be taken literally. Instead, it compares things in an unusual way. It creates mental images that help the readers see ideas in new ways, too.

Symbolism and personification are two more types of figurative language. **Symbolism** is figurative language in which an object, a person, or an event represents something else. For example, a country's flag usually symbolizes its pride and its people. **Personification** takes symbolism one step further. When an object is personified, it is given human qualities.

Just remember: PERSONIFICATION = LIKE A PERSON.

For example, a building doesn't experience feelings and emotions. Still, a writer might say, "The old building stood its ground bravely against the wrecking ball."

Imagery is the poet's appeal to our senses: the smell of perfume, the thrill of a roller coaster ride, the sound of a cat's meow, and the feel of rain on your face. Words that express these images call up sensations that are much greater than the words themselves. When you see a verbal image in a poem, try to feel, to sense, to experience the image as you read it. Okay, we know you won't have that much time while you take your exam, but now you know all about figurative language.

And, speaking of language, let move on to a quick review of word parts and how they work. After all, without words, there'd be no reading on which to test you!

How Word Parts Work

Your exit-level reading or language arts exam isn't a spelling test, and it isn't a "vocabulary bee," but you should be aware of the parts of words and how they work. This chapter will help you figure out the meanings of unfamiliar words you come across in your exam. You'll learn the basics of how words are built, what word parts mean, and how they work together. You'll also get a crash-course list of common word parts that will help you understand the meanings of words you may encounter (maybe for the first time).

HOW WORDS ARE BUILT

Knowing what the parts of words mean is the key to deciphering words you've never seen before. Let's take a look at the word *biography* and its parts. You know that a biography is something written about a person's life. How do the word parts tell you this? Well, the second part of the word, *graphy*, comes from a Greek word that means "writing." The first part of the word, *bio*, is also from Greek and it means "life." Put them both together and you get... *biography*, the story of a person's life. If you add the Latin word for "self"—*auto*—you get ... *autobiography*, a story you write about your own life. Think about some other words that use one or more of these parts, like *automobile*, *biochemistry*, and *autograph*. Can you see how the meaning fits the word parts?

When you know some common word parts and how they work, then you'll have a formula for figuring out the meanings of unfamiliar words.

THE THREE BASIC WORD PARTS AND HOW THEY WORK

Different kinds of word parts work together to make a fully functioning word. Think about it: If your car is going to do more than just sit there, it needs a collection of parts put together in the right way. Two steering wheels won't do you any good if you don't have a gas tank.

Each kind of word part has a specific purpose. There are three basic types of word parts:

1. **Prefixes**—These parts attach to the beginning of a root word to alter its meaning or create a new word.

2. **Suffixes**—These parts attach to the end of a root word to change its meaning, help make it grammatically correct in context, or form a new word.

3. **Roots**—The basic element of a word that determines its meaning. Groups of words from the same root word are called word families.

PT/HSPA, FCAT, MEAP HST, MCAS, GEE21, Regents Exams, SOL, NCCT, AHSGE, GHSGT, BS
NCCT, AHSGE, GHSGT, BST, BSAP, WASL, CAHSEE, TAAS, OGT, /HSPA, FCAT, MEAP
GT, HSPT/HSPA, FCAT, MEAP HST, MCAS, GEE21, Regents Exams, NCCT, AHSGE, GHS
T, GHSGT, BST, BSAP, WASL, CAHSEE, TAAS, OGT, HSPT/HSPA, FCAT, MEAP HST, MCAS, C

CHAPTER
6

A word can have a root, a prefix, and a suffix; it can have a root and two suffixes or a root and one prefix. The possibilities are endless (almost), but you must always have a root.

Use the word list that follows to expand your word horizons. Once you begin to learn the word parts on the list, you'll be able to take apart unfamiliar words like a master mechanic. As you make your way through the list, try to think of other words with the same parts. If you have time, check their meanings in a dictionary and take a look at the word origins in the entry.

LIST OF COMMON WORD PARTS

Prefixes

Prefix	Meaning	Example
a-	in, on, of, to	*abed*—in bed
a-, ab-, abs-	from, away	*abrade*—wear off *absent*—away, not present
a-, an-	lacking, not	*asymptomatic*—showing no symptoms *anaerobic*—able to live without air
ac-, ad-, af-, ag-, al-, an-, ap-, ar-, as-, at-	to, toward	*accost*—approach and speak to *adjunct*—something added to *aggregate*—bring together
ambi-, amphi-	around, both	*ambidextrous*—using both hands equally *amphibious*—living both in water and on land
ana-	up, again, anew, throughout	*analyze*—loosen up, break up into parts *anagram*—word spelled by mixing up letters of another word
ante-	before	*antediluvian*—before the Flood
anti-	against	*antiwar*—against war
arch-	first, chief	*archetype*—first model
auto-	self	*automobile*—self-moving vehicle
bene-, ben-	good, well	*benefactor*—one who does good deeds

bi-	two	*bilateral*—two-sided
circum-	around	*circumnavigate*—sail around
com-, co-, col-, con-, cor-	with, together	*concentrate*—bring closer together *cooperate*—work with *collapse*—fall together
contra-, contro-, counter-	against	*contradict*—speak against *counterclockwise*—against the clock
de-	away from, down, opposite of	*detract*—draw away from
demi-	half	*demitasse*—half cup
di-	twice, double	*dichromatic*—having two colors
dia-	across, through	*diameter*—measurement across
dis-, di-	not, away from	*dislike*—to not like *digress*—turn away from the subject
dys-	bad, poor	*dyslexia*—poor reading
equi-	equal	*equivalent*—of equal value
ex-, e-, ef-	from, out	*expatriate*—one who lives outside his or her native country *emit*—send out
extra-	outside, beyond	*extraterrestrial*—from beyond the earth
fore-	in front of, previous	*forecast*—tell ahead of time *foreleg*—front leg
geo-	earth	*geography*—science of the earth's surface
homo-	same, like	*homophonic*—sounding the same
hyper-	too much, over	*hyperactive*—overly active
hypo-	too little, under	*hypothermia*—state of having too little body heat
in-, il-, ig-, im-, ir-	not	*innocent*—not guilty *ignorant*—not knowing *illogical*—not logical *irresponsible*—not responsible

T/HSPA, FCAT, MEAP HST, MCAS, GEE21, Regents Exams, SOL, NCCT, AHSGE, GHSGT, BST
NCCT, AHSGE, GHSGT, BST, BSAP, WASL, CAHSEE, TAAS, OGT HST/HSPA, FCAT, MEAP
GT, HSPT/HSPA, FCAT, MEAP HST, MCAS, GEE21, Regents Exams NCCT, AHSGE, GHSC
GHSGT BST BSAP WASL CAHSEE TAAS OGT HSPT/HSPA FCAT MEAP HST MCAS

CHAPTER
6

in-, il-, im-, ir-	on, into, in	*impose*—place on *invade*—go into
intra-, intro-	within, inside	*intrastate*—within a state
inter-	between, among	*interplanetary*—between planets
mal-, male-	bad, wrong, poor	*maladjust*—adjust poorly *malevolent*—ill-wishing
mis-	badly, wrongly	*misunderstand*—understand wrongly
mis-, miso-	hatred	*misogyny*—hatred of women
mono-	single, one	*monorail*—train that runs on a single rail
neo-	new	*neolithic*—of the New Stone Age
non-	not	*nonentity*—a nobody
ob-	over, against, toward	*obstruct*—stand against
omni-	all	*omnipresent*—present in all places
pan-	all	*panorama*—a complete view
peri-	around, near	*periscope*—device for seeing all around
poly-	many	*polygonal*—many-sided
post-	after	*postmortem*—after death
pre-	before, earlier than	*prejudice*—judgment in advance
pro-	in favor of, forward, in front of	*proceed*—go forward *prowar*—in favor of war
re-	back, again	*rethink*—think again *reimburse*—pay back
retro-	backward	*retrospective*—looking backward
se-	apart, away	*seclude*—keep away
semi-	half	*semiconscious*—half conscious
sub-, suc-, suf-, sug-, sus-	under, beneath	*subscribe*—write underneath *suspend*—hang down *suffer*—undergo
super-	above, greater	*superfluous*—overflowing, beyond what is needed
syn-, sym-, syl-, sys-	with, at the same time	*synthesis*—a putting together *sympathy*—a feeling with

tele-	far	*television*—machine for seeing far
trans-	across	*transport*—carry across a distance
un-	not	*uninformed*—not informed
vice-	acting for, next in rank to	*viceroy*—one acting for the king

Suffixes

Suffix	Meaning	Example
-able, -ble	able, capable	*acceptable*—able to be accepted
-acious, -cious	characterized by, having the quality of	*fallacious*—having the quality of a fallacy
-age	sum, total	*mileage*—total number of miles
-al	of, like, suitable for	*theatrical*—suitable for theater
-ance, -ancy	act or state of	*disturbance*—act of disturbing
-ant, -ent	one who	*defendant*—one who defends him- or herself
-ary, -ar	having the nature of, concerning	*military*—relating to soldiers *polar*—concerning the pole
-cy	act, state, or position of	*presidency*—position of president *ascendancy*—state of being raised up
-dom	state, rank, that which belongs to	*wisdom*—state of being wise
-ence	act, state, or quality of	*dependence*—state of depending
-er, -or	one who, that which	*doer*—one who does *conductor*—that which conducts
-escent	becoming	*obsolescent*—becoming obsolete
-fy	to make	*pacify*—make peaceful
-hood	state, condition	*adulthood*—state of being adult
-ic, -ac	of, like	*demonic*—of or like a demon
-il, -ile	having to do with, like, suitable for	*civil*—having to do with citizens *tactile*—having to do with touch
-ion	act or condition of	*operation*—act of operating

CHAPTER 6

-ious	having, characterized by	*anxious*—characterized by anxiety
-ish	like, somewhat	*foolish*—like a fool
-ism	belief or practice of	*racism*—belief in racial superiority
-ist	one who does, makes, or is concerned with	*scientist*—one concerned with science
-ity, -ty, -y	character or state of being	*amity*—friendship *jealousy*—state of being jealous
-ive	of, relating to, tending to	*destructive*—tending to destroy
-logue, -loquy	speech or writing	*monologue*—speech by one person *colloquy*—conversation
-logy	speech, study of	*geology*—study of the earth
-ment	act or state of	*abandonment*—act of abandoning
-mony	a resulting thing, condition, or state	*patrimony*—property inherited from one's father
-ness	act or quality	*kindness*—quality of being kind
-ory	having the quality of; a place or thing for	*compensatory*—having the quality of a compensation *lavatory*—place for washing
-ous, -ose	full of, having	*glamorous*—full of glamour
-ship	skill, state of being	*horsemanship*—skill in riding *ownership*—state of being an owner
-some	full of, like	*frolicsome*—playful
-tude	state or quality of	*rectitude*—state of being morally upright
-ward	in the direction of	*homeward*—in the direction of home
-y	full of, like, somewhat	*wily*—full of wiles

Roots

Root	Meaning	Examples
acr	bitter	*acrid, acrimony*
act, ag	do, act, drive	*action, react, agitate*
acu	sharp, keen	*acute, acumen*

High Stakes: Reading

agog	leader	*pedagogue, demagogic*
agr	field	*agronomy, agriculture*
ali	other	*alias, alienate, inalienable*
alt	high	*altitude, contralto*
alter, altr	other, change	*alternative, altercation, altruism*
am, amic	love, friend	*amorous, amiable*
anim	mind, life, spirit	*animism, animate, animosity*
annu, enni	year	*annual, superannuated, biennial*
anthrop	man	*anthropoid, misanthropy*
apt, ept	fit	*apt, adapt, ineptitude*
aqu	water	*aquatic, aquamarine*
arbit	judge	*arbiter, arbitrary*
arch	chief	*anarchy, matriarch*
arm	arm, weapon	*army, armature, disarm*
art	skill, a fitting together	*artisan, artifact, articulate*
aster, astr	star	*asteroid, disaster, astral*
aud, audit, aur	hear	*auditorium, audition, auricle*
aur	gold	*aureate, aureomycin*
aut	self	*autism, autograph*
bell	war	*antebellum, belligerent*
ben, bene	well, good	*benevolent, benefit*
bibli	book	*bibliography, bibliophile*
bio	life	*biosphere, amphibious*
brev	short	*brevity, abbreviation*
cad, cas, cid	fall	*cadence, casualty, occasion, accident*
cand	white, shining	*candid, candle, incandescent*
cant, chant	sing, charm	*cantor, recant, enchant*
cap, capt, cept, cip	take, seize, hold	*capable, captive, accept, incipient*
capit	head	*capital, decapitate, recapitulate*
carn	flesh	*carnal, incarnate*

17/HSPA, FCAT, MEAP HST, MCAS, GEE21, Regents Exams, SOL, AHSGE, GHSGT, BS
NCCT, AHSGE, GHSGT, BST, BSAP, WASL, CAHSEE, TAAS, OGT, ST/HSPA, FCAT, MEAP
GT, HSPT/HSPA, FCAT, MEAP HST, MCAS, GEE21, Regents Exams, NCCT, AHSGE, GHS
E GHSGT, BST, BSAP, WASL, CAHSEE, TAAS, OGT, HSPT/HSPA, FCAT, MEAP HST, MCAS

CHAPTER
6

READING

cede, ceed, cess	go, yield	*secede, exceed, process, intercession*
cent	hundred	*percentage, centimeter*
cern, cert	perceive, make certain, decide	*concern, certificate, certain*
chrom	color	*monochrome, chromatic*
chron	time	*chronometer, anachronism*
cide, cis	cut, kill	*genocide, incision*
cit	summon, impel	*cite, excite, incitement*
civ	citizen	*uncivil, civilization*
clam, claim	shout	*clamorous, proclaim, claimant*
clar	clear	*clarity, clarion, declare*
clin	slope, lean	*inclination, recline*
clud, clus, clos	close, shut	*seclude, recluse, closet*
cogn	know	*recognize, incognito*
col, cul	till	*colony, cultivate, agriculture*
corp	body	*incorporate, corpse*
cosm	order, world	*cosmetic, cosmos, cosmopolitan*
crac, crat	power, rule	*democrat, theocracy*
cre, cresc, cret	grow	*increase, crescent, accretion*
cred	trust, believe	*credit, incredible*
crux, cruc	cross	*crux, crucial, crucifix*
crypt	hidden	*cryptic, cryptography*
culp	blame	*culprit, culpability*
cur, curr, curs	run, course	*occur, current, incursion*
cura	care	*curator, accurate*
cycl	wheel, circle	*bicycle, cyclone*
dec	ten	*decade, decimal*
dem	people	*demographic, demagogue*
dent	tooth	*dental, indentation*
derm	skin	*dermatitis, pachyderm*
di, dia	day	*diary, quotidian*

dic, dict	say, speak	*indicative, edict, dictation*
dign	worthy	*dignified, dignitary*
doc, doct	teach, prove	*indoctrinate, docile, doctor*
domin	rule	*predominate, domineer, dominion*
dorm	sleep	*dormitory, dormant*
du	two	*duo, duplicity, dual*
duc, duct	lead	*educate, abduct, ductile*
dur	hard, lasting	*endure, obdurate, duration*
dyn	force, power	*dynamo, dynamite*
ego	I	*egomania, egotist*
equ	equal	*equation, equitable*
erg, urg	work, power	*energetic, metallurgy, demiurge*
err	wander	*error, aberrant*
ev	time, age	*coeval, longevity*
fac, fact, fect, fic	do, make	*facility, factual, perfect, artifice*
fer	bear, carry	*prefer, refer, conifer, fertility*
ferv	boil	*fervid, effervesce*
fid	belief, faith	*infidelity, confidant, perfidious*
fin	end, limit	*finite, confine*
firm	strong	*reaffirm, infirmity*
flect, flex	bend	*reflex, inflection*
flor	flower	*florescent, floral*
flu, fluct, flux	flow	*fluid, fluctuation, influx*
form	shape	*formative, reform, formation*
fort	strong	*effort, fortitude*
frag, fract	break	*fragility, infraction*
fug	flee	*refuge, fugitive*
fus	pour, join	*infuse, transfusion*
gam	marry	*exogamy, polygamous*
ge, geo	earth	*geology, geode, perigee*
gen	birth, kind, race	*engender, general, generation*

gest	carry, bear	*gestation, ingest, digest*
gon	angle	*hexagonal, trigonometry*
grad, gress	step, go	*regress, gradation*
gram	writing	*grammar, cryptogram*
graph	writing	*telegraph, graphics*
grat	pleasing, agreeable	*congratulate, gratuitous*
grav	weight, heavy	*gravamen, gravity*
greg	flock, crowd	*gregarious, segregate*
habit, hibit	have, hold	*habitation, inhibit, habitual*
heli	sun	*helium, heliocentric, aphelion*
hem	blood	*hemoglobin, hemorrhage*
her, hes	stick, cling	*adherent, cohesive*
hydr	water	*dehydration, hydrofoil*
iatr	heal, cure	*pediatrics, psychiatry*
iso	same, equal	*isotope, isometric*
it	journey, go	*itinerary, exit*
ject	throw	*reject, subjective, projection*
jud	judge	*judicial, adjudicate*
jug, junct	join	*conjugal, juncture, conjunction*
jur	swear	*perjure, jurisprudence*
labor	work	*laborious, belabor*
leg	law	*legal, illegitimate*
leg, lig, lect	choose, gather, read	*illegible, eligible, select, lecture*
lev	light, rise	*levity, alleviate*
liber	free	*liberal, libertine*
liter	letter	*literate, alliterative*
lith	rock, stone	*eolithic, lithograph*
loc	place	*locale, locus, allocate*
log	word, study	*logic, biology, dialogue*
loqu, locut	talk, speech	*colloquial, loquacious, interlocutor*

luc, lum	light	*translucent, pellucid, illumine, luminous*
lud, lus	play	*allusion, ludicrous, interlude*
magn	large, great	*magnificent, magnitude*
mal	bad, ill	*malodorous, malinger*
man, manu	hand	*manifest, manicure, manuscript*
mar	sea	*maritime, submarine*
mater, matr	mother	*matriarchal, maternal*
medi	middle	*intermediary, medieval*
mega	large, million	*megaphone, megacycle*
ment	mind	*demented, mental*
merg, mers	plunge, dip	*emerge, submersion*
meter, metr, mens	measure	*chronometer, metronome, geometry, commensurate*
micr	small	*microfilm, micron*
min	little	*minimum, minute*
mit, miss	send	*remit, admission, missive*
mon, monit	warn	*admonish, monument, monitor*
mor	custom	*mores, immoral*
mor, mort	death	*mortify, mortician*
morph	shape	*amorphous, anthropomorphic*
mov, mob, mot	move	*removal, automobile, motility*
multi	many	*multiply, multinational*
mut	change	*mutable, transmute*
nasc, nat	born	*native, natural, nascent, innate*
nav	ship, sail	*navy, navigable*
necr	dead, die	*necropolis, necrosis*
neg	deny	*renege, negative*
neo	new	*neologism, neoclassical*
nomen, nomin	name	*nomenclature, cognomen, nominate*
nomy	law, rule	*astronomy, antinomy*

nov	new	*novice, innovation*
ocul	eye	*binocular, oculist*
omni	all	*omniscient, omnibus*
onym	name	*pseudonym, eponymous*
oper	work	*operate, cooperation, inoperable*
ora	speak, pray	*oracle, oratory*
orn	decorate	*adorn, ornate*
orth	straight, correct	*orthodox, orthopedic*
pan	all	*panacea, pantheon*
pater, patr	father	*patriot, paternity*
path, pat, pass	feel, suffer	*telepathy, patient, compassion, passion*
ped	child	*pedagogue, pediatrics*
ped, pod	foot	*pedestrian, impede, tripod*
pel, puls	drive, push	*impel, propulsion*
pend, pens	hang	*pendulous, suspense*
pet, peat	seek	*petition, impetus, repeat*
phil	love	*philosopher, Anglophile*
phob	fear	*phobic, agoraphobia*
phon	sound	*phonograph, symphony*
phor	bearing	*semaphore, metaphor*
phot	light	*photograph, photoelectric*
pon, pos	place, put	*component, repose, postpone*
port	carry	*report, portable, deportation*
pot	power	*potency, potential*
press	press	*pressure, impression*
prim	first	*primal, primordial*
proto, prot	first	*proton, protagonist*
psych	mind	*psychic, metempsychosis*
pyr	fire	*pyrite, pyrophobia*
quer, quir, quis, ques	ask, seek	*query, inquiry, inquisitive, quest*
reg, rig, rect	straight, rule	*regulate, dirigible, corrective*

rid, ris	laugh	*deride, risible, ridiculous*
rog	ask	*rogation, interrogate*
rupt	break	*erupt, interruption, rupture*
sanct	holy	*sacrosanct, sanctify, sanction*
sci, scio	know	*nescient, conscious, omniscience*
scop	watch, view	*horoscope, telescopic*
scrib, script	write	*scribble, proscribe, description*
sed, sid, sess	sit, seat	*sedate, residence, session*
seg, sect	cut	*segment, section, intersect*
sent, sens	feel, think	*nonsense, sensitive, sentient, dissent*
sequ, secut	follow	*sequel, consequence, consecutive*
sign	sign, mark	*signature, designate, assign*
sol	alone	*solitary, solo, desolate*
solv, solu, solut	loosen	*dissolve, soluble, absolution*
somn	sleep	*insomnia, somnolent*
son	sound	*sonorous, unison*
soph	wise, wisdom	*philosophy, sophisticated*
spec, spic, spect	look	*specimen, conspicuous, spectacle*
spir	breathe	*spirit, conspire, respiration*
stab, stat	stand	*unstable, status, station, establish*
stead	place	*instead, steadfast*
string, strict	bind	*astringent, stricture, restrict*
stru, struct	build	*construe, structure, destructive*
sum, sumpt	take	*presume, consumer, assumption*
tang, ting, tact, tig	touch	*tangent, contingency, contact, tactile, contiguous*
tax, tac	arrange, arrangement	*taxonomy, tactic*
techn	skill, art	*technique, technician*
tele	far	*teletype, telekinesis*
tempor	time	*temporize, extemporaneous*
ten, tain, tent	hold	*tenant, tenacity, retention, contain*

tend, tens, tent	stretch	*contend, extensive, intent*
tenu	thin	*tenuous, attenuate*
term	end	*terminal, terminate*
terr, ter	land, earth	*inter, terrain*
test	witness	*attest, testify*
the	god	*polytheism, theologist*
therm	heat	*thermos, isotherm*
tom	cut	*atomic, appendectomy*
tort, tors	twist	*tortuous, torsion, contort*
tract	pull, draw	*traction, attract, protract*
trib	assign, pay	*attribute, tribute, retribution*
trud, trus	thrust	*obtrude, intrusive*
turb	agitate	*perturb, turbulent, disturb*
umbr	shade	*umbrella, penumbra, umbrage*
uni	one	*unify, disunity, union*
urb	city	*urbane, suburb*
vac	empty	*vacuous, evacuation*
vad, vas	go	*invade, evasive*
val, vail	strength, worth	*valid, avail, prevalent*
ven, vent	come	*advent, convene, prevention*
ver	true	*aver, veracity, verity*
verb	word	*verbose, adverb, verbatim*
vert, vers	turn	*revert, perversion*
vest	dress	*vestment*
vid, vis	see	*video, evidence, vision, revise*
vinc, vict	conquer	*evince, convict, victim*
viv, vit	life	*vivid, revive, vital*
voc, vok	call	*vociferous, provocative, revoke*
vol	wish	*involuntary, volition*
voly, volut	roll, turn	*involve, convoluted, revolution*
vulg	common	*divulge, vulgarity*
zo	animal	*zoologist, paleozoic*

Summary: What You Need To Know about Word Parts

☑ Words have three basic parts: *roots*, *suffixes*, and *prefixes*

☑ Each word part has a specific purpose

☑ Word parts work together to form the meaning and function of the word in which they occur

☑ When you recognize common word parts you can deconstruct any word to determine its meaning.

Pop Quiz B

Directions: In each of the following exercises, the words in the left-hand column are built on roots given in the word-part list. Match each word with its definition from the right-hand column. Refer to the list if necessary. Can you identify the roots of each word? If you can't figure out a word, look it up in a dictionary.

1.	mutable	A.	able to be touched
2.	culpable	B.	laughable
3.	interminable	C.	empty of meaning or interest
4.	amiable	D.	of the first age
5.	vacuous	E.	holding firmly
6.	vital	F.	necessary to life
7.	primeval	G.	unending
8.	tenacious	H.	stable, not able to be loosened or broken up
9.	tangible	I.	changeable
10.	inoperable	J.	friendly
11.	risible	K.	blameworthy
12.	indissoluble	L.	not working, out of order

NCCT, AHSGE, GHSGT, BST, BSAP, WASL, CAHSEE, TAAS, OGT   /HSPA, FCAT, MEAP
GT, HSPT/HSPA, FCAT, MEAP HST, MCAS, GEE21, Regents Exams,   NCCT, AHSGE, GHS

CHAPTER

6

READING

Solutions for Pop Quiz B

1. I	4. J	7. D	9. A	11. B
2. K	5. C	8. E	10. L	12. H
3. G	6. F			

CHAPTER 7

PRACTICE ONE

It's an old story—so old, in fact, that you may not have heard it. A man standing on a street-corner in New York City is trying to find his way to Carnegie Hall, because he has tickets to a concert there. A taxicab is stopped at a light, and the man figures nobody would know his way around the city better than the cab driver, so he decides to ask the cabbie for directions.

"Excuse me, sir," the man says to the cab driver, "but can you tell me how to get to Carnegie Hall?"

The cabbie looks at him for a moment, nods his head, and just as the light turns green replies: "Practice, practice, practice."

Practice, practice, practice is what the rest of this book is about. No matter how much you study about *how* things work, you still need to practice *doing* what needs to be done. Practicing a musical instrument may or may not get you to Carnegie Hall, but practicing for your high-stakes exam will help you to get a better grade.

In this chapter, you will find different sets of questions. Some of these sets will require you to read a passage, and some will not. Each has its own directions, and each section is followed by the solutions for that section, including (where feasible) explanations of how the answers were determined. Enjoy yourself, and knock 'em dead!

Practicing Sentence Completions

Directions: Each of the following questions consists of an incomplete sentence followed by five words or pairs of words. Choose that word or pair of words that, when substituted for the blank space or spaces, best completes the meaning of the sentence and mark the letter of your choice either in the book or on a separate sheet of scrap paper.

Example of a Sentence Completion Question:

In view of the extenuating circumstances and the defendant's youth, the judge recommended _____.

(A) conviction

(B) a defense

(C) a mistrial

(D) leniency

(E) life imprisonment

Ⓐ Ⓑ Ⓒ ● Ⓔ

Now, begin the Sentence Completion practice.

1. Because the elder Johnson was regarded with much _____ by an appreciative public, the younger quite naturally received _____.

(A) disdain .. kudos

(B) awe .. respect

(C) curiosity .. familiarity

(D) contemplation .. abandonment

(E) pleasantry .. laughs

Ⓐ Ⓑ Ⓒ Ⓓ Ⓔ

s, GEE 21, Regents Exams, SOL, NCCT, AHSGE, GHSGT, BST, BSAP, WASL, CAHSEE, TAAS, C
AP, WASL, CAHSEE, TAAS, OGT, HSPT/HSPA, FCAT, MEAP HST, MCAS, GEE 21, Regents Exar
MC gents Exams, SOL, NCCT, AHSGE, GHSGT, BST, BSAP, WASL, CAHSEE, T
SEE TAAS OCT HSPT/HSPA ECAT MEAP HST MCAS GEE 21 SOL NCC

PRACTICE ONE

HIGH STAKES

2. Her temperament was exceedingly _____, angry one minute but serene the next.
   (A) mercurial
   (B) steadfast
   (C) distraught
   (D) archetypal
   (E) circumspect

   Ⓐ Ⓑ Ⓒ Ⓓ Ⓔ

3. Traveling by automobile was _____ to him, but he thought nothing of bobsledding, which had been his _____ for many years.
   (A) tiresome .. profession
   (B) tiring .. outlet
   (C) harrowing .. hobby
   (D) a threat .. relief
   (E) exciting .. fun

   Ⓐ Ⓑ Ⓒ Ⓓ Ⓔ

4. Perennial flowers, such as irises, remain _____ every winter, but they _____ in the spring.
   (A) fertile .. wither
   (B) arable .. congeal
   (C) dormant .. burgeon
   (D) distended .. contract
   (E) attenuated .. rebound

   Ⓐ Ⓑ Ⓒ Ⓓ Ⓔ

5. The _____ customer was _____ by the manager's prompt action and apology.
   (A) pecuniary .. appalled
   (B) weary .. enervated
   (C) sedulous .. consoled
   (D) intrepid .. mortified
   (E) irate .. mollified

   Ⓐ Ⓑ Ⓒ Ⓓ Ⓔ

SPT/HSPA, FCAT, MEAP HST, MCAS, GEE21, Regents Exams, SOL, NCCT, AHSGE, GHSGT, B
L, NCCT, AHSGE, GHSGT, BST, BSAP, WASL, CAHSEE, TAAS, OGT, T/HSPA, FCAT, MEA
OGT, HSPT/HSPA, FCAT, MEAP HST, MCAS, GEE21, Regents Exams, OL, NCCT, AHSGE, GH
GE, GHSGT, BST, BSAP, WASL, CAHSEE, TAAS, OGT, HSPT/HSPA, FCAT, MEAP HST, MCAS

CHAPTER
7
READING

6. His _____ manner served to hide the fact that
he secretly indulged in the very vices he publicly
_____.

(A) sedulous .. dispelled

(B) sanctimonious .. condemned

(C) dogmatic .. espoused

(D) stentorian .. prescribed

(E) candid .. promulgated

Ⓐ Ⓑ Ⓒ Ⓓ Ⓔ

7. Because of the _____ caused by the flood,
living conditions in the area have _____; many
people have lost all their belongings.

(A) trepidation .. augmented

(B) morass .. careened

(C) censure .. abated

(D) devastation . .deteriorated

(E) vertigo .. ameliorated

Ⓐ Ⓑ Ⓒ Ⓓ Ⓔ

8. Propaganda is a(n) _____ of truth—a mixture of
half-truths and half-lies calculated to deceive.

(A) revision

(B) perversion

(C) dissension

(D) perception

(E) invasion

Ⓐ Ⓑ Ⓒ Ⓓ Ⓔ

9. Though brilliantly presented, the report was
_____, since the information on which it was
based was erroneous.

(A) informative

(B) erudite

(C) laudable

(D) worthless

(E) verbose

Ⓐ Ⓑ Ⓒ Ⓓ Ⓔ

SOLUTIONS FOR SENTENCE COMPLETIONS

1. **The correct answer is (B).** An "appreciative public" is likely to give *respect* to the elder Johnson's son. (Think about it.)

2. **The correct answer is (A).** A person who is angry one minute but serene the next is said to be *mercurial* (changeable). [Imagine liquid mercury sliding all over the place.]

3. **The correct answer is (C).** Irony, or paradox, is indicated by the phrase "but he thought nothing of..." It is ironic that automobile travel should be *harrowing* (frightening) to someone whose hobby is bobsledding, which is a dangerous sport.

4. **The correct answer is (C).** A *perennial* flower is one that blooms every year. In the winter, it lies *dormant* (inactive), but the following spring it *burgeons* (sprouts) anew. This is in contrast to an annual, which blooms for one year only.

5. **The correct answer is (E).** A manager who apologizes must be dealing with an *irate* (angry) customer. As a result of the apology, the customer was *mollified* (soothed and pacified).

6. **The correct answer is (B).** Ordinarily, vices are publicly condemned. Secret indulgence in them might, however, be hidden by a *sanctimonious* (excessively righteous) manner.

7. **The correct answer is (D)** A flood that destroys people's belongings causes *devastation*. Living conditions in the area can be said to have *deteriorated* (worsened).

8. **The correct answer is (B).** A *perversion* of the truth is a deviation from the truth, in other words, the half-truths and half-lies that are mentioned in the second half of the sentence.

9. **The correct answer is (D).** As indicated by the word *though*, the sentence requires a contrast. Since the presentation was positive, you should put a negative word in the blank; *worthless* is the best choice to describe a report full of errors.

And now for something completely different, let's move on to Analogies.

SPT/HSPA, FCAT, MEAP HST, MCAS, GEE21, Regents Exams, SOL, NCCT, AHSGE, GHSGT, BS
NCCT, AHSGE, GHSGT, BST, BSAP, WASL, CAHSEE, TAAS, OGT, /HSPA, FCAT, MEAP
OGT, HSPT/HSPA, FCAT, MEAP HST, MCAS, GEE21, Regents Exams, OL, NCCT, AHSGE, GHS
GHSGT, BST, BSAP, WASL, CAHSEE, TAAS, OGT, HSPA, FCAT, MEAP HST, MCAS

CHAPTER
7

READING

Practicing Solving Analogies

Directions: Each of the following questions consists of a capitalized pair of words followed by five pairs of word, lettered (A) to (E). The capitalized words bear some meaningful relationship to one another. Choose the lettered pair of words whose relationship is most similar to that expressed by the capitalized pair and mark its letter either in the book or on a separate sheet of scrap paper.

Example of an Analogy Question:

DAY : SUN ::

(A) sunlight : daylight   (D) heat : cold

(B) ray : sun   (E) moon : star

(C) night : moon

Ⓐ Ⓑ ● Ⓓ Ⓔ

Now, begin the Analogies practice.

10. NOSE : HEAD ::

(A) hand : arm   (D) wrist : finger

(B) foot : toe   (E) teeth : gums

(C) eye : lid

Ⓐ Ⓑ Ⓒ Ⓓ Ⓔ

11. WHEAT : GRAIN ::

(A) cow : beef   (D) coconut : palm

(B) orange : lime   (E) hamburger : steak

(C) carrot : vegetable

Ⓐ Ⓑ Ⓒ Ⓓ Ⓔ

12. COTTAGE : CASTLE ::

(A) house : apartment   (D) man : family

(B) puppy : dog   (E) poet : gentleman

(C) dory : liner

Ⓐ Ⓑ Ⓒ Ⓓ Ⓔ

PRACTICE ONE

13. OLD : ANTIQUE ::

   (A) new : modern   (D) wanted : needed

   (B) cheap : expensive   (E) rich : valuable

   (C) useless : useful

   Ⓐ Ⓑ Ⓒ Ⓓ Ⓔ

14. POSSIBLE : PROBABLE ::

   (A) likely : unlikely   (D) quick : fast

   (B) best : better   (E) frightened : worried

   (C) willing : eager

   Ⓐ Ⓑ Ⓒ Ⓓ Ⓔ

15. DIGRESS : RAMBLE ::

   (A) muffle : stifle   (D) rest : stir

   (B) rust : weld   (E) find : explain

   (C) introduce : conclude

   Ⓐ Ⓑ Ⓒ Ⓓ Ⓔ

SOLUTIONS FOR SOLVING ANALOGIES

10. **The correct answer is (A).** The *nose* is part of the *head*, and the *hand* is part of the *arm*.

11. **The correct answer is (C).** *Wheat* is a type of *grain*; *carrot* is a type of *vegetable*. Both are foodstuffs, and both are specific items that belong to larger groups.

12. **The correct answer is (C).** A *cottage* is a small house; a *castle* is a large and luxurious one. A *dory* is a small rowboat; a *liner* is a large and luxurious passenger ship. See the connection? That was *not* an easy question, especially if you don't know the meaning of the word *dory*.

13. **The correct answer is (A).** Something *antique* is necessarily *old*, and something *modern* is necessarily *new*. The words are essentially synonyms.

14. **The correct answer is (C).** Something that's *possible* might be—but is not necessarily—*probable*. Someone who is *willing* might be—but is not necessarily—*eager*.

15. **The correct answer is (A).** To *digress* from a topic is to *ramble*, and to *muffle* a sound is to *stifle* it. The relationship is again one of synonyms.

Are you still with us? Great; now let's try analyzing some reading passages.

Practicing Reading Passages

Directions: Each passage below is followed by a set of questions. Read each passage, then answer the accompanying questions, basing your answers on what is stated or implied in the passage and in any introductory material provided. Mark the letter of your choice either in the book or on a separate sheet of scrap paper.

Passage 1

Questions 16–22 are based on the following passage.

This passage is taken from the first book of short stories published by Willa Cather (1873-1947), better known for her novels of the western past such as 0 Pioneers! *"Paul's Case" is subtitled "A Study in Temperament."*

Line   It was Paul's afternoon to appear before the faculty of the Pittsburgh High School
        to account for his various misdemeanors. He had been suspended a week ago,
        and his father had called at the Principal's office and confessed his perplexity
        about his son. Paul entered the faculty room suave and smiling. His clothes
    5   were a trifle outgrown, and the tan velvet on the collar of his open overcoat was
        frayed and worn; but for all that there was something of the dandy in him, and
        he wore an opal pin in his neatly knotted black four-in-hand and a red carna-
        tion in his button hole. This latter adornment the faculty somehow felt was not
        properly significant of the contrite spirit befitting a boy under the ban of sus-
    10 pension.

        Paul was tall for his age and very thin, with high, cramped shoulders and a
        narrow chest. His eyes were remarkable for a certain hysterical brilliancy, and
        he continually used them in a conscious, theatrical sort of way, peculiarly offen-
        sive in a boy. The pupils were abnormally large, as though he was addicted to
    15 belladonna, but there was a glassy glitter about them which that drug does not
        produce.

        When questioned by the Principal as to why he was there, Paul stated, politely
        enough, that he wanted to come back to school. This was a lie, but Paul was
        quite accustomed to lying; found it, indeed, indispensable for overcoming fric-
    20 tion. His teachers were asked to state their respective charges against him, which
        they did with such a rancor and aggrievedness as evinced that this was not a

usual case. Disorder and impertinence were among the offenses named, yet each of his instructors felt that it was scarcely possible to put into words the cause of the trouble, which lay in a sort of hysterically defiant manner of the
25 boy's; in the contempt which they all knew he felt for them, and which he seemingly made not the least effort to conceal. Once, when he had been making a synopsis of a paragraph at the blackboard, his English teacher had stepped to his side and attempted to guide his hand.

Paul had started back with a shudder and thrust his hands violently behind
30 him. The astonished woman could scarcely have been more hurt and embarrassed had he struck at her. The insult was so involuntary and definitely personal as to be unforgettable. In one way and another he had made all of his teachers, men and women alike, conscious of the same feeling of physical aversion. In one class he habitually sat with his hand shading his eyes; in another he
35 always looked out the window during the recitation; in another he made a running commentary on the lecture, with humorous intention.

His teachers felt this afternoon that his whole attitude was symbolized by his shrug and his flippantly red carnation flower, and they fell upon him without mercy, his English teacher leading the pack. He stood through it smiling, his
40 pale lips parted over his white teeth. (His lips were constantly twitching, and he had a habit of raising his eyebrows that was contemptuous and irritating to the last degree.) Older boys than Paul had broken down and shed tears under that baptism of fire, but his set smile did not once desert him, and his only sign of discomfort was the nervous trembling of the fingers that toyed with the buttons
45 of his overcoat, and an occasional jerking of the other hand that held his hat. Paul was always smiling, always glancing about him, seeming to feel that people might be watching him and trying to detect something. This conscious expression, since it was as far as possible from boyish mirthfulness, was usually attributed to insolence or "smartness."

16. The subtitle "A Study in Temperament" suggests that Cather wants to examine

(A) a certain type of character

(B) reactions under pressure

(C) how people change over time

(D) people and their settings

(E) inner rage

17. Cather makes it clear in the first paragraph that the faculty of the high school

   (A) are perplexed by Paul's actions

   (B) find Paul's demeanor inappropriate

   (C) cannot understand Paul's words

   (D) want only the best for Paul

   (E) are annoyed at Paul' s disruption of their day

Ⓐ Ⓑ Ⓒ Ⓓ Ⓔ

18. As it is used in lines 12 and 24, the word *hysterical* seems to imply

   (A) hilarious   (D) frothing

   (B) raving   (E) delirious

   (C) uncontrolled

Ⓐ Ⓑ Ⓒ Ⓓ Ⓔ

19. To keep the reader from sympathizing with the faculty, Cather compares them metaphorically to

   (A) rabbits   (D) comedians

   (B) wolves   (E) warships

   (C) dictators

Ⓐ Ⓑ Ⓒ Ⓓ Ⓔ

20. The word *smartness* as used in line 49 is used to mean

   (A) wit   (D) reasonableness

   (B) intelligence   (E) resourcefulness

   (C) impudence

Ⓐ Ⓑ Ⓒ Ⓓ Ⓔ

21. Which adjective *does not* describe Paul as Cather presents him here?

   (A) paranoid   (D) flippant

   (B) defiant   (E) candid

   (C) proud

Ⓐ Ⓑ Ⓒ Ⓓ Ⓔ

22. By the end of the selection, we find that the faculty

(A) resent and loathe Paul

(B) admire and trust Paul

(C) struggle to understand Paul

(D) are physically revolted by Paul

(E) may learn to get along with Paul

Ⓐ Ⓑ Ⓒ Ⓓ Ⓔ

SOLUTIONS FOR PASSAGE 1

16. **The correct answer is (A).** Choice (A) is the only choice that explains the subtitle. The other choices may be included under the idea "A Study in Temperament," but they are not the main idea.

17. **The correct answer is (B).** The faculty members may be perplexed, choice (A), but the first paragraph focuses on their feeling that Paul's dress and behavior are not properly contrite.

18. **The correct answer is (C).** Paul seems to be unable to control his odd mannerisms, but he is not actually frenzied, as choices (B), (D), or (E) would suggest.

19. **The correct answer is (B).** The faculty members "fell upon him without mercy, his English teacher leading the pack" (lines 38-39). The comparison is to a pack of wolves.

20. **The correct answer is (C).** All of the choices could mean "smartness," but only *impudence* makes sense in the context of the passage.

21. **The correct answer is (E).** There is evidence for every other choice in the descriptions of Paul's actions. The point is made in lines 18–20 that Paul often lies, so he cannot be called "candid," which means frank and truthful.

22. **The correct answer is (A).** Paul is physically revolted by the faculty, not vice versa, as in choice (D). The faculty's attack on Paul indicates their hatred for him.

That was certainly a good start, but now that we've gotten our feet wet, so to speak, let's plunge into another pool of words.

Passage 2

Questions 23-31 are based on the following passage.

Thomas Jefferson wrote in 1787 to his nephew, Peter Carr, a student at the College of William and Mary. Here, Jefferson gives advice about Peter's proposed course of study.

Line   Paris, August 10,1787

Dear Peter,

I have received your two letters of Decemb. 30. and April 18. and am very happy to find by them, as well as by letters from Mr. Wythe, that you have been
5 so fortunate as to attract his notice and good will: I am sure you will find this to have been one of the more fortunate events of your life, as I have ever been sensible it was of mine. I inclose you a sketch of the sciences to which I would wish you to apply in such order as Mr. Wythe shall advise: I mention also the books in them worth your reading, which submit to his correction. Many of
10 these are among your father's books, which you should have brought to you. As I do not recollect those of them not in his library, you must write to me for them, making out a catalogue of such as you think you shall have occasion for in 18 months from the date of your letter, and consulting Mr. Wythe on the subject. To this sketch I will add a few particular observations.

15 *1. Italian.* I fear the learning of this language will confound your French and Spanish. Being all of them degenerated dialects of the Latin, they are apt to mix in conversation. I have never seen a person speaking the three languages who did not mix them. It is a delightful language, but late events having rendered the Spanish more useful, lay it aside to prosecute that:

20 *2. Spanish.* Bestow great attention on this, and endeavor to acquire an accurate knowledge of it. Our future connections with Spain and Spanish America will render that language a valuable acquisition. The ancient history of a great part of America too is written in that language. I send you a dictionary.

3. Moral philosophy. I think it lost time to attend lectures in this branch. He
25 who made us would have been a pitiful bungler if he had made the rules of our moral conduct a matter of science. For one man of science, there are thousands who are not. What would have become of them? Man was destined for society. His morality therefore was to be formed to this object. He was endowed with a

sense of right and wrong merely relative to this. This sense is as much a part of
30 his nature as the sense of hearing, seeing, feeling; it is the true foundation of
morality …The moral sense, or conscience, is as much a part of man as his leg
or arm. It is given to all human beings in a stronger or weaker degree, as force of
members is given them in a greater or less degree…State a moral case to a
ploughman and a professor. The former will decide it as well, and often better
35 than the latter, because he has not been led astray by artificial rules…

23. As he refers to Mr. Wythe, Jefferson seems to

(A) affect an air of condescension

(B) reject many of that man's opinions

(C) warn his nephew not to repeat his mistakes

(D) relive pleasant memories from his youth

(E) dispute his nephew' s preconceived notions

Ⓐ Ⓑ Ⓒ Ⓓ Ⓔ

24. Jefferson uses the word *sciences* (line 7) to mean

(A) Italian and Spanish only

(B) moral philosophy and the physical sciences

(C) school subjects in general

(D) the subjects treated in his father's books

(E) biology and chemistry

Ⓐ Ⓑ Ⓒ Ⓓ Ⓔ

25. Jefferson's numbered points refer to

(A) subjects in order of importance

(B) academic courses

(C) languages of the world

(D) topics discussed in an earlier letter

(E) items from a catalogue

Ⓐ Ⓑ Ⓒ Ⓓ Ⓔ

26. Jefferson uses the word *confound* (line 15) to mean

    (A) fluster

    (B) misunderstand

    (C) curse

    (D) muddle

    (E) clarify

          Ⓐ Ⓑ Ⓒ Ⓓ Ⓔ

27. Jefferson encourages his nephew to study Spanish because

    (A) it is related to Latin

    (B) it will prove useful in international relations

    (C) there are many good dictionaries available

    (D) it will prove helpful in learning Italian

    (E) it is the language of history

          Ⓐ Ⓑ Ⓒ Ⓓ Ⓔ

28. By "lost time" (line 24), Jefferson means

    (A) wasted time

    (B) the past

    (C) missing time

    (D) youth

    (E) about time

          Ⓐ Ⓑ Ⓒ Ⓓ Ⓔ

29. Jefferson's main objection to attending lectures in moral philosophy is that

    (A) it could be taught as well by farmers

    (B) it is innate and cannot be taught

    (C) it is better practiced outside school

    (D) very few people understand what it means

    (E) parents, not professors, should be the instructors

          Ⓐ Ⓑ Ⓒ Ⓓ Ⓔ

30. The example of the ploughman and the professor is used to

(A) illustrate the uselessness of education

(B) demonstrate the path to true knowledge

(C) explain the universality of morality

(D) define the nature of conscience

(E) disprove Mr. Wythe's theory of moral conduct

Ⓐ Ⓑ Ⓒ Ⓓ Ⓔ

31. Jefferson compares conscience to a physical limb of the body to show

(A) that it is natural and present in all human beings

(B) how easily we take it for granted

(C) that without it, men are powerless

(D) how mental and physical states are integrated

(E) what is meant by "the arm of the law"

Ⓐ Ⓑ Ⓒ Ⓓ Ⓔ

SOLUTIONS FOR PASSAGE 2

23. **The correct answer is (D).** Jefferson is "ever sensible" that meeting and attracting the good will of Mr. Wythe was "one of the more fortunate events" of his life (line 5).

24. **The correct answer is (C).** Jefferson uses the word *sciences* as a general term covering Italian, Spanish, and moral philosophy. Clearly, he is referring to school subjects in general.

25. **The correct answer is (B).** The numbered points are (1) Italian, (2) Spanish, and (3) Moral philosophy—courses that Peter proposes taking.

26. **The correct answer is (D).** This is part of Jefferson's argument, in which he states that since Italian, French, and Spanish are related, people who speak all three mix or muddle them in conversation.

27. **The correct answer is (B).** Jefferson says, "Our future connections with Spain and Spanish America will render that language a valuable acquisition."

28. **The correct answer is (A).** Point 3 is all about the fact that no one needs to study moral philosophy. In other words, to study it is a waste of time.

29. **The correct answer is (B).** Lines 24–26 explain this reasoning.

30. **The correct answer is (C).** Jefferson's point is that either one is as likely to decide a moral argument fairly; morality is bred into everyone and does not require an advanced degree.

31. **The correct answer is (A).** Choices (B), (C), and (D) may be true, but Jefferson only covers the first point, that morality is as natural as an arm or leg, and is given to all "in a stronger or weaker degree" (line 32).

Let's change gears, and try some critical reasoning, for a refreshing change of pace.

Practice with Critical Reasoning, AKA: More Sentence Completions

Directions: Each of the following questions consists of an incomplete sentence followed by five words or pairs of words. Choose that word or pair of words that, when substituted for the blank space or spaces, best completes the meaning of the sentence and mark the letter of your choice either in the book or on a separate sheet of scrap paper.

Example of Sentence Completion Question:

In view of the extenuating circumstances and the defendant's youth, the judge recommended _____.

(A) conviction

(B) a defense

(C) a mistrial

(D) leniency

(E) life imprisonment

Ⓐ Ⓑ Ⓒ ● Ⓔ

AS, GEE 21, Regents Exams, SOL, NCCT, AHSGE, GHSGT, BST, BSAP, WASL, CAHSEE, TAAS,
AP, WASL, CAHSEE, TAAS, OGT, HSPT/HSPA, FCAT, MEAP HST, MCAS, GEE 21, Regents Exa
ST, M... ...egents Exams, SOL, NCCT, AHSGE, GHSGT, BST, BSAP, WASL, CAHSEE,
...SEE, TAAS, OGT, HSPT/HSPA, FCAT, MEAP HST, MCAS, GEE 21, ... SOL, NC

PRACTICE ONE

1. He dashed into the house, ran for the phone, and answered _____, tripping over the cord.

   (A) hesitantly   (D) distantly

   (B) nobly   (E) breathlessly

   (C) soothingly

Ⓐ Ⓑ Ⓒ Ⓓ Ⓔ

2. The criminal record of the witness caused the jury to_____ his testimony.

   (A) affirm   (D) acquit

   (B) belie   (E) discredit

   (C) retract

Ⓐ Ⓑ Ⓒ Ⓓ Ⓔ

3. Although the storm left the family _____, it could not _____ their spirits.

   (A) discordant .. raise   (D) sodden .. excite

   (B) moribund .. drench   (E) indolent .. inhibit

   (C) destitute .. dampen

Ⓐ Ⓑ Ⓒ Ⓓ Ⓔ

4. By a stroke of luck, the troops _____ a crushing _____.

   (A) converged .. blow   (D) retrenched .. retreat

   (B) prevailed .. defeat   (E) interceded .. assault

   (C) diverged .. siege

Ⓐ Ⓑ Ⓒ Ⓓ Ⓔ

5. You must act with_____ if you want to buy your airline ticket before tomorrow's price increase.

   (A) celerity   (D) lassitude

   (B) clemency   (E) laxity

   (C) facility

Ⓐ Ⓑ Ⓒ Ⓓ Ⓔ

High Stakes: Reading

PT/HSPA, FCAT, MEAP HST, MCAS, GEE21, Regents Exams, SOL, NCCT, AHSGE, GHSGT, BST
NCCT, AHSGE, GHSGT, BST, BSAP, WASL, CAHSEE, TAAS, OGT T/HSPA, FCAT, MEAP
GT, HSPT/HSPA, FCAT, MEAP HST, MCAS, GEE21, Regents Exams, SOL NCCT, AHSGE, GHS

CHAPTER
7

READING

6. The _____ background music hinted of the
dangers threatening the movie's heroine.

   (A) trenchant

   (B) ebullient

   (C) sardonic

   (D) portentous

   (E) precocious

   Ⓐ Ⓑ Ⓒ Ⓓ Ⓔ

7. Nineteenth-century advances in women's rights were
gradual and _____; years might separate one
advance from the next.

   (A) reticent

   (B) onerous

   (C) incumbent

   (D) docile

   (E) sporadic

   Ⓐ Ⓑ Ⓒ Ⓓ Ⓔ

8. Since several offices have been_____ across the
street, the old directory is now _____.

   (A) refurbished .. adequate

   (B) relocated .. obsolete

   (C) deployed .. reserved

   (D) transmuted .. oblivious

   (E) removed .. upgraded

   Ⓐ Ⓑ Ⓒ Ⓓ Ⓔ

9. The junta's promise of free elections was _____, a mere
sop to world opinion.

   (A) spurious

   (B) contentious

   (C) unctuous

   (D) lucid

   (E) presumptuous

   Ⓐ Ⓑ Ⓒ Ⓓ Ⓔ

10. The woman acted in a _____ manner, pretending not to
notice the nearby celebrities.

   (A) convivial

   (B) doleful

   (C) nonchalant

   (D) cogent

   (E) vicarious

   Ⓐ Ⓑ Ⓒ Ⓓ Ⓔ

SOLUTIONS FOR MORE SENTENCE COMPLETIONS

1. **The correct answer is (E).** If he "dashed into the house," then he was in a hurry and was probably out of breath.

2. **The correct answer is (E).** A criminal record may indeed cause a jury to *discredit* (disbelieve) a witness's testimony.

3. **The correct answer is (C).** A catastrophic storm might leave a family *destitute* (living in poverty). For the second blank, the word *although* indicates a shift in mood from negative to positive; poverty could not *dampen* (depress) the family's spirits.

4. **The correct answer is (B).** "By a stroke of luck" implies good fortune; the troops likely *prevailed* (were victorious), thereby avoiding a crushing *defeat*.

5. **The correct answer is (A).** If the price is going up tomorrow, you must do your buying with *celerity* (swiftness).

6. **The correct answer is (D).** If danger threatens, the music would likely be *portentous* (ominous).

7. **The correct answer is (E).** If years separated one advance from the next, progress in women's rights was *sporadic* (occasional or scattered over time).

8. **The correct answer is (B).** Offices that are now across the street have been *relocated* (moved). As a result, the directory is *obsolete* (out of date).

9. **The correct answer is (A).** Since the promise—a mere sop to world opinion—was unlikely to be kept, it was *spurious* (false).

10. **The correct answer is (C).** Pretending not to notice nearby celebrities is acting in a *nonchalant* (casually indifferent) manner.

How about another round with analogies?

FT/HSPA, FCAT, MEAP HST, MCAS, GEE21, Regents Exams, SOL, NCCT, AHSGE, GHSGT, BST
NCCT, AHSGE, GHSGT, BST, BSAP, WASL, CAHSEE, TAAS, OGT, /HSPA, FCAT, MEAP H
GT, HSPT/HSPA, FCAT, MEAP HST, MCAS, GEE21, Regents Exams, OL, NCCT, AHSGE, GHSC
GHSGT, BST, BSAP, WASL, CAHSEE, TAAS, OGT, HSPA, FCAT, MEAP HST, MCAS, C

CHAPTER
7

READING

More Practice Solving Analogies

Directions: Each of the following questions consists of a capitalized pair of words followed by five pairs of words lettered (A) to (E). The capitalized words bear some meaningful relationship to each other. Choose the lettered pair of words whose relationship is most similar to that expressed by the capitalized pair and mark its letter either in the book or on a separate sheet of scrap paper.

Example of an Analogy Question:

DAY: SUN ::

(A) sunlight : daylight   (D) heat : cold

(B) ray : sun   (E) moon: star

(C) night : moon

Ⓐ ● Ⓒ Ⓓ Ⓔ

11. LIBRARY : BOOKS ::

(A) hotel : children   (D) park : cars

(B) zoo : animals   (E) school: buses

(C) office : sales

Ⓐ Ⓑ Ⓒ Ⓓ Ⓔ

12. TINY : HUGE ::

(A) small : little   (D) sad : gloomy

(B) great : grand   (E) chaotic : confuse

(C) weak : strong

Ⓐ Ⓑ Ⓒ Ⓓ Ⓔ

13. FRIGHTEN : SCARE ::

(A) question : ask   (D) brave : fear

(B) look : see   (E) upset : calm

(C) terrorize : startle

Ⓐ Ⓑ Ⓒ Ⓓ Ⓔ

14. SEARCH : FIND ::

(A) fight : win   (D) write : read

(B) obey : believe   (E) listen : talk

(C) look : seek

Ⓐ Ⓑ Ⓒ Ⓓ Ⓔ

PRACTICE ONE

15. DOOR : OPEN ::

   (A) cap : remove   (D) gift : take

   (B) knife : cut   (E) car : speed

   (C) blackboard : eras

Ⓐ Ⓑ Ⓒ Ⓓ Ⓔ

16. DASTARD : COWARDICE ::

   (A) cipher : importance

   (B) scoundrel : immorality

   (C) native : intimacy

   (D) refugee : nationality

   (E) client : independence

Ⓐ Ⓑ Ⓒ Ⓓ Ⓔ

17. TOE : FOOT ::

   (A) elbow : wrist   (D) pupil : eye

   (B) fist : hand   (E) arm : leg

   (C) shoe : sock

Ⓐ Ⓑ Ⓒ Ⓓ Ⓔ

18. STRUM : GUITAR ::

   (A) tune : instrument   (D) pedal : organ

   (B) tighten : drum   (E) hum : song

   (C) polish : bugle

Ⓐ Ⓑ Ⓒ Ⓓ Ⓔ

19. PUERILE : MATURITY ::

   (A) pungent : poignancy

   (B) poised : serenity

   (C) obscure : clarity

   (D) ostentatious : pretension

   (E) profuse : extravagance

Ⓐ Ⓑ Ⓒ Ⓓ Ⓔ

20. HURTLE : TOSS ::

  (A) strike : tap

  (B) throw : bite

  (C) squelch : crush

  (D) quarrel : squabble

  (E) murmur : mumble

Ⓐ Ⓑ Ⓒ Ⓓ Ⓔ

21. INFINITE : BOUNDS ::

  (A) intangible : property (D) ponderous : bulk

  (B) kinetic : motion   (E) propitious : favor

  (C) nebulous : clarity

Ⓐ Ⓑ Ⓒ Ⓓ Ⓔ

22. TIME : MINUTES ::

  (A) month : calendar   (D) yard : square

  (B) clock : faces   (E) arms : legs

  (C) race : laps

Ⓐ Ⓑ Ⓒ Ⓓ Ⓔ

23. MOUNTAIN : TUNNEL ::

  (A) window : frame   (D) charcoal : fire

  (B) river : bridge   (E) wall : window

  (C) door : handle

Ⓐ Ⓑ Ⓒ Ⓓ Ⓔ

SOLUTIONS FOR MORE PRACTICE SOLVING ANALOGIES

11. **The correct answer is (B).** A *library* is a place for *books*, just as a *zoo* is a place for *animals*.

12. **The correct answer is (C).** Something *tiny* is much smaller in size than something *huge*. Something *weak* is much less in strength than something *strong*. Sometimes, it's just a matter of degree.

13. **The correct answer is (A).** To *frighten* someone is to *scare* that person; to *question* someone is to *ask* that person. (See, it's synonyms again.) You might have been confused by choice (C), but *terrorize* is a much more extreme word than *startle*. That extreme does not exist between the original two words.

14. **The correct answer is (A).** *Finding* is a result of *searching*, and *winning* is a result of *fighting*. (Both are cause and effect.)

15. **The correct answer is (B).** By means of a *door*, we can *open* something. By means of a *knife*, we can *cut* into something. (Each is a means to an end.)

16. **The correct answer is (B).** A *dastard* is characterized by *cowardice*, just as a *scoundrel* is characterized by *immorality*.

17. **The correct answer is (D).** A *toe* is part of the *foot*, and the *pupil* is part of the *eye*.

18. **The correct answer is (D).** *Strumming* and *pedaling* are methods of playing an instrument. We *strum* the guitar and *pedal* the organ.

19. **The correct answer is (C).** *Puerile* means childish or lacking in *maturity*. *Obscure* means vague or lacking in *clarity*.

20. **The correct answer is (A).** To *hurtle* is to throw with force; to *toss* is to throw lightly. Similarly, to *strike* is to hit with force and to *tap* is to hit lightly.

21. **The correct answer is (C).** Something *infinite* (endless) lacks *limits* or bounds, just as something *nebulous* (vague) lacks *clarity*.

22. **The correct answer is (C).** *Time* is measured in *minutes* as a *race* is measured in *laps*.

23. **The correct answer is (B).** A *tunnel* is a roadway through a *mountain* and a *bridge* is a roadway over a *river*.

Let's round off this first practice chapter with a couple of additional reading passages.

More Practice With Reading Interpretation and Analysis

Directions: The reading passage below is followed by a set of questions. Read the passage and answer the accompanying questions, basing your answers on what is stated or implied in the passage. Mark the letter of your choice either in the book or on a separate sheet of scrap paper.

Passage 3

Questions 24–35 are based on the following passage.

A major step forward in the history of the novel, Don Quixote *was penned by Miguel de Cervantes and first published in Spain in 1605. Driven mad by his constant perusal of tales of chivalry, Alonso Quijano changes his name to Don Quixote and rides off to seek adventure. This passage describes his First Expedition.*

Line Once these preparations were completed, he was anxious to wait no longer before putting his ideas into effect, impelled to this by the thought of the loss the world suffered by his delay, seeing the grievances there were to redress, the wrongs to right, the injuries to amend, and the debts to discharge. So, telling
5   nobody of his intentions, and quite unobserved, one morning before dawn—it was on one of those sweltering July days—he armed himself completely, mounted Rocinante, put on his badly-mended headpiece, slung on his shield, seized his lance and went out into the plain through the back gate of his yard, pleased and delighted to see with what ease he had started on his fair design. But scarcely
10   was he in open country when he was assailed by a thought so terrible that it almost made him abandon the enterprise he had just begun. For he suddenly remembered that he had never received the honor of knighthood, and so, according to the laws of chivalry, he neither could nor should take arms against any knight, and even if he had been knighted he was bound, as a novice, to wear
15   plain armour without a device on his shield until he should gain one by his prowess. These reflections made him waver in his resolve, but as his madness outweighed any other argument, he made up his mind to have himself knighted

by the first man he met, in imitation of many who had done the same, as he had read in the books which had so influenced him. As to plain armor, he decided
20 to clean his own, when he had time, till it was whiter than ermine. With this he quieted his mind and went on his way, taking whatever road his horse chose, in the belief that in this lay the essence of adventure.

As our brand-new adventurer journeyed along, he talked to himself, saying: "Who can doubt that in ages to come, when the authentic story of my famous
25 deeds comes to light, the sage who writes of them will say when he comes to tell of my first expedition so early in the morning: 'Scarce had the ruddy Apollo spread the golden threads of his lovely hair over the broad and spacious face of the earth, and scarcely had the forked tongues of the little painted birds greeted with mellifluous harmony the coming of the rosy Aurora who, leaving the soft
30 bed of her jealous husband, showed herself at the doors and balconies of the Manchegan horizon, when the famous knight, Don Quixote de la Mancha, quitting the slothful down, mounted his famous steed Rocinante and began to journey across the ancient and celebrated plain of Montiel'?" That was, in fact, the road that our knight actually took as he went on: "Fortunate the age and
35 fortunate the times in which my famous deeds will come to light, deeds worthy to be engraved in bronze, carved in marble and painted on wood, as a memorial for posterity. And you, sage enchanter, whoever you may be, to whose lot it falls to be the chronicler of this strange history, I beg you not to forget my good Rocinante, my constant companion on all my rides and journeys!" And pres-
40 ently he cried again, as if he had really been in love: "0 Princess Dulcinea, mistress of this captive heart! You did me great injury in dismissing me and inflicting on me the cruel rigour of your command not to appear in your beau- teous presence. Deign, lady, to be mindful of your captive heart, which suffers such griefs for love of you."

45 He went on stringing other nonsense on to this, all after the fashion he had learnt in his reading, and imitating the language of his books as best he could. And all the while he rode so slowly and the sun's heat increased so fast that it would have been enough to turn his brain, if he had had any.

PT/HSPA, FCAT, MEAP HST, MCAS, GEE21, Regents Exams, SOL, NCCT, AHSGE, GHSGT, BS
NCCT, AHSGE, GHSGT, BST, BSAP, WASL, CAHSEE, TAAS, OGT HSPA, FCAT, MEAP
GT, HSPT/HSPA, FCAT, MEAP HST, MCAS, GEE21, Regents Exams, SOL, NCCT, AHSGE, GHS
GHSGT, BST, BSAP, WASL, CAHSEE, TAAS, OGT, HSPT/HSPA, FCAT, MEAP HST, MCAS

CHAPTER
7

READING

24. The word *redress* in line 3 most nearly means

   (A) to locate a residence

   (B) to put on clothes

   (C) to downplay

   (D) to correct

   (E) to confuse

   Ⓐ Ⓑ Ⓒ Ⓓ Ⓔ

25. As described in lines 9–16, Don Quixote was hesitant to fight because he

   (A) was afraid for his life

   (B) didn't believe in violence

   (C) would break the established code of chivalry

   (D) he would lose his wife if he fought for what he truly believed

   (E) he was indifferent to the cause

   Ⓐ Ⓑ Ⓒ Ⓓ Ⓔ

26. The word *device* in line 15 probably means

   (A) emblem   (D) trick

   (B) tool   (E) metal

   (C) gadget

   Ⓐ Ⓑ Ⓒ Ⓓ Ⓔ

27. The words that best describe the first speech Cervantes has Don Quixote make (lines 24–33) might be

   (A) informative and deliberate

   (B) profound and resolute

   (C) dull and ill-conceived

   (D) shocking and defamatory

   (E) flowery and overwrought

   Ⓐ Ⓑ Ⓒ Ⓓ Ⓔ

28. What does Don Quixote mean when he says "quitting the slothful down" (line 32)?

(A) leaving the farm

(B) climbing into the saddle

(C) feeling happier and more energetic

(D) recovering from illness

(E) getting out of bed

Ⓐ Ⓑ Ⓒ Ⓓ Ⓔ

29. The phrase "as if he had really been in love" (line 40) is used to illuminate Don Quixote's

(A) need for attention

(B) starved spirit

(C) dementia

(D) unhappy childhood

(E) inability to emote

Ⓐ Ⓑ Ⓒ Ⓓ Ⓔ

30. Cervantes has his hero address his remarks to

(A) God

(B) the reader

(C) his horse

(D) a mythical historian and a princess

(E) an unknown knight

Ⓐ Ⓑ Ⓒ Ⓓ Ⓔ

31. The last line of the selection reminds us that

(A) the story takes place in Spain

(B) Don Quixote is mad

(C) Rocinante has no destination in mind

(D) other knights have taken this same route

(E) the long day is about to end

Ⓐ Ⓑ Ⓒ Ⓓ Ⓔ

SPT/HSPA, FCAT, MEAP HST, MCAS, GEE21, Regents Exams, SOL, NCCT, AHSGE, GHSGT, BS NCCT, AHSGE, GHSGT, BST, BSAP, WASL, CAHSEE, TAAS, OGT, /HSPA, FCAT, MEAP GT, HSPT/HSPA, FCAT, MEAP HST, MCAS, GEE21, Regents Exams SOL, NCCT, AHSGE, GH

CHAPTER **7**

32. We first suspect that Don Quixote is not quite the hero he seems when he recalls that

   (A) he left his armor at home

   (B) his horse is named Rocinante

   (C) he is not a real knight

   (D) Dulcinea holds him captive

   (E) he started his journey with ease

   Ⓐ Ⓑ Ⓒ Ⓓ Ⓔ

33. According to the author, Don Quixote's speech is affected by

   (A) romantic books he has read

   (B) the language of seventeenth-century Spain

   (C) letters received from Dulcinea

   (D) the speeches of Alfonso X

   (E) his night visions

   Ⓐ Ⓑ Ⓒ Ⓓ Ⓔ

34. Cervantes's opinion of the literature of his day seems to be that it is

   (A) written by madmen

   (B) argumentative and controversial

   (C) not up to the standards of the previous century

   (D) sentimental drivel

   (E) derivative

   Ⓐ Ⓑ Ⓒ Ⓓ Ⓔ

35. The best word to describe Cervantes's feeling toward his hero might be

   (A) disdainful

   (B) revolted

   (C) indifferent

   (D) mocking

   (E) appreciative

   Ⓐ Ⓑ Ⓒ Ⓓ Ⓔ

PRACTICE ONE

SOLUTIONS FOR PASSAGE 3

24. **The correct answer is (D).** In the text, the author discusses Quixote's desire to change wrongs to right and redress grievances. In this context, *redress* means to fix, change, or correct for the better.

25. **The correct answer is (C).** Because Don Quixote is not a knight, to take up arms against another knight would be a breach in the code of chivalry. (Chivalry is from the French, *cheval*, which means horse. The code covered how knights were to behave during the Middle Ages.)

26. **The correct answer is (A).** Don Quixote is worried that he cannot wear armor with a *device* on his shield that denotes his knighthood. The only appropriate answer is choice (A).

27. **The correct answer is (E).** With such malapropisms as "forked tongues" of birds, Cervantes imbues his hero with language that mimics the flowery language of the romance stories that he reads.

28. **The correct answer is (E).** In his florid, overblown language, Don Quixote tells of getting out of bed to ride off on his adventure. "The slothful down" seems to refer to the down mattress on which he sleeps.

29. **The correct answer is (C).** Don Quixote is talking to himself and calling on a woman who may or may not exist. His speech cries out for his love for Dulcinea, but Cervantes pulls the reader back with this line to show that Quixote is mad.

30. **The correct answer is (D).** Don Quixote speaks first to the "sage enchanter" who might chronicle his tale (lines 37–39) and then to Dulcinea, "mistress of this captive heart" (lines 40–44).

31. **The correct answer is (B).** The sun's heat "would have been enough to turn his brain, if he had had any." Cervantes is again reminding the reader that Don Quixote is out of his mind.

32. **The correct answer is (C).** The story up to this point might be the tale of any knight somewhat down on his luck, but in lines 11–16, Cervantes jolts the reader into realizing that Don Quixote is out of his mind—he is not even a real knight.

33. **The correct answer is (A).** Cervantes refers to the romantic books that fill Don Quixote's head in line 19 and in lines 45–46.

34. **The correct answer is (D).** Although he never comes right out and says so, Cervantes's mocking reproduction of the language of romantic books makes it clear that he does not think much of the writing styles he imitates. The fact that the hero who speaks the way such writers write is completely mad is another ironic twist that reveals Cervantes's opinion.

35. **The correct answer is (D).** Throughout, Cervantes uses a gently mocking tone to show Don Quixote's ridiculousness. Examples such as lines 10–11, 15–16, and line 40 show that Cervantes is amused by his hero but not contemptuous as choice (A) would suggest.

I hope you had as much fun with that passage as I did. Cervantes was ultra cool. Let's wrap up the chapter with a pair of related passages. The following 12 questions will refer to passages 4 and 5.

Directions: The two passages below deal with a related topic. Following the passages are questions about the content of each passage or about the relationship between the two passages. Answer the questions based upon what is stated or implied in the passages and in any introductory material provided. Mark the letter of your choice either in the book or on a separate sheet of scrap paper.

Passages 4 and 5

The struggle of African Americans to make economic and political progress within the socioeconomic structure of the United States has been long filled with setbacks. These two passages document some of the events in that long struggle and seek to explain why the struggle was so difficult.

Questions 36–42 refer to Passage 4.

Passage 4—The Economic Scene

Line   Because of slavery, which lasted until 1865, and undereducation, African Americans have been at a disadvantage in terms of socioeconomic progress until well into the twentieth century. Segregated schools were often not on a par with the schools in which whites were educated; consequently, when African Americans
5   competed for jobs with whites, they often found they could not.

Increased opportunities for African Americans followed in the wake of the civil rights movement, and as a result, African Americans were able to gain higher levels of education and achieve more managerial positions within the various professions. In the 1980s, African Americans moved into the upper middle
10 class in large numbers.

Consistently in the last five decades, African Americans have moved into higher-status jobs, have opened their own businesses, and have increased their levels of education. Because of such progress, it is safe to assume that those African Americans who have become upwardly mobile would not be able to tolerate
15 racial discrimination as it existed prior to the civil rights movement.

While progress has been made in some segments of the African-American population, less progress has occurred among low-income African Americans. Many low-income African Americans do not have a place in the class structure because of racial segregation and poverty, particularly in urban areas. When segre-
20 gation and poverty prevail, urban neighborhoods become places of high crime, poor schools, and poorly maintained homes.

Thus, what has emerged in the 1990s is a widening socioeconomic gap between low-income African Americans and the African Americans who have been able to improve their socioeconomic status.

Questions 43–49 refer to Passage 2.

Passage 2—The Political Scene

Line Only with the enforcement of the Reconstruction Act of 1867 and the ratification of the Fifteenth Amendment to the Constitution did African Americans first win seats in Congress. Hiram Revels of Mississippi became the first African American to serve in Congress when he took his seat in the Senate on February
5 25,1870. Joseph Rainey of South Carolina became the first African American member of the House of Representatives later in 1870.

African Americans throughout the South became politically active soon after emancipation and the close of the Civil War. A generation of African-American leaders emerged who nearly unanimously adhered to the Repub-
10 lican Party because it had championed the rights of African Americans. African Americans elected to Congress during Reconstruction found the national legislature an effective forum for the advocacy of political equality.

SPT/HSPA, FCAT, MEAP HST, MCAS, GEE21, Regents Exams, SOL, NCCT, AHSGE, GHSGT, BS
L, NCCT, AHSGE, GHSGT, BST, BSAP, WASL, CAHSEE, TAAS, OGT, /HSPA, FCAT, MEAP
OGT, HSPT/HSPA, FCAT, MEAP HST, MCAS, GEE21, Regents Exams, OL, NCCT, AHSGE, GHS

CHAPTER
7

Following the end of federal Reconstruction in 1877, African Americans continued to win election to Congress, and carried on the struggle for civil
15 rights and economic opportunity.

During the 1890s and early 1900s, no African American won election to Congress, in part because of restrictive state election codes in some southern states. During World War I and in the following decade, however, African-American migration to northern cities established the foundations for political organiza-
20 tion in urban centers. Over the next three decades African Americans won congressional seats in New York City, Detroit, and Philadelphia. In the wake of the civil rights movement and the enforcement of the Voting Rights Act of 1965, African Americans regained seats in the South. Since the 1930s, nearly all African-American representatives have been Democrats.

25 Since the nineteenth century, African American members of Congress have served as advocates for all African Americans as well as representatives for their constituencies. During Reconstruction and the late nineteenth century, African American representatives called on their colleagues to protect the voting rights of African Americans. They also called for expanded educational opportunities
30 and land grants for freed African Americans. In the mid-twentieth century, African-American representatives turned to the needs of urban communities and urged federal programs for improved housing and job training. These representatives served as defenders of the civil rights movement and proponents of legislation to end segregation. The Congressional Black Caucus demonstrated a
35 special concern for the protection of civil rights; the guarantee of equal opportunity in education, employment, and housing; and a broad array of foreign and domestic policy issues.

Since the victories of the civil rights movement in the 1960s, African-American men and women have won election to Congress from increasingly diverse re-
40 gions of the country. Whether from largely urban districts, suburban areas, or more recently from rural Mississippi, these members of Congress have maintained their common concern with economic issues that affect African Americans with the protection of civil rights.

The collected biographies of African Americans who served in the House and
45 Senate provide an important perspective on the history of the Congress and the role of African Americans in American politics. Their stories offer eloquent testimony to the long struggle to extend the ideals of the founders to encompass all citizens of the United States.

High Stakes: Reading

36. The author's attitude in Passage 1 is primarily one of
    (A) complete detachment
    (B) unbridled outrage
    (C) indifference
    (D) disinterest
    (E) objectivity

    Ⓐ Ⓑ Ⓒ Ⓓ Ⓔ

37. Passage 1 indicates that socioeconomic progress for African Americans has been slow because of
    (A) prejudice
    (B) insurmountable poverty
    (C) slavery and undereducation
    (D) generally slow economic progress in the United States
    (E) immigrants from Central America

    Ⓐ Ⓑ Ⓒ Ⓓ Ⓔ

38. The phrase "on a par" (line 3) means
    (A) in the same location
    (B) at odds with
    (C) in competition with
    (D) on the same level
    (E) on a different level

    Ⓐ Ⓑ Ⓒ Ⓓ Ⓔ

39. According to the passage, African Americans have done all of the following in the last five decades EXCEPT
    (A) move into higher-status jobs
    (B) open their own businesses
    (C) tolerate more racial discrimination
    (D) achieve more managerial positions
    (E) increase their level of education

    Ⓐ Ⓑ Ⓒ Ⓓ Ⓔ

40. While not directly stated, the passage implies that the civil rights movement

   (A) had no effect on African-American upward mobility

   (B) caused a setback for African-American socioeconomic progress

   (C) was not supported by African Americans

   (D) had very little strong leadership

   (E) helped African Americans in their struggle to achieve economic goals

   Ⓐ Ⓑ Ⓒ Ⓓ Ⓔ

41. The conclusion that the author ultimately reaches in Passage 1 is that

   (A) all African Americans have made socioeconomic progress

   (B) upward mobility is no longer an issue with African Americans

   (C) the civil rights movement was not a success as far as most African Americans are concerned

   (D) poverty in the inner cities of the United States is insurmountable

   (E) the 1990s have seen a widening of the gap between low-income African Americans and those who have made economic progress

   Ⓐ Ⓑ Ⓒ Ⓓ Ⓔ

42. According to Passage 2, the first African American to serve in the House of Representatives was

   (A) a former slave

   (B) Hiram Revels

   (C) from Chicago

   (D) Joseph Rainey

   (E) Oscar DePriest

   Ⓐ Ⓑ Ⓒ Ⓓ Ⓔ

PRACTICE ONE

43. One difference between African-American congressional representatives in the nineteenth century and those in the mid-twentieth century was

(A) their commitment to education for African Americans

(B) the political party to which they were likely to belong

(C) the strength of their ties to the African-American community as a whole

(D) the extent to which they represented all African Americans

(E) their ability to influence other congressional members

Ⓐ Ⓑ Ⓒ Ⓓ Ⓔ

44. When the African-American representatives "turned to" certain issues in the mid-twentieth century (line 31), they

(A) became antagonistic toward those issues

(B) reversed their positions on those issues

(C) referred to those issues

(D) devoted themselves to those issues

(E) listened to criticisms of those issues

Ⓐ Ⓑ Ⓒ Ⓓ Ⓔ

45. One reason cited in the passage for the election of African Americans to Congress from both southern states after Reconstruction and northern states after World War I is

(A) strength of local African-American political organizations

(B) success of the civil rights movement

(C) passage and enforcement of the Fifteenth Amendment

(D) predominance of African Americans in certain districts

(E) elimination of regional differences

Ⓐ Ⓑ Ⓒ Ⓓ Ⓔ

46. The author expresses admiration for the African-American congressional representatives discussed in the passage for their

(A) political acumen

(B) attempts to ensure the rights of all Americans

(C) single-minded devotion to the struggle for civil rights

(D) focus on providing economic opportunity for African Americans

(E) ability to regularly secure reelection

Ⓐ Ⓑ Ⓒ Ⓓ Ⓔ

47. The author of Passage 1 connects increased opportunity for African Americans with the civil rights movement of the 1960s, while the author of Passage 2

(A) believes that African-American empowerment didn't occur until the 1980s

(B) argues that since the American revolution, blacks have had significant political opportunities

(C) states that since the end of the Civil War, African Americans have enjoyed a steady rise in political power

(D) points out that although political empowerment started in 1867, there have been bumps in the road to progress

(E) claims that not until World War I did African Americans come to power

Ⓐ Ⓑ Ⓒ Ⓓ Ⓔ

SOLUTIONS FOR PASSAGES 4 AND 5

36. **The correct answer is (E).** Most of the choices are extremes, either extreme outrage or extreme lack of interest. The author takes more of an objective middle ground in outlining the history of African-American economics.

37. **The correct answer is (C).** In the first sentence of the passage, the author indicates that slavery and undereducation hindered economic progress for African Americans until well into the twentieth century.

38. **The correct answer is (D).** The context of the sentence indicates that the best answer is "on the same level."

39. **The correct answer is (C).** On the contrary, in the last five decades African Americans have become much less tolerant of racial discrimination.

40. **The correct answer is (E).** The passage generally implies that the civil rights movement did help African Americans in their quest for economic and political equality.

41. **The correct answer is (E).** The passage acknowledges that progress has been made in some segments of the African-American population but that the gap is widening between lower-income and higher-income African Americans.

42. **The correct answer is (D).** See lines 3–5. Hiram Revels was the first African American in Congress, but he was elected to the Senate. Choice (A) may be true, but it is not mentioned in the passage.

43. **The correct answer is (B).** Compare lines 8–10 and 23–24.

44. **The correct answer is (D).** The context makes it clear that "turned to" means "concentrated on" or "devoted themselves to."

45. **The correct answer is (A).** Political organizations in southern states in the nineteenth century are mentioned in lines 28–30; political organizations in northern states in the twentieth century are cited in lines 34–37.

46. **The correct answer is (B).** In this passage, the author expresses admiration only in the last paragraph, where the representatives' "long struggle to extend the ideals of the founders to encompass all citizens of the United States" is cited.

47. **The correct answer is (D).** Although the author of Passage 2 points out that political gain occurred immediately following the Civil War, he also indicates that African Americans suffered political powerlessness from 1890-1900. Therefore, there were bumps in the road.

CHAPTER 8

GRAMMA(R) SAID THERE'D BE DAYS LIKE THIS

Okay, so the song goes "*Mamma* said there'd be days like this." But you have to make some allowance for poetic license! In this chapter, we take a break from the ordinary reading passages, sentence completions, and analogies practiced in Chapter 7 and try our hand at something a little different.

Trying not to be repetitious of the directions that are just ahead, these exercises deal with grammar and style, which we talked about in Chapter 5. Feel free to go back and look at Chapter 5 if you don't remember this. There are only four answer choices for each of these questions, so your chance of guessing the correct one has improved from one in five to one in four. There are other questions too, but we'll leave the rest to the rather formal directions. Make sure that you understand them before you proceed. There are four different sets of exercises, each with one reading passage and a group of 15 questions. Enjoy!

Directions: This exercises consists of a passage in which particular words or phrases are underlined and numbered. Following the passage, you will see alternative words and phrases that could be substituted for the underlined part. You must select the alternative that expresses the idea most clearly and correctly or that best fits the style and tone of the entire passage. If the original version is best, select "NO CHANGE."

The exercises also include questions about entire paragraphs and the passage as a whole. These questions are identified by a number in a box, like 1 , 2 , etc.

After you select the correct answer for each question, mark the oval representing the correct answer on your answer sheet.

Exercise 1: The Magic of Special Effects

The movies are one place where magic can come true. You can see sights you might never <u>under any circumstances</u> hope to see in real life—ocean liners
                 1
sinking, earthquakes swallowing cities, planets exploding. You can also see sights that might never exist at <u>all; such as</u> rampaging monsters, battles in outer space,
                   2
and sky-high cities of the future.

All of these are examples of the movie magic known as special effects.
<u>Its the work of</u> amazingly clever and skilled effects artists. <u>And</u> the real magic
    3   4
lies in how they're able to make a man in a gorilla suit into King Kong . . . tiny . . . plastic models into huge space ships . . . and instructions in a computer into images of a world that no one <u>have ever imagined</u> before.
                  5

Effects artists have developed many tricks and techniques over the years. Working closely with movie directors, producers, and actors, <u>a growing role in moviemaking today is played by them.</u>

6

[1] They can be used <u>to save money, some movie scenes</u> would be impossibly

7

costly to produce using ordinary methods. [2] Special effects techniques are useful to moviemakers in several ways. [3] Clever use of special effects can cut those costs dramatically. [4] For example, to show an imaginary city, it would cost millions of dollars to build real buildings, roads, and so on. 8

9 Battle or disaster scenes involving explosions, floods, or avalanches can be very dangerous to film. Effects artists can simulate <u>such</u> in ways that give audiences the

10

thrill of witnessing a dangerous event without <u>the exposing of actors</u> to real

11

hazards. <u>Most important,</u> special effects allow moviemakers to film scenes that

12

would otherwise be impossible. They let movies show non-existent, even impossible worlds. 13 Special effects are a <u>moviemakers</u> tool for communicating a

14

unique imaginative experience. <u>And after all—that's</u> one of the reasons we all

15

go to the movies.

1. (A) NO CHANGE
   (B) normally
   (C) in daily life
   (D) OMIT the underlined portion

Ⓐ Ⓑ Ⓒ Ⓓ

2. (A) NO CHANGE
   (B) all, such as
   (C) all. Such as
   (D) all—such as

Ⓐ Ⓑ Ⓒ Ⓓ

3. **(A)** NO CHANGE

   (B) It's the work of

   (C) They're by

   (D) They are the work of

   Ⓐ Ⓑ Ⓒ Ⓓ

4. **(A)** NO CHANGE

   (B) Nonetheless,

   (C) Although

   (D) Because

   Ⓐ Ⓑ Ⓒ Ⓓ

5. **(A)** NO CHANGE

   (B) could ever imagine

   (C) has ever imagined

   (D) ever had been imagining

   Ⓐ Ⓑ Ⓒ Ⓓ

6. **(A)** NO CHANGE

   (B) moviemaking today requires them to play a growing role.

   (C) they play a growing role in moviemaking today.

   (D) their role in moviemaking today is a growing one.

   Ⓐ Ⓑ Ⓒ Ⓓ

7. **(A)** NO CHANGE

   (B) to save money. Some movie scenes

   (C) for saving money, some movie scenes

   (D) to save money; since some movie scenes

   Ⓐ Ⓑ Ⓒ Ⓓ

8. Which of the following sequences of sentences will make the paragraph most logical?

   (A) 2,1,4,3

   (B) 3,1,4,2

   (C) 2,4,3,1

   (D) 1,4,3,2

   Ⓐ Ⓑ Ⓒ Ⓓ

9. Which of the following sentences would provide the best transition here from the topic of the previous paragraph to the new topic of this paragraph?

(A) Today's moviemakers are highly budget conscious.

(B) Some of the most exciting special effects involve computer-simulated imagery.

(C) There is a long history to the use of special effects in movies.

(D) Special effects can also make moviemaking safer.

Ⓐ Ⓑ Ⓒ Ⓓ

10. (A) NO CHANGE

(B) these events

(C) those

(D) it

Ⓐ Ⓑ Ⓒ Ⓓ

11. (A) NO CHANGE

(B) exposing actors

(C) actors being exposed

(D) actors having to be exposed

Ⓐ Ⓑ Ⓒ Ⓓ

12. (A) NO CHANGE

(B) To summarize,

(C) On the other hand,

(D) Nevertheless,

Ⓐ Ⓑ Ⓒ Ⓓ

13. At this point, the writer is considering the addition of the following sentence:

Visions of unknown, unseen worlds have long stimulated the imaginations of human beings the world over.

Would this be a logical and relevant addition to the essay?

(A) Yes, because it emphasizes the important role that special effects play in the movies.

(B) No, because it does not directly relate to the topic of movie special effects.

(C) Yes, because it underscores the universal appeal of works of the imagination.

(D) No, because most of the world's most popular movies are produced in the United States, not "the world over."

Ⓐ Ⓑ Ⓒ Ⓓ

14. (A) NO CHANGE

(B) moviemaker's

(C) moviemakers'

(D) OMIT the underlined portion

Ⓐ Ⓑ Ⓒ Ⓓ

15. (A) NO CHANGE

(B) And—after all, that's

(C) And, after all, that's

(D) And that after all, is

Ⓐ Ⓑ Ⓒ Ⓓ

SOLUTIONS FOR EXERCISE 1

1. **The correct answer is (D).** The underlined phrase is redundant, since the phrase "under no circumstances" adds nothing to the meaning conveyed by the word *never*. It can be omitted with no loss of meaning, making the sentence more concise.

2. **The correct answer is (B).** The semicolon in the underlined portion is wrong, since the phrase that follows the semicolon cannot stand alone as a sentence. Instead, a comma should be used.

3. **The correct answer is (B).** When the word *its* is used in place of the words *it is*, the correct spelling is *it's*; the apostrophe stands for the omitted letter "i" in the contraction.

4. **The correct answer is (A).** Choice (A), *and*, is the most logical conjunction to connect this sentence with the previous one. The other answer choices all imply a contraction or some other shift in meaning, which in fact doesn't exist.

5. **The correct answer is (C).** The subject of the verb "have . . . imagined" is the pronoun *no one*, which is singular. Therefore, the singular verb "has . . . imagined" is necessary to make the subject and verb agree in number.

6. **The correct answer is (C).** The modifying phrase with which the sentence begins, "Working closely . . . ," describes the effects artists. In order to keep the modifier from "dangling," what follows the phrase should be a word naming the people being described. Thus, it's correct for the word *they* (meaning, of course, the effects artists) to immediately follow the comma. Choice (C) is also more concise and graceful than the other answer choices.

7. **The correct answer is (B).** As originally written, the sentence is a run-on—two complete sentences jammed together with a comma between them. Choice (B) corrects the error by breaking the two sentences apart at the logical place.

8. **The correct answer is (A).** It makes sense to start with sentence 2, which makes the general point about the usefulness of special effects that the rest of the paragraph then explains in more detail. And it makes sense for sentence 3 to follow sentence 4, since sentence 3 refers to "those costs" that are described in sentence 4.

9. **The correct answer is (D).** This sentence introduces the topic around which the other sentences in the paragraph are organized.

10. **The correct answer is (B).** The pronoun *such* is vague, so it leaves the reader slightly uncertain as to what it refers to. It is also awkward and "weird sounding." The phrase "these events" refers back to the previous sentence clearly and understandably.

11. **The correct answer is (B).** This wording is the simplest and most concise of the answer choices.

12. **The correct answer is (A).** The phrase "most important" introduces the point made in the final paragraph in a logical fashion—which is the idea that special effects free moviemakers to depict impossible worlds is the "most important" or at least most remarkable idea in the passage. The other alternative connecting words or phrases don't make as much sense in this context.

13. **The correct answer is (B).** Since this sentence adds nothing to our understanding of movie special effects or how they are used, it can be omitted without losing anything.

14. **The correct answer is (B).** The word *maker's* is a possessive; the sentence refers to something (the "tool" of special effects) that belongs to the moviemakers. Therefore, it should be spelled with an apostrophe s.

15. **The correct answer is (C).** The parenthetical phrase "after all" should be surrounded by commas to set it off from the rest of the sentence.

Breathing Space Number One

Wasn't that fun? Well, at least you'll have to admit that it was different. Speaking of different, you'll notice that the next passage has numbers preceding each paragraph. That's so you can be asked questions about specific paragraphs at the end, and not have to rely on your counting them. They're pre-numbered for your convenience.

Take a deep breath and let it out slowly. Now, do it a second time. You may or may not feel better as a result of that exercise, but at least I kept my word and gave you some breathing space. Now, let's get on with it.

Exercise 2: Cities on the Sea

[1]

Hunger has long plagued millions of the world's people, especially in the vast cities of the underdeveloped nations of Africa, Asia, and India. The food to feed the world's growing population may come largely from ocean resources. 16

[2]

Three quarter's of the earth's surface is covered with water. Many scientists are now
   17
looking at these vast watery regions for solutions to some pressing human dilemmas.

[3]

Minerals such as iron, nickel, copper, aluminum, and tin are in limited supply on the earth. Undersea mines are expected to yield fresh supplies of many of these resources. Oil and gas deposits, have been discovered under the ocean floor 19.
            18

[4]

To take advantage of these ocean-based resources, some scientists foresee entire cities on the ocean. At first, it will be built close to the shore. Later, floating cities
            20

might be located hundreds of miles out at sea. These cities could serve many functions, <u>playing a variety of roles</u>.
21
Some of the people living there could harvest fish and sea plants, like farmers of the ocean. Others could operate oil and gas wells or work in undersea enclosures mining the ocean floors. <u>Also</u> the floating cities could serve as terminals or stations
22
for international travel, where ships could stop for refueling or repairs.

[5]
Much of the technology needed to build such cities <u>have already been developed</u>. Oil
23
drilling on a large scale is already conducted at sea. Rigs as large as small towns built on floating platforms or on platforms anchored into the seabed <u>serving as homes</u> to scores
24
of workers for months at a time. The same principles, on a larger scale, could be used to create ocean-going cities.

[6]
<u>The cities</u> would have to be virtually self-sufficient, <u>although</u> shipping supplies
25   26
from the mainland would be costly. Each city would be a multistory structure with room for <u>many kinds of facilities needed by the inhabitants</u>. The ocean itself could
27
provide much of the needed food and other raw <u>materials: while</u> solar panels and
28
generators running on water power could provide energy.

[7]
Many thousands of men, women, and children might inhabit such a city. They would probably visit the mainland from time to time, but otherwise would spend their lives at sea as ocean-dwelling pioneers.

16. Which of the following sentences, if added here, would most effectively support the assertion made in the previous sentence?

(A) Fish, sea-grown plants, and even food-stuffs synthesized from algae are all examples.

(B) If population growth can be brought under control, the problem of hunger may well be alleviated.

(C) Pollution of the seas has not yet reached a level where it endangers the use of saltwater fish by humans.

(D) For thousands of years, humans have drawn nourishment from the seas around us.

Ⓐ Ⓑ Ⓒ Ⓓ

17. (A) NO CHANGE

(B) Three quarters

(C) Three fourth's

(D) Three-quarter's

Ⓐ Ⓑ Ⓒ Ⓓ

18. (A) NO CHANGE

(B) deposits has

(C) deposits have

(D) deposits, has

Ⓐ Ⓑ Ⓒ Ⓓ

19. The writer wishes to add another relevant example to Paragraph 3. Which of the following sentences does that best?

(A) Exploration of the deepest reaches of the ocean floors has only recently begun.

(B) And the tides and thermal currents—water movements caused by temperature variations—may be future energy sources.

(C) Solar energy, too, is expected to become a major supplier of the world's future energy needs.

(D) The sea, after all, is the ultimate source of all life on Earth.

Ⓐ Ⓑ Ⓒ Ⓓ

20. (A) NO CHANGE
    (B) they will be built
    (C) they will build them
    (D) it will be

ⒶⒷⒸⒹ

21. (A) NO CHANGE
    (B) and play many roles.
    (C) with a variety of roles to play.
    (D) OMIT the underlined portion

ⒶⒷⒸⒹ

22. (A) NO CHANGE
    (B) (Place after could)
    (C) (Place after serve)
    (D) (Place after travel)

ⒶⒷⒸⒹ

23. (A) NO CHANGE
    (B) has already been developed.
    (C) have been developed already.
    (D) is already developed.

ⒶⒷⒸⒹ

24. (A) NO CHANGE
    (B) serving for homes
    (C) have served like homes
    (D) serve as homes

ⒶⒷⒸⒹ

25. (A) NO CHANGE
    (B) (Begin new paragraph) The cities, however,
    (C) (Do NOT begin new paragraph) Furthermore, the cities
    (D) (Do NOT begin new paragraph) And, these cities

ⒶⒷⒸⒹ

26. (A) NO CHANGE
    (B) since
    (C) when
    (D) whereas

ⒶⒷⒸⒹ

PT/HSPA, FCAT, MEAP HST, MCAS, GEE21, Regents Exams, SOL, NCCT, AHSGE, GHSGT, BS
NCCT, AHSGE, GHSGT, BST, BSAP, WASL, CAHSEE, TAAS, OGT, VHSPA, FCAT, MEAP
GT, HSPT/HSPA, FCAT, MEAP HST, MCAS, GEE21, Regents Exam, NCCT, AHSGE, GHS

CHAPTER
8

27. (A) NO CHANGE

(B) apartments, small factories, offices, schools, and stores.

(C) various living and other quarters to be used by the town's citizens.

(D) people to live and engage in other activities as in a land-based city.

Ⓐ Ⓑ Ⓒ Ⓓ

28. (A) NO CHANGE

(B) materials. While

(C) materials, while

(D) materials,

Ⓐ Ⓑ Ⓒ Ⓓ

Items 29 and 30 pose questions about the essay as a whole.

29. The writer wishes to include the following sentence in the essay:

Tourists might find the floating cities attractive vacation spots for boating, swimming, and fishing.

That sentence will fit most smoothly and logically into Paragraph

(A) 3, after the last sentence.

(B) 4, before the first sentence.

(C) 4, after the last sentence.

(D) 6, after the last sentence.

Ⓐ Ⓑ Ⓒ Ⓓ

30. For the sake of the unity and coherence of this essay, Paragraph 1 should be placed

(A) where it is now.

(B) after Paragraph 2.

(C) after Paragraph 3.

(D) after Paragraph 4.

Ⓐ Ⓑ Ⓒ Ⓓ

HIGH STAKES

SOLUTIONS FOR EXERCISE 2

16. **The correct answer is (A).** We're looking for a sentence that will support the idea that the hungry people of the world may be fed from resources in the sea. The sentence in choice (A) does this by giving several concrete examples of foods derived from the oceans.

17. **The correct answer is (B).** The phrase "three quarters" is neither a possessive nor a contraction; it's a simple plural, and therefore should be spelled without an apostrophe.

18. **The correct answer is (C).** There's no reason to separate the subject (deposits) from the verb (have been discovered) with a comma.

19. **The correct answer is (B).** Only the sentence given in choice (B) offers an additional example of important resources that may be provided by the oceans.

20. **The correct answer is (B).** Since the sentence is talking about the "cities on the ocean" mentioned in the previous sentence, the logical pronoun to use is "they" (a plural pronoun to match the plural antecedent). Choice (C) is incorrect because it seems to refer to a "they" we can't identify—some unnamed group of people who will build the futuristic cities on the sea.

21. **The correct answer is (D).** The phrase "playing a variety of roles" means exactly the same thing as the phrase "could serve many functions" that precedes it. Since the underlined phrase adds no new information to the sentence, it can and should be eliminated.

22. **The correct answer is (B).** In general, it is best for the adverb to be as close as possible to the word it modifies—in this case, the verb "could serve." It should be graceful and natural to insert it in the middle of the verb phrase: "could also serve."

23. **The correct answer is (B).** The subject of the verb phrase "have . . . been developed" is the singular pronoun *much*. Therefore, the verb phrase should also be singular: "has been developed."

24. **The correct answer is (D).** As originally written, the sentence is a fragment; it has no independent verb. Choice (D) corrects the problem by turning the gerund *serving* into the verb *serve*, whose subject is the word *rigs* that appears way back at the start of the sentence.

PT/HSPA, FCAT, MEAP HST, MCAS, GEE21, Regents Exams, SOL, NCCT, AHSGE, GHSGT, BST
NCCT, AHSGE, GHSGT, BST, BSAP, WASL, CAHSEE, TAAS, OGT, T/HSPA, FCAT, MEAP
GT, HSPT/HSPA, FCAT, MEAP HST, MCAS, GEE21, Regents Exams, NCCT, AHSGE, GHS
F, GHSGT, BST, BSAP, WASL, CAHSEE, TAAS, OGT, HSPT/HSPA, FCAT, MEAP HST, MCAS, G

CHAPTER
8

READING

25. **The correct answer is (A)**. It makes sense to start a new paragraph here. The previous paragraph talks about the existing oil-rig technology that could be used to build cities on the sea, and this paragraph talks about what these new cities would be like. The ideas are distinct and deserve separate paragraphs.

26. **The correct answer is (B)**. The logical relationship between the two clauses in this sense is best expressed by the word *since*—the fact that shipping supplies from the mainland would be costly is the reason why the cities would have to be self-sufficient. *Since* states this relationship.

27. **The correct answer is (B)**. The original phrase is vague, as are choices (C) and (D). Choice (B) names the kinds of facilities to be included in the new cities rather than merely alluding to them.

28. **The correct answer is (C)**. The phrase that follows the semicolon can't stand alone as a sentence, so the semicolon is incorrect. It must be changed to a comma.

29. **The correct answer is (C)**. Paragraph 4 is devoted to describing the various purposes that cities on the sea might serve. The new sentence, which adds an extra example of these purposes, would be best if placed at the end of that paragraph.

30. **The correct answer is (B)**. Paragraph 1 describes an example of the "human dilemmas" introduced in paragraph 2. Therefore, it makes sense to have paragraph 1 follow paragraph 2.

Breathing Space Number Two

I certainly hope that that last passage didn't make you seasick. If you have any SCUBA gear, this might be a good time to try it out. Sorry, but that was another obligatory allusion to the "breathing space" thing, and if you don't understand "obligatory" or "allusion" this would be an excellent time to stretch your mind and use your dictionary.

Since you may well have taken a longer than a few minute break between the last passage and the next, we are going to provide you with a full-sized repetition of the directions. Get ready, because here they come.

Directions: These exercises consist of a passage in which particular words or phrases are underlined and numbered. Following the passage, you will see alternative words and phrases that could be substituted for the underlined part. You must select the alternative that expresses the idea most clearly and correctly or that best fits the style and tone of the entire passage. If the original version is best, select "NO CHANGE." The exercises also include questions about entire paragraphs and the passage as a whole. These questions are identified by a number in a box, like ⬚1, ⬚2, etc.

After you select the correct answer for each question, mark the oval representing the correct answer on your answer sheet.

Exercise 3: The Devastation of El Niño

[1]

Throughout 1998, it seemed, whenever anything went wrong, someone could be heard exclaiming, "Blame it on El Niño!" This unusually powerful weather system received so much attention in the news media around the world that El Niño came to seem <u>like a good</u> scapegoat for almost any mishap. |32|
          31

[2]

Every year, in late December—around Christmas time—oceanic winds from the West tend to shift, causing warm water from the western Pacific to move toward South America, heating the waters along its coast. These hot currents and the weather disturbances they cause <u>has been dubbed</u> El Niño—Spanish for "the
          33
child"—because of their annual association with the Christmas holiday.

[3]

Usually, the temperature of the water increases for six months, then returns to normal. <u>In 1998 however</u>, the wind shifts occurred around April and didn't peak
          34
until January, lasting substantially longer than usual. The resulting storms and other climatic changes produced widespread flooding and <u>erosion. And,</u> among
          35
other problems, devastated Peru's population of seals and birds.

[4]

When El Niño hit, vast schools of small fish, such as anchovies and sardines,

sought cooler temperatures <u>furthest</u> down in the depths of the Pacific than the
                                  36

levels where they are usually found. While this protected the fish from the unsea-
sonable weather conditions, their predators were unable to reach them at these
new, greater <u>depths, thus</u> the predators had no food readily available.
              37

[5]
Aquatic mammals were hit <u>especially hardly</u>. Along one Peruvian beach, the Punta
                           38
San Juan, a whole season's pup production of fur seals and sea lions died, <u>as well as</u>
                                            39

thousands of juveniles and breeding adults. By May 13, 1998, only 15 fur seals
were counted, when there are usually hundreds. <u>On the other hand</u>, only 1,500 sea
                                    40
lions were found in an area that usually houses 8,000.

[6]
The Humboldt penguins also faced population losses due to El Niño. These
penguins normally breed twice a <u>year: but</u> in 1998, their second breeding ground
                         41
was flooded by 52 consecutive hours of rain. Only 50 of the 3,500 to 5,000
penguins that usually lay eggs were <u>able to do so.</u>
                         42

[7]
Because Peru is <u>so close in distance</u> to the Pacific regions where the wind shifts and
                    43
water warming of El Niño originate, it experiences the harshest effects of this
unpredictable weather phenomenon. <u>Two or three more such years may spell an</u>
                           44
<u>end to many species of wildlife that once thrived on Peruvian shores.</u>
                    44

31. (A) NO CHANGE

    (B) as a good

    (C) as if it was a good

    (D) as a

                                          Ⓐ Ⓑ Ⓒ Ⓓ

32. Which of the choices best introduces a central theme of the essay and provides the most appropriate transition between the first and second paragraphs?

   (A) Yet the underlying meteorological causes of El Niño remain obscure.

   (B) Unfortunately, the problems it really caused for creatures living on the Pacific coast of Peru were all too real.

   (C) All over the United States, people found their lives disrupted by the violent effects of El Niño.

   (D) But the real effects of El Niño proved to be surprisingly mild.

   Ⓐ Ⓑ Ⓒ Ⓓ

33. (A) NO CHANGE

   (B) have been dubbed

   (C) was dubbed

   (D) is known as

   Ⓐ Ⓑ Ⓒ Ⓓ

34. (A) NO CHANGE

   (B) However in 1998,

   (C) In 1998, however,

   (D) In 1998—however,

   Ⓐ Ⓑ Ⓒ Ⓓ

35. (A) NO CHANGE

   (B) erosion; and,

   (C) erosion, and,

   (D) erosion and

   Ⓐ Ⓑ Ⓒ Ⓓ

36. (A) NO CHANGE

   (B) more far

   (C) farther

   (D) farthest

   Ⓐ Ⓑ Ⓒ Ⓓ

T/HSPA, FCAT, MEAP HST, MCAS, GEE21, Regents Exams, SOL, NCCT, AHSGE, GHSGT, BS
NCCT, AHSGE, GHSGT, BST, BSAP, WASL, CAHSEE, TAAS, OGT, /HSPA, FCAT, MEAP
GT, HSPT/HSPA, FCAT, MEAP HST, MCAS, GEE21, Regents Exams, NCCT, AHSGE, GHS
GHSGT, BST, BSAP, WASL, CAHSEE, TAAS, OGT, HSPT/HSPA, FCAT, MEAP HST, MCAS

CHAPTER
8

37. **(A)** NO CHANGE
    (B) depths: thus
    (C) depths—thus
    (D) depths. Thus,

Ⓐ Ⓑ Ⓒ Ⓓ

38. **(A)** NO CHANGE
    (B) hard, especially.
    (C) especially hard.
    (D) specially hardly.

Ⓐ Ⓑ Ⓒ Ⓓ

39. **(A)** NO CHANGE
    (B) as also
    (C) at the same time as
    (D) so did

Ⓐ Ⓑ Ⓒ Ⓓ

40. **(A)** NO CHANGE
    (B) Yet
    (C) Similarly,
    (D) Likewise,

Ⓐ Ⓑ Ⓒ Ⓓ

41. **(A)** NO CHANGE
    (B) year, but
    (C) year. And
    (D) year, however

Ⓐ Ⓑ Ⓒ Ⓓ

42. **(A)** NO CHANGE
    (B) capable of this.
    (C) able to lay them.
    (D) possible.

Ⓐ Ⓑ Ⓒ Ⓓ

43. **(A)** NO CHANGE
    (B) very close in distance
    (C) not distant
    (D) so close

Ⓐ Ⓑ Ⓒ Ⓓ

Items 44 and 45 pose questions about the passage as a whole.

44. Which of the following sentences, if added, would best conclude the passage and effectively summarize its main idea? If you feel the original conclusion is best, select choice (A).

   (A) Two or three more such years may spell an end to many species of wildlife that once thrived on Peruvian shores.

   (B) Fortunately, other countries in South America do not suffer the ill effects of El Niño to the same extent as does Peru.

   (C) Government officials in Peru are currently at work to develop plans for dealing with the problems caused by El Niño the next time it strikes.

   (D) However, aid from foreign countries has helped Peru to save certain of the endangered species whom El Niño has decimated.

Ⓐ Ⓑ Ⓒ Ⓓ

45. Suppose the writer were to eliminate Paragraph 4. This omission would cause the essay as a whole to lose primarily

   (A) relevant details about how Pacific fish are destroyed by the effects of El Niño.

   (B) irrelevant facts about feeding patterns among creatures in the southern Pacific ocean.

   (C) relevant information about how El Niño affects aquatic animals on the shores of Peru.

   (D) irrelevant details about the kinds of fish that live off the shores of Peru.

Ⓐ Ⓑ Ⓒ Ⓓ

Solutions for Exercise 3

31. **The correct answer is** (A). The conjunction *like* is correct, because it's idiomatic to say that something "seems like" something else, rather than "seems as" something else.

32. **The correct answer is** (B). The first paragraph discusses in a somewhat light-hearted way how people blamed all kinds of problems on El Niño. But since the rest of the passage describes the very serious problems El Niño really caused in Peru, a transitional sentence is needed that says to the reader, "All kidding aside—El Niño produced some real headaches." The sentence in choice (B) does just that.

33. **The correct answer is** (B). The subject of the verb phrase "has been dubbed" is plural—it's the two things, "hot currents" and "weather disturbances" (a compound subject). Therefore, the plural verb "have been dubbed" is needed.

34. **The correct answer is** (C). The parenthetical word *however* needs to be set off from the rest of the sentence by a pair of commas, one before it and one after it.

35. **The correct answer is** (C). The last sentence of the paragraph, as originally written, is a fragment that lacks any real subject. By changing the period before it into a comma, the sentence is merged with the previous one, and "storms and . . . climatic changes" becomes the subject of the verb *devastated*.

36. **The correct answer is** (C). Two things are being compared: the greater depths the fish sought during El Niño and the lesser depths at which they normally swim. Since only two things are being compared, the comparative adjective "farther" is wanted rather than the superlative *farthest*.

37. **The correct answer is** (D). Break this sentence into two, since it's a run-on as it stands originally.

38. **The correct answer is** (C). The adverb form of the adjective *hard* looks the same as the adjective: *hard*. The *-ly* suffix isn't used in this case.

39. **The correct answer is** (A). The conjunction "as well as" is the most graceful and idiomatic of the answer choices. Note that choice (D) would turn the sentence into a run-on: "So did thousands of juveniles and breeding adults" could and should stand on its own as a complete sentence.

40. **The correct answer is (C).** The word *similarly* makes the most sense here, since what's being described in the sentence is a phenomenon that resembles the one described in the previous sentence. *Likewise* sounds awkward in this context.

41. **The correct answer is (B).** When two potentially complete sentences are linked with a coordinating conjunction (in this case, *but*), it's normally correct to use a comma before the conjunction rather than some other punctuation mark.

42. **The correct answer is (A).** The original wording is the most clear and concise choice. Choices (B) and (D) are vague and confusing, and choice (C) sounds clumsy.

43. **The correct answer is (D).** The words "in distance" are redundant, since the word *close* obviously refers to distance; they should be eliminated.

44. **The correct answer is (A).** This sentence neatly ties together the various destructive effects of El Niño on wildlife living on the shores of Peru.

45. **The correct answer is (C).** Paragraph 4 explains the indirect way El Niño affects the Peruvian mammals by reducing the availability of their food, the schools of anchovies and sardines. It's necessary if we are to understand how El Niño affected the seals and sea lions in Peru.

Breathing Space Number Three

Wow! That last passage could have taken your breath away, so I'll wait while you catch up with it. Got it? All right then; we'll try one more of these passages.

When you see the title, you might think that it's going to turn out to be a real turkey, but that certainly isn't the case. In fact, it's kind of amusing, if you like that sort of thing. No, seriously, I think you're going to enjoy it, but, at any rate (as they say), better you than I.

Actually, they usually say "Better you than me," but that's not correct. I'll bet you really feel better now that you know that!

CHAPTER 8

Exercise 4: The First Thanksgiving—Turkey Day and a Whole Lot More

Every autumn, when Thanksgiving rolls around, anxiety and stress levels in millions of American families rise. Hosting friends and relatives from all over the country and then <u>to prepare</u> one of the largest meals of the year is not an easy job.

46

But, when the typical Thanksgiving dinner of today <u>is compared with</u> the

47

celebration of the first Thanksgiving, it doesn't seem like <u>quite a feat.</u>

48

<u>First consider the menu.</u> At a typical modern-day Thanksgiving, there is a roast

49

turkey, baked yams, stuffing, cranberry sauce, gravy, and some sort of dessert—maybe ice cream and some pie or cake. Of course, you can fix everything yourself, from scratch, if you like; but if you prefer, all of the food can be purchased at a local <u>supermarket: just one trip</u> and you have all you need for your dinner. Today's

50

menu seems stingy by comparison to <u>the Pilgrims meal</u> enjoyed on the first

51

Thanksgiving in 1621. According to contemporary records, the list of foods included five deer; wild turkeys, geese, and duck; eels, lobsters, clams, and mussels fished from the ocean; pumpkin; an assortment of biscuits; hoe and ash cakes <u>(whatever those were)</u>; popcorn balls made with corn and maple syrup; pudding;

52

berries of several kinds—gooseberries, cranberries, strawberries—plums, cherries, and bogbeans; beer made from barley; and wine spiked with brandy. Just in case <u>this wasn't</u> enough, you could fill in the corners with "flint corn," a rock-hard

53

corn ground into a mush. $\boxed{54}$ And once the dinner was served, the meal didn't last a few hours, <u>but a few days —and</u> with no football on TV to distract the

55

Pilgrims and their friends from the serious business of eating.

The other major difference was the guest list. Nowadays, in many households, the whole family comes for Thanksgiving, <u>this provokes</u> many groans from besieged

56

hosts. Statistics show that the average Thanksgiving dinner boasts twenty-three total guests—no tiny gathering, at that. [57] At the first Thanksgiving,

when Squanto, the Indian-in-residence, decided to invite Massasoit,

<u>the leader of the Wampanoags</u>, for a little pot-luck supper, the Pilgrims weren't

58

expecting him to bring along the other ninety person guest list. I guess

<u>they weren't overdoing it</u>, after all.

59

So, when the next Thanksgiving rolls around, and <u>your tempted</u> to complain

60

about "all this cooking—all this food—all these people!"—just be thankful it isn't
1621 and you aren't hosting the first Thanksgiving!

46. (A) NO CHANGE

   (B) preparing

   (C) working on preparation of

   (D) doing preparation for

   Ⓐ Ⓑ Ⓒ Ⓓ

47. (A) NO CHANGE

   (B) is compared against

   (C) is viewed in reference to

   (D) compares with

   Ⓐ Ⓑ Ⓒ Ⓓ

48. (A) NO CHANGE

   (B) as great a feat.

   (C) all that much of a feat.

   (D) such a feat.

   Ⓐ Ⓑ Ⓒ Ⓓ

49. (A) NO CHANGE

   (B) Start by thinking about the food that was served.

   (C) The menu is the first thing we shall discuss.

   (D) The food at the first Thanksgiving was incredible.

   Ⓐ Ⓑ Ⓒ Ⓓ

50. (A) NO CHANGE
    (B) supermarket, just one trip
    (C) supermarket. One trip;
    (D) supermarket; one trip is all,

Ⓐ Ⓑ Ⓒ Ⓓ

51. (A) NO CHANGE
    (B) what the Pilgrims'
    (C) the meal that the Pilgrim's
    (D) the dinner the Pilgrims

Ⓐ Ⓑ Ⓒ Ⓓ

52. (A) NO CHANGE
    (B) (what they are is unknown to me)
    (C) (unheard-of today)
    (D) OMIT the underlined portion

Ⓐ Ⓑ Ⓒ Ⓓ

53. (A) NO CHANGE
    (B) this weren't
    (C) all of the above weren't
    (D) one didn't find this

Ⓐ Ⓑ Ⓒ Ⓓ

54. At this point, the writer is considering the addition of the following sentence:

Everything, of course, was prepared by hand; there were no food processors, microwave ovens, or other appliances to help.

Would this be a logical and relevant addition to the essay?

   (A) Yes, because it emphasizes how difficult it was to prepare the first Thanksgiving dinner.

   (B) Yes, because many readers may not be aware that the Pilgrims lived in a time when technology was relatively primitive.

   (C) No, because the rest of the passage does not focus on technological differences between 1621 and today.

   (D) No, because it is unconnected to the list of foodstuffs that occupies most of the rest of the paragraph.

Ⓐ Ⓑ Ⓒ Ⓓ

55. (A) NO CHANGE
    (B) rather a few days—
    (C) but instead a few days:
    (D) a few days, rather;

Ⓐ Ⓑ Ⓒ Ⓓ

56. (A) NO CHANGE
    (B) so as to provoke
    (C) the provocation of
    (D) provoking

Ⓐ Ⓑ Ⓒ Ⓓ

57. Which of the following sentences, if inserted here, would provide the best transition between the first half and the second half of the paragraph?
    (A) We rarely have that many guests in my house.
    (B) It could be a lot worse, however.
    (C) Both family and friends are included in this number.
    (D) And, all of them show up hungry.

Ⓐ Ⓑ Ⓒ Ⓓ

58. (A) NO CHANGE
    (B) the Wampanoag's leader,
    (C) who was leading the Wampanoag's
    (D) Wampanoag leader,

Ⓐ Ⓑ Ⓒ Ⓓ

59. (A) NO CHANGE
    (B) the repast served was not, in fact, excessive,
    (C) that dinner menu wasn't overdoing it,
    (D) it wasn't too much,

Ⓐ Ⓑ Ⓒ Ⓓ

60. (A) NO CHANGE
    (B) your feeling a temptation
    (C) you're tempted
    (D) there's a temptation

Ⓐ Ⓑ Ⓒ Ⓓ

Solutions for Exercise 4

46. **The correct answer is (B).** Choice (B) is correct because it is grammatically parallel with the word *hosting*; the present participle *preparing* is better than the infinitive *to prepare*.

47. **The correct answer is (A).** The correct idiomatic phrase is "compared with," not "compared against" or any of the other answer choices.

48. **The correct answer is (D).** In this rather casual, mildly humorous essay, the phrase "such a feat" sounds both idiomatic and appropriate. The other answer choices either sound a bit awkward or are verbose by comparison.

49. **The correct answer is (A).** The original sentence is clear and concise. The alternatives add words without adding anything to the meaning or tone of the essay.

50. **The correct answer is (A).** Note that what follows the colon restates or summarizes what precedes it. This is a good example of the proper use of a colon.

51. **The correct answer is (D).** Choice (D) states the idea most clearly of all the answer choices. The original wording is wrong, among other reasons, because the phrase "Pilgrims meal" would have to be written as the possessive "Pilgrims' meal."

52. **The correct answer is (A).** The parenthetical phrase is appropriate in this light-hearted look back at a long-ago, slightly amazing, and mysterious holiday celebration. Choices (B) and (C) say almost the same thing, but less gracefully and idiomatically.

53. **The correct answer is (A).** The original wording is more concise and clear than the alternatives.

54. **The correct answer is (A).** The proposed addition fits logically into the overall theme of the essay. Note, too, that it picks up on the idea that the original Thanksgiving dinner was much harder to prepare than today's Thanksgiving dinners, which can be purchased ready-made at the supermarket (as mentioned in the second paragraph).

55. **The correct answer is (A).** The original wording is correctly parallel to the phrase it's paired with: not "a few hours, but a few days."

56. **The correct answer is (D).** As it is originally written, the sentence is a run-on. By changing the subject-verb pair *this provokes* into the present participle, *provoking*, the second half of the sentence is tightly and correctly linked with the first half, and the run-on problem is eliminated.

57. **The correct answer is (B).** The first half of the paragraph talks about the many guests who show up at today's Thanksgiving dinners, while the second half talks about how many more guests there were at the first Thanksgiving. The sentence in choice (B) deftly links the two ideas.

58. **The correct answer is (A).** The original word is both perfectly correct and idiomatic.

59. **The correct answer is (C).** As originally worded, the underlined phrase is pretty vague; it's hard to tell what the writer is getting at. Choice (C) clarifies the point: the huge menu described in the previous paragraph makes sense when you consider how many people attended the dinner.

60. **The correct answer is (C).** The contraction *you're* is necessary in this sentence, since what's intended is the same meaning as the two words "you are."

Breathing Space Number Four

There is no breathing space number four. For goodness sakes, it's the end of the chapter. What more could you ask for? Go out and shoot some hoops.

CHAPTER 9

PRACTICE TOO (OR TWO)

Suppose you required surgery for some condition or another. You certainly wouldn't want to be worked on by a surgeon who was inexperienced at the procedure that you were about to undergo. Well, it just so happens that surgeons are never done learning their profession—neither is any other type of physician, for that matter. Not a day goes by when doctors do not *practice* medicine. Actually, that's not quite true, since some don't practice on weekends. Come to think of it, some don't practice on Wednesdays either, because then they're out playing golf. Well then, at least, they're practicing golf.

Needless to say, practicing medicine and practicing golf are not exactly comparable to one another, although the latter is somewhat comparable to learning to do something well. With that in mind, this chapter is presented for your personal entertainment and personal improvement. Don't expect it to do anything for your golf, however—a sport for which I personally have no use and that Mark Twain called a hell of a way to ruin a good walk.

Practicing Sentence Completions

Directions: Each of the following questions consists of an incomplete sentence followed by five words or pairs of words. Choose that word or pair of words that, when substituted for the blank space or spaces, best complete the meaning of the sentence. Then, mark the letter of your choice either in the book or on a separate sheet of scrap paper.

Example of a Sentence Completion Question:

In view of the extenuating circumstances and the defendant's youth, the judge recommended _____.

(A) conviction

(B) a defense

(C) a mistrial

(D) leniency

(E) life imprisonment

Ⓐ Ⓑ Ⓒ ● Ⓔ

1. Unsure of her skills in English , the young girl was _____ when called on to speak in class.

(A) remunerative

(B) transient

(C) reticent

(D) sartorial

(E) resilient

Ⓐ Ⓑ Ⓒ Ⓓ Ⓔ

2. Anyone familiar with the facts could _____ his arguments, which seemed logical but were actually _____.

(A) refute ... specious

(B) support ... protracted

(C) repeat ... recumbent

(D) review ... cogent

(E) elicit ... prodigious

Ⓐ Ⓑ Ⓒ Ⓓ Ⓔ

3. Each spring the _____ tree put out fewer and fewer leaves.

(A) ambient

(B) malignant

(C) desultory

(D) moribund

(E) reclusive

Ⓐ Ⓑ Ⓒ Ⓓ Ⓔ

4. The building had been _____; she could not even be sure exactly where it had stood.

(A) jettisoned

(B) debilitated

(C) mitigated

(D) berated

(E) obliterated

Ⓐ Ⓑ Ⓒ Ⓓ Ⓔ

5. The bully's menacing, _____ manner was actually just for show; in reality it was entirely _____ .

(A) imperturbable ... vapid

(B) truculent ... affected

(C) stringent ... credulous

(D) supercilious ... blatant

(E) parsimonious ... contentious

Ⓐ Ⓑ Ⓒ Ⓓ Ⓔ

6. The municipality attracted the country's scientific elite and _____ them, insulating them entirely from the problems of ordinary civilian life.

(A) cajoled

(B) muted

(C) mused

(D) cosseted

(E) impeded

Ⓐ Ⓑ Ⓒ Ⓓ Ⓔ

SPT/HSPA, FCAT, MEAP HST, MCAS, GEE21, Regents Exams, SOL, NCCT, AHSGE, GHSGT, B
, NCCT, AHSGE, GHSGT, BST, BSAP, WASL, CAHSEE, TAAS, OGT, HSPT/HSPA, FCAT, MEAP
GT, HSPT/HSPA, FCAT, MEAP HST, MCAS, GEE21, Regents Exams, NCCT, AHSGE, GH

CHAPTER
9

7. Although the bank executive gave the appearance of a
_____ businessman, he was really a _____.

   (A)   dedicated ... capitalist

   (B)   respectable ... reprobate

   (C)   depraved ... profligate

   (D)   empathetic ... philanthropist

   (E)   churlish ... miscreant

Ⓐ Ⓑ Ⓒ Ⓓ Ⓔ

8. During a campaign, politicians often engage in _____
debate, attacking each other's proposals in a torrent of
_____ words.

   (A)   acerbic ... amiable

   (B)   acrimonious ... angry

   (C)   intensive ... nebulous

   (D)   garrulous ... inarticulate

   (E)   impassioned ... vapid

Ⓐ Ⓑ Ⓒ Ⓓ Ⓔ

9. He was uneven in his approach to the problem, at once
_____ and _____.

   (A)   surly ... unwilling

   (B)   sincere ... well-meaning

   (C)   harmonious ... foolhardy

   (D)   conscientious ... frivolous

   (E)   careless ... insouciant

Ⓐ Ⓑ Ⓒ Ⓓ Ⓔ

SOLUTIONS FOR SENTENCE COMPLETIONS

1. **The correct answer is (C).** If the young girl was unsure of her English skills, she was likely to be *reticent* (shy and restrained) when asked to speak.

2. **The correct answer is (A).** Arguments that only seemed logical were likely to be *specious* (false), and anyone familiar with the facts could *refute* (disprove) them.

3. **The correct answer is (D).** A tree that puts out fewer and fewer leaves is probably *moribund* (dying).

4. **The correct answer is (E).** If no trace of the building remained, it had been *obliterated* (destroyed completely).

5. **The correct answer is (B).** A manner that is menacing or threatening is said to be *truculent*. If, however, it is put on only for show, it is merely *affected*.

6. **The correct answer is (D).** Those who are protected from the harsh world around them are pampered, or *cosseted*. The other choices make no sense.

7. **The correct answer is (B).** The transitional word *although* sets up a contrast suggesting that one choice will be positive and one choice will be negative. The only possible answer is choice (B). Someone only appearing to be a respectable businessman may in reality be a *reprobate*, or a scoundrel.

8. **The correct answer is (B).** The word *attacking* indicates the need for two strong negative words. Only choice (B) satisfies this requirement with *acrimonious*, meaning harsh or bitter, and *angry*.

9. **The correct answer is (D).** Uneven means inconsistent. *Conscientious* (extremely careful) and *frivolous* (silly) are opposing characteristics.

Analogies, Not Analgesics! (Look it up if you need to.)

Directions: Each of the following questions consists of a capitalized pair of words followed by five pairs of words lettered (A) to (E). The capitalized words bear some meaningful relationship to each other. Choose the lettered pair of words whose relationship is most similar to that expressed by the capitalized pair and mark its letter either in the book or on a separate sheet of scrap paper.

Example of an Analogy Question:

DAY : SUN ::

(A) sunlight : daylight

(B) ray : sun

(C) night : moon

(D) heat : cold

(E) moon : star

Ⓐ Ⓑ ● Ⓓ Ⓔ

CHAPTER 9

READING

10. PEEL : APPLE ::

    (A) skin : knee

    (B) sail : boat

    (C) shell : lobster

    (D) pit : grape

    (E) coat : fur

    Ⓐ Ⓑ Ⓒ Ⓓ Ⓔ

11. FINGER : RING ::

    (A) neck : necklace

    (B) bandage : wound

    (C) bracelet : wrist

    (D) glove : hand

    (E) lip : tune

    Ⓐ Ⓑ Ⓒ Ⓓ Ⓔ

12. ADULT : CHILD ::

    (A) mother : baby

    (B) sheep : lamb

    (C) cow : calf

    (D) puppy : baby

    (E) buck : fawn

    Ⓐ Ⓑ Ⓒ Ⓓ Ⓔ

13. PEPPER : SEASON ::

    (A) cinnamon : prepare

    (B) sugar : sweeten

    (C) celery : plant

    (D) accent : cook

    (E) salt : taste

    Ⓐ Ⓑ Ⓒ Ⓓ Ⓔ

14. BEEF : JERKY ::

    (A) corn : flake

    (B) ham : pork

    (C) grape : raisin

    (D) meat : sausage

    (E) flesh : bone

    Ⓐ Ⓑ Ⓒ Ⓓ Ⓔ

15. SCHOOL : FISH ::

(A) herd : cows

(B) cars : traffic

(C) dog : puppy

(D) bird : wing

(E) pig : barn

Ⓐ Ⓑ Ⓒ Ⓓ Ⓔ

SOLUTIONS FOR ANALOGIES

10. **The correct answer is (C).** The *peel* is the outer layer of an *apple,* just as the *shell* is the outer covering of a *lobster.*

11. **The correct answer is (A).** A *ring* is worn around the *finger,* and a *necklace* is worn around the *neck.*

12. **The correct answer is (B).** A *child,* on becoming a fully mature person, is an *adult.* A *lamb* becomes a *sheep* on reaching full maturity. (*Cow* and *buck,* other mature animals, are specifically female and male, respectively. Pretty tricky, eh?!)

13. **The correct answer is (B).** *Pepper* is added to food to *season* it and *sugar* to *sweeten* it. That's pretty straightforward.

14. **The correct answer is (C).** *Beef* can be dried to make *jerky,* and *grapes* can be dried to make *raisins.* I was tempted to go for choice (D), before I thought it through more carefully.

15. **The correct answer is (A).** A group of *fish* is called a *school,* and a group of *cows* is called a *herd.* This one's about as easy as it gets.

SPT/HSPA, FCAT, MEAP HST, MCAS, GEE21, Regents Exams, SOL, NCCT, AHSGE, GHSGT, B
L, NCCT, AHSGE, GHSGT, BST, BSAP, WASL, CAHSEE, TAAS, OGT, ST/HSPA, FCAT, MEAP
OGT, HSPT/HSPA, FCAT, MEAP HST, MCAS, GEE21, Regents Exams, NCCT, AHSGE, GH
SE, GHSGT, BST, BSAP, WASL, CAHSEE, TAAS, OGT, HSPT/HSPA, FCAT, MEAP HST, MCAS

CHAPTER
9

READING

Now Analyze This

Directions: Each passage below is followed by a set of questions. Read each passage, then answer the accompanying questions, basing your answers on what is *stated* or *implied* in the passage and in any introductory material provided. Mark the letter of your choice either in the book or on a separate sheet of scrap paper.

Questions 16–23 are based on the following passage.

The following speech was delivered at the height of the 1960s civil rights movement by Dr. Martin Luther King Jr., head of the Southern Christian Leadership Conference and the movement's most eloquent spokesperson.

Line We have come to this hallowed spot to remind America of the fierce urgency of now. This is no time to engage in the luxury of cooling off or to take the tranquilizing drug of gradualism. Now is the time to make real the promises of democracy. Now is the time to rise from the dark and desolate valley of segrega-

5 tion to the sunlit path of racial justice. Now is the time to lift our nation from the quicksand of racial injustice to the solid rock of brotherhood. Now is the time to make justice a reality for all of God's children.

It would be fatal for the nation to overlook the urgency of the moment. This sweltering summer of the Negro's legitimate discontent will not pass until there

10 is an invigorating autumn of freedom and equality. Those who hope that the Negro needed to blow off steam and will now be content will have a rude awakening if the nation returns to business as usual. There will be neither rest nor tranquility in America until the Negro is granted his citizenship rights. The whirlwinds of revolt will continue to shake the foundations of our nation until

15 the bright day of justice emerges.

But that is something that I must say to my people who stand on the warm threshold that leads into the palace of justice. In the process of gaining our rightful place, we must not be guilty of wrongful deeds. Let us not seek to satisfy our thirst for freedom by drinking from the cup of bitterness and hatred.

20 We must forever conduct our struggle on the high plane of dignity and discipline. We must not allow our creative protest to degenerate into physical violence. Again and again we must rise to the majestic heights of meeting physical force with soul force. The marvelous new militancy that has engulfed the Negro

25 community must not lead us to a distrust of all white people, for many of our white brothers, as evidenced by their presence here today, have come to realize

that their destiny is tied up with our destiny. And they have come to realize that their freedom is inextricably bound to our freedom. We cannot walk alone.

30 As we walk, we must make the pledge that we shall always march ahead. We cannot turn back. There are those who are asking the devotees of civil rights, "When will you be satisfied?" We can never be satisfied as long as the Negro is the victim of the unspeakable horrors of police brutality. We can never be satisfied as long as the Negro's basic mobility is from a smaller ghetto to a larger one. We can never be satisfied as long as our children are stripped of their selfhood 35 and robbed of their dignity by signs stating "For Whites Only." We cannot be satisfied as long as a Negro in Mississippi cannot vote and a Negro in New York believes he has nothing for which to vote. No, no, we are not satisfied, and we will not be satisfied until justice rolls down like waters and righteousness like a mighty stream.

40 I am not unmindful that some of you have come out of great trials and tribulations. Some of you have come fresh from narrow jail cells. Some of you have come from areas where your quest for freedom left you battered by the storms of persecution and staggered by the winds of police brutality. You have been the veterans of creative suffering. Continue to work with the faith that unearned 45 suffering is redemptive.

Go back to Mississippi, go back to Alabama, go back to South Carolina, go back to Louisiana, go back to the slums and ghettos of our Northern cities, knowing that somehow this situation can and will be changed. Let us not wallow in the valley of despair.

16. When King says in lines 44–45 that "unearned suffering is redemptive," he means that it
    (A) provokes police brutality
    (B) confers sanctity, or holiness, upon the sufferer
    (C) is bound to continue forever
    (D) strips children of their dignity or self-worth
    (E) will never be repaid

    Ⓐ Ⓑ Ⓒ Ⓓ Ⓔ

17. In the passage, King's attitude is generally
    (A) prejudiced
    (B) cynical

PT/HSPA, FCAT, MEAP HST, MCAS, GEE21, Regents Exams, SOL, NCCT, AHSGE, GHSGT, BS
NCCT, AHSGE, GHSGT, BST, BSAP, WASL, CAHSEE, TAAS, OGT, HSPT/HSPA, FCAT, MEAP
OGT, HSPT/HSPA, FCAT, MEAP HST, MCAS, GEE21, Regents Exams, NCCT, AHSGE, GHS
GHSGT, BST, BSAP, WASL, CAHSEE, TAAS, OGT, HSPT/HSPA, FCAT, MEAP HST, MCAS

CHAPTER
9

READING

(C) fearful

(D) optimistic

(E) neutral

Ⓐ Ⓑ Ⓒ Ⓓ Ⓔ

18. Which quotation best suggests the main idea of the speech?

(A) "...we must not be guilty of wrongful deeds."

(B) "We cannot walk alone."

(C) "We can never be satisfied as long as the Negro's basic mobility is from a smaller ghetto to a larger one."

(D) "...to remind America of the fierce urgency of now."

(E) "...this situation can and will be changed."

Ⓐ Ⓑ Ⓒ Ⓓ Ⓔ

19. The tone of this speech can best be described as

(A) inspirational

(B) boastful

(C) defiant

(D) sad

(E) buoyant

Ⓐ Ⓑ Ⓒ Ⓓ Ⓔ

20. King's attitude toward white Americans appears to be based on

(A) noncommitment

(B) contempt for authority

(C) mutual distrust

(D) mutual respect

(E) negativism

Ⓐ Ⓑ Ⓒ Ⓓ Ⓔ

21. King's remarks indicate that he considers the racial problem a national problem because

(A) all white Americans are prejudiced

(B) African Americans are moving to the suburbs

(C) all areas of American life are affected

(D) the U.S. Constitution supports segregation

(E) laws will be broken if the problem is left unattended

Ⓐ Ⓑ Ⓒ Ⓓ Ⓔ

22. In the passage, King implies that the struggle for racial justice can be best won through

   (A) marching on Washington

   (B) civil disorder

   (C) creative protest

   (D) challenging unjust laws

   (E) doing nothing

Ⓐ Ⓑ Ⓒ Ⓓ Ⓔ

23. In this speech, King specifically recommends

   (A) nonviolent resistance

   (B) faith in God

   (C) Communist ideas

   (D) social turmoil

   (E) turbulent revolt

Ⓐ Ⓑ Ⓒ Ⓓ Ⓔ

KINGLY SOLUTIONS

16. **The correct answer is (B).** King urges his listeners to "continue to work with the faith that unearned suffering is redemptive." Even if you did not know the meaning of *redemptive*, you could infer that it promised something positive. Of the choices, only choice (B) satisfies this condition.

17. **The correct answer is (D).** The last paragraph gives King's belief that "...this situation can and will be changed." That's hopeful, therefore, *optimistic*.

18. **The correct answer is (E).** This is stated in the last paragraph and sums up the point of the entire speech.

19. **The correct answer is (A).** King is attempting to inspire his listeners.

20. **The correct answer is (D).** Lines 25–27 state that this new attitude "...must not lead us to a distrust of all white people, for many of our white brothers...have come to realize that their destiny is tied up with our destiny."

21. **The correct answer is (C).** King states, in lines 12–13, "There will be neither rest nor tranquility in America until the Negro is granted his citizenship rights."

22. **The correct answer is (C).** Paragraph 4 specifically mentions *creative protest*.

23. **The correct answer is (A).** The second paragraph discusses "the whirl-winds of revolt" that will continue until justice prevails; the third paragraph urges listeners to obey the law, as "…we must not be guilty of wrongful deeds." Thus, nonviolent resistance is the best response.

Now, try your hand at the next passage. Be forewarned, it is very poetical, and therefore very different from what we've become accustomed to dealing with.

Questions 24–31 are based on the following passage.

Agustin Yáñez was the author of many short stories, most of them based in or around Guadalajara, Mexico, his hometown. "Alda," from which this passage is excerpted, is from a collection entitled Archipiélago de Mujeres.

Line I never met my first love. She must have been a sweet and sad child. Her photographs inspire my imagination to reconstruct the outlines of her soul simple and austere as a primitive church, extensive as a castle, stately as a tower, deep as a well. Purity of brow, which, like the throat, the hands, the entire body must

5 have been carved in crystal or marble; the very soft lines of the face; the deep-set eyes with a look of surprise, sweet and sad, beneath the veil of the eyelashes; a brief mouth with fine lips, immune to sensuality; docile hair, harmonious and still; simply dressed in harmony with the obvious distinction and nobility of her bearing; all of her, aglow with innocence and a certain gravity in which are

10 mixed the delights of childhood and the reverie of first youth. Her photographs invite one to try to imagine the timbre and rhythm of her voice, the ring of her laughter, the depth of her silences, the cadence of her movements, the direction and intensity of her glances. Her arms must have moved like the wings of a musical and tranquil bird; her figure must have yielded with the gentleness of a

15 lily in an April garden. How many times her translucent hands must have trimmed the lamps of the vigilant virgins who know not the day or the hour; in what moments of rapture did her mouth and eyes accentuate their sadness? When did they emphasize her sweet smile?

No, I never met her. And yet, even her pictures were with me for a long time

20 after she died. Long before then, my life was filled with her presence, fashioned of unreal images, devoid of all sensation; perhaps more faithful, certainly more

vivid, than these almost faded photographs. Hers was a presence without volume, line or color; an elusive phantom, which epitomized the beauty of all faces without limiting itself to any one, and embodied the delicacy of the best and
25 loftiest spirits, indefinitely.

I now believe that an obscure feeling, a fear of reality, was the cause of my refusal to exchange the formless images for a direct knowledge of her who inspired them. How many times, just when the senses might have put a limit to fancy did I avoid meeting her; and how many others did Fate intervene! On one
30 of the many occasions that I watched the house in which my phantom lived, I decided to knock; but the family was out.

24. What does Yáñez mean when he says "I never met my first love" (line 1)?
   (A) He loved unconditionally.
   (B) His first love died young.
   (C) He never fell in love.
   (D) He fell in love with someone he never really knew.
   (E) His first love was not a human being.

ⒶⒷⒸⒹⒺ

25. The description in Paragraph 1 moves from
   (A) sound to sight
   (B) smell to sight to sound
   (C) sight to touch
   (D) sight to sound to movement
   (E) touch to sound to sight

ⒶⒷⒸⒹⒺ

26. The word *docile* (line 7) is used to imply
   (A) wildness
   (B) conformity
   (C) manageability
   (D) indifference
   (E) willingness

ⒶⒷⒸⒹⒺ

27. In Paragraph 1, to what does Yáñez compare Alda's soul?
   (A) A series of buildings
   (B) Crystal and marble
   (C) The wings of a bird

(D) A flower in a garden

(E) A photograph

Ⓐ Ⓑ Ⓒ Ⓓ Ⓔ

28. When Yáñez says he is "devoid of all sensation" (line 21), he means that he

(A) has no sense of who Alda might be

(B) does not see, hear, or touch Alda

(C) cannot be sensible where Alda is concerned

(D) has little judgment

(E) feels nothing for Alda

Ⓐ Ⓑ Ⓒ Ⓓ Ⓔ

29. The word *faithful* (line 21) is used to mean

(A) loyal

(B) constant

(C) devoted

(D) firm

(E) reliable

Ⓐ Ⓑ Ⓒ Ⓓ Ⓔ

30. Unlike the previous paragraphs, Paragraph 3

(A) suggests an explanation for the author's behavior

(B) describes the author's photographs of Alda

(C) mentions the elusive qualities of Alda

(D) compares Alda to someone the author loved later

(E) expresses regret for losing Alda's love

Ⓐ Ⓑ Ⓒ Ⓓ Ⓔ

31. How might you reword the phrase "the senses might have put a limit to fancy" (lines 28–29)?

(A) "if I were sensible, I would not have fantasized"

(B) "my good taste enabled me to dream without limits"

(C) "good sense would have made things plainer"

(D) "I could sense that she wanted to end my dreams"

(E) "seeing her might have stopped my fantasies"

Ⓐ Ⓑ Ⓒ Ⓓ Ⓔ

High Stakes: Reading

POETICAL SOLUTIONS

This was, as promised, a very different type of passage from what you've been used to reading. Poetical images are not always easy to make sense of.

24. **The correct answer is (D).** This is a completely literal statement. As the rest of the passage makes clear, the narrator never really knew Alda.

25. **The correct answer is (D).** To answer this synthesis/analysis question will require looking back at the paragraph and tracing its structure. The narrator describes what Alda looked like, speculates on what she sounded like, and guesses what she moved like, in that order.

26. **The correct answer is (C).** *Docile* has several connotations, but a look back at the citation in question will tell you that only two of the choices could easily be applied to hair, and choice (A) is exactly opposite to the meaning the narrator intends.

27. **The correct answer is (A).** He compares her brow to choice (B), and he speaks of a flower, choice (D), and a photograph, choice (E). However, he compares her soul to a church, castle, and tower as well as to a well (see lines 3–4).

28. **The correct answer is (B).** Reread the surrounding text to remind yourself of the author's main point. Her presence has no sensation for him, because he has not really met her.

29. **The correct answer is (E).** Each choice is a possible synonym, but only choice (E) suits the idea of memory being more faithful than faded photographs.

30. **The correct answer is (A).** In the first sentence of Paragraph 3, the author suggests that his fear of reality was the reason he failed to meet Alda. This is the time he has made such a suggestion. Paragraph 3 might also be said to support choice (C), but so do paragraphs 1 and 2. Choices (D) and (E) are not supported anywhere in the passage.

31. **The correct answer is (E).** Here is an example of an oddly worded phrase that cannot be easily deciphered. By testing the choices in place of the phrase in context, however, the reasonable translation is clear.

Now wasn't that a hoot? Take a minute to catch your breath, and we'll change the pace again. Let's continue with a different allusion to poetry—a rather strange one at that. Hope your grammar skills are sharp!

Directions: This exercise consists of a passage in which particular words or phrases are underlined and numbered. Following the passage, you will see alternative words and phrases that could be substituted for the underlined part. You must select the alternative that expresses the idea most clearly and correctly or that best fits the style and tone of the entire passage. If the original version is best, select "NO CHANGE." The exercises also include questions about entire paragraphs and the passage as a whole. These questions are identified by a number in a box, like ⌐1⌐, ⌐2⌐, etc.

After you select the correct answer for each question, mark the oval representing the correct answer on your answer sheet.

The Poetry of Economics

"The poetry of economics?" a reader might ask. "How can 'the dismal science' be associated with the subtlety and creativity of poetry?" <u>You're</u> skepticism is

32

understandable, <u>and</u> perhaps a story from an economist's life can sketch the poetry

33

of economics at work.

Shortly after the Second World War, the agricultural economist Theodore Schultz, later to win a Nobel prize, spent a term based at Auburn University in <u>Alabama, he interviewed</u> farmers in the neighborhood. One day he interviewed an

34

old and poor farm <u>couple. And was struck</u> by how contented they seemed. "Why

35

are you so contented," he asked, "though very poor?" They answered: "You're wrong, Professor. We're not poor. We've used up our farm to educate four children through college, <u>remaking</u> fertile land and well-stocked pens into knowledge of

36

law and Latin. We are rich."

The parents had told Schultz that the *physical* capital, <u>which economists think they</u>

37

<u>understand,</u> is in some sense just like the human capital of education. The children now owned it, and so the parents did, too. Once it had been rail fences and hog

pens and <u>it was also their</u> mules. Now it was in the children's brains, this human
        38
capital. The farm couple was rich. <u>The</u> average economist was willing to accept the
        39
discovery of human capital as soon as he understood it, which is in fact how many
scientific and scholarly discoveries <u>get received.</u> It was an argument in a metaphor
        40
(or, if you like, an analogy, a simile, a model). A hog pen, Schultz would say to
another economist, is "just like" Latin 101.

The other economist would have to admit that there was something to it.
<u>Both the hog pen, and the Latin instruction,</u> are paid for by saving. Both are
        41
valuable assets <u>for the earning of income,</u> understanding "income" to mean, as
        42
economists put it, "a stream of satisfaction." Year after year, the hog pen and the
Latin <u>cause</u> satisfaction to stream out <u>as</u> water from a dam. Both last a long time,
        43   44
but finally wear out—when the pen falls down and the Latin-learned brain dies.
And the one piece of "capital" can be made into the other. An educated farmer,
<u>because of his degree in agriculture from Auburn,</u> can get a bank loan to build a
        45
hog pen; and when his children grow up he can sell off the part of the farm with
the hog pen to pay for another term for Junior and Sis up at Auburn, too. 46

32. (A) NO CHANGE
    (B) Your
    (C) One's
    (D) A reader's

Ⓐ Ⓑ Ⓒ Ⓓ

33. (A) NO CHANGE
    (B) but
    (C) therefore
    (D) so

Ⓐ Ⓑ Ⓒ Ⓓ

34. (A) NO CHANGE
    (B) Alabama. Where he interviewed

(C) Alabama, interviewing

(D) Alabama so as to interview

Ⓐ Ⓑ Ⓒ Ⓓ

35. **(A)** NO CHANGE

(B) couple, and was struck

(C) couple; struck

(D) couple. Struck

Ⓐ Ⓑ Ⓒ Ⓓ

36. **(A)** NO CHANGE

(B) so remaking

(C) this remade

(D) and to remake

Ⓐ Ⓑ Ⓒ Ⓓ

37. **(A)** NO CHANGE

(B) understood by economists (or so they think),

(C) that is thought by economists to be understood,

(D) OMIT the underlined portion

Ⓐ Ⓑ Ⓒ Ⓓ

38. **(A)** NO CHANGE

(B) also

(C) as well

(D) OMIT the underlined portion

Ⓐ Ⓑ Ⓒ Ⓓ

39. **(A)** NO CHANGE

(B) (Begin new paragraph) The

(C) (Begin new paragraph) So the

(D) (Do NOT begin new paragraph) Yet the

Ⓐ Ⓑ Ⓒ Ⓓ

40. **(A)** NO CHANGE

(B) are received.

(C) become received.

(D) have their reception

Ⓐ Ⓑ Ⓒ Ⓓ

41. **(A)** NO CHANGE

(B) Both the hog pen and the Latin instruction

High Stakes: Reading

www.petersons.com   241

(C) The hog pen, and the Latin instruction as well,

(D) Both the hog pen, and also the Latin instruction,

Ⓐ Ⓑ Ⓒ Ⓓ

42. (A) NO CHANGE

(B) for income's earning,

(C) for earning income,

(D) with which income may be earned,

Ⓐ Ⓑ Ⓒ Ⓓ

43. (A) NO CHANGE

(B) causes

(C) produce

(D) makes

Ⓐ Ⓑ Ⓒ Ⓓ

44. (A) NO CHANGE

(B) similarly to

(C) as with

(D) like

Ⓐ Ⓑ Ⓒ Ⓓ

45. (A) NO CHANGE

(B) due to having a degree from Auburn in agriculture,

(C) as a result of a degree in agriculture from Auburn

(D) OMIT the underlined portion

Ⓐ Ⓑ Ⓒ Ⓓ

46. The writer wants to link the essay's opening and conclusion. If inserted at the end of the essay, which of the following sentences best achieves this effect?

(A) The wisdom of the farmer is greater, in the end, than the wisdom of the economics professor.

(B) Human capital is a concept based on a metaphor—and metaphor is the essential tool of poetry.

(C) Thus, education is the most valuable form of human capital, even for the farmer.

(D) Physical capital and human capital are ultimately not so different after all.

Ⓐ Ⓑ Ⓒ Ⓓ

Solutions for the Poetry of Economics

32. **The correct answer is (B).** In this context, what's needed is the posses-sive *your* rather than the contraction *you're* (you are).

33. **The correct answer is (B).** The logical conjunction here is *but*, since there is a contrast in meaning between the skepticism referred to in the first half of the sentence and the explanation offered in the second half, which is intended to disarm that skepticism.

34. **The correct answer is (C).** The sentence is a run-on as it is written; the second half of the sentence that begins with "he interviewed" could stand alone as a sentence. Choice (C) corrects this by making the last five words into a modifying phrase that explains what Schultz did in Alabama, tacked neatly on to the rest of the sentence.

35. **The correct answer is (B).** It's incorrect to handle this as two sentences, since what follows the period is lacking a subject for the verb "was struck." As shown in choice (B), the two should be unified, so that the pronoun *he* becomes the subject for both verbs: *interviewed* and *was struck*.

36. **The correct answer is (A).** The original word is grammatically correct and logical in meaning.

37. **The correct answer is (A).** The original wording is more clear and idi-omatic than either choice (B) or choice (C). It would be wrong to de-lete the phrase altogether, choice (D), since it ties into one of the main ideas of the essay: how Schultz used a poetic metaphor to explain a new economic idea through analogy with an old, familiar idea.

38. **The correct answer is (D).** For the sake of parallelism, eliminate these words. The list should simply read, "rail fences and hog pens and mules."

39. **The correct answer is (B).** It makes sense to begin a new paragraph here, since the main idea has changed. The previous paragraph summa-rizes the old farm couple's concept of "human capital"; the new para-graph, which begins at this point, discusses how metaphors can help to explain new theoretical concepts.

40. **The correct answer is (B).** The phrase "get received" is very slangy, too much so for the context of this fairly serious, formal essay on econom-ics. "Are received," which means much the same thing, is more appro-priate.

PRACTICE TOO (OR TWO)

41. **The correct answer is (B).** The commas in the original are needless; among other flaws, they separate the subject of the sentence (it's the compound subject "hog pen" and "Latin instruction") from its verb ("are paid for"). The subject and the verb shouldn't be separated by commas unless it's unavoidable.

42. **The correct answer is (C).** The wording in choice (C) is the most concise and graceful of the four alternatives.

43. **The correct answer is (A).** The plural verb *cause* is necessary, since the compound subject *hog pen* and *Latin* is plural.

44. **The correct answer is (D).** The noun phrase "water from a dam" follows the underlined word. Therefore, the preposition *like* is correct. (The conjunction "as" would be correct only if what followed was a clause, such as "water pours from a dam.")

45. **The correct answer is (A).** All three alternatives mean much the same thing, but the original wording is clearest and most graceful. To omit the underlined words would obscure the point of the sentence, which is that the educated farmer can use his knowledge to produce concrete wealth (a hog pen).

46. **The correct answer is (B).** This sentence serves the stated purpose best because it summarizes the main point of the essay by linking its opening and closing paragraphs, using the concept of "the poetry of economics" as the connecting theme.

That was absolutely refreshing. What? You need to take a deep breath anyway? Well, go ahead and take one; in fact, take two. I'm feeling particularly generous. All right, that's enough.

The title of the next section speaks for itself.

PT/HSPA, FCAT, MEAP HST, MCAS, GEE21, Regents Exams, SOL, N... AHSGE, GHSGT, BS
NCCT, AHSGE, GHSGT, BST, BSAP, WASL, CAHSEE, TAAS, OGT... ...HSPA, FCAT, MEAP
GT, HSPT/HSPA, FCAT, MEAP HST, MCAS, GEE21, Regents Exams... NCCT, AHSGE, GHS
...HSGT, BST, BSAP, WASL, CAHSEE, TAAS, OGT, HSPT/HSPA, FCAT, MEAP HST, MCAS

CHAPTER
9

What the ?

Directions: Each of the following questions consists of an incomplete sentence followed by five words or pairs of words. Choose that word or pair of words that, when substituted for the blank space or spaces, best completes the meaning of the sentence and mark the letter of your choice either in the book or on a separate sheet of scrap paper.

Example of a Sentence Completion Question:

In view of the extenuating circumstances and the defendant's youth, the judge recommended _____.

(A) conviction

(B) a defense

(C) a mistrial

(D) leniency

(E) life imprisonment

(Of course he or she recommended leniency, although life-imprisonment would have run a close second. After all, jay-walking is a pretty serious crime.)

47. Her clear _____ of the situation kept the meeting from breaking up into _____.

(A) grasp ... chaos

(B) vision ... anarchy

(C) knowledge ... uproar

(D) control ... harmony

(E) idea ... laughter

(A) (B) (C) (D) (E)

48. The mayor remained _____ in her commitment to _____ the rise of unemployment among her constituents.

(A) firm ... uphold

(B) wavering ... identify

(C) steadfast ... stem

(D) uncertain ... staunch

(E) alone ... approach

(A) (B) (C) (D) (E)

49. A _____ old stone farmhouse, it had been a landmark since before the Civil War.

(A) corrupt

(B) sturdy

(C) rickety

(D) ramshackle

(E) vital

Ⓐ Ⓑ Ⓒ Ⓓ Ⓔ

50. Because she thought her hateful cousin's behavior was _____, it _____ her to hear the adults praise him.

(A) intangible ... thrilled

(B) putative ... baffled

(C) laconic ... encouraged

(D) insipid ... demeaned

(E) obnoxious ... galled

Ⓐ Ⓑ Ⓒ Ⓓ Ⓔ

51. A public official must be _____ in all his or her actions to avoid even the appearance of impropriety.

(A) redolent

(B) unctuous

(C) baleful

(D) circumspect

(E) propitious

Ⓐ Ⓑ Ⓒ Ⓓ Ⓔ

52. So many people turned out for the meeting that there were not enough seats to _____ them all.

(A) count

(B) ascertain

(C) accommodate

(D) delineate

(E) delegate

Ⓐ Ⓑ Ⓒ Ⓓ Ⓔ

53. The editorial accused the mayor of _____ for making promises he knew he could not _____.

(A) hypocrisy ... fulfill

(B) revulsion ... condone

(C) impunity ... reprise

(D) liability ... improve

(E) petulance ... verify

Ⓐ Ⓑ Ⓒ Ⓓ Ⓔ

54. She was _____ as a child, accepting without question everything she was told.

(A) obstreperous

(B) recalcitrant

(C) credulous

(D) truculent

(E) tearful

Ⓐ Ⓑ Ⓒ Ⓓ Ⓔ

55. Warned by an anonymous phone call that an explosion was _____, the police _____ the building immediately.

(A) expected ... filled

(B) ubiquitous ... purged

(C) eminent ... checked

(D) imminent ... evacuated

(E) insidious ... obviated

Ⓐ Ⓑ Ⓒ Ⓓ Ⓔ

56. Route 71 has always been known to wind its _____ way through steep mountain passes and coarse terrain.

(A) neat

(B) indirect

(C) evasive

(D) tortuous

(E) deceitful

Ⓐ Ⓑ Ⓒ Ⓓ Ⓔ

SOLUTIONS FOR WHAT THE ?

47. **The correct answer is (A).** Keeping a meeting from breaking up requires more than a clear *idea* or *vision*; it requires control, or a *grasp* of the situation.

48. **The correct answer is (C).** The word *commitment* signals the appropriate actions of the mayor; to be *steadfast* in her commitment, she must *stem*, or check, the increase of economic problems for the people who voted her into office.

49. **The correct answer is (B).** For the farmhouse to have been a landmark since before the Civil War, it must have been well built, or *sturdy*.

50. **The correct answer is (E).** If she thought her cousin was hateful, it is most likely that she found his behavior *obnoxious* (offensive) and that she was *galled*, or irritated, to hear him praised.

51. **The correct answer is (D).** *Circumspect*, meaning "watchful or wary," is the only choice that makes sense.

52. **The correct answer is (C).** *Accommodate*, meaning "to provide space for," is the only answer that makes sense.

53. **The correct answer is (A).** To make promises you know you cannot *fulfill* is *hypocrisy*. No other choice correctly fills both blanks. Try them if you haven't yet, and see for yourself.

54. **The correct answer is (C).** One who accepts without question is *credulous* (tending to believe readily).

55. **The correct answer is (D).** If the police know an explosion is *imminent* (about to happen), they are likely to *evacuate* (empty) the building quickly. [Don't confuse *imminent* with choice (C)'s *eminent*, meaning prominent, or lofty.]

56. **The correct answer is (D).** The key word is *wind*. A road that winds is *tortuous*, choice (D). Choices (C) and (E) are wrong because they refer to other meanings of *tortuous*. Choices (A) and (B) make no sense.

Keep your thinking cap on, because brain-exercises are about to resume.

SPT/HSPA, FCAT, MEAP HST, MCAS, GEE21, Regents Exams, SOL, NCCT, AHSGE, GHSGT, BS
L, NCCT, AHSGE, GHSGT, BST, BSAP, WASL, CAHSEE, TAAS, OGT, HSPA, FCAT, MEAP
DGT, HSPT/HSPA, MEAP HST, MCAS, GEE21, Regents Exams, NCCT, AHSGE, GHS
ST, GHSGT, BST, BSAP, WASL, CAHSEE, TAAS, OGT, HSPT/HSPA, FCAT, MEAP HST, MCAS

CHAPTER
9

Analogy versus Digital

A *digital* clock is one where the numbers flip minute by minute; an *analogy* one has a minute and an hour hand, which turn clockwise to show … Wait a second; that's *analogue*! Oh, is my clock-face red! Never mind.

Directions: Each of the following questions consists of a capitalized pair of words followed by five pairs of words lettered (A) to (E). The capitalized words bear some meaningful relationship to each other. Choose the lettered pair of words whose relationship is most similar to that expressed by the capitalized pair and mark its letter either in the book or on a separate sheet of scrap paper.

Example of an Analogy Question:

DAY : SUN ::

(A) sunlight : daylight

(B) ray : sun

(C) night : moon

(D) heat : cold

(E) moon : star

Ⓐ Ⓑ ● Ⓓ Ⓔ

57. CRACK : SMASH ::

(A) merge : break

(B) run : hover

(C) whisper : scream

(D) play : work

(E) tattle : tell

Ⓐ Ⓑ Ⓒ Ⓓ Ⓔ

58. SURGEON : DEXTEROUS ::

(A) clown : fat

(B) actress : beautiful

(C) athlete : tall

(D) acrobat : agile

(E) man : strong

Ⓐ Ⓑ Ⓒ Ⓓ Ⓔ

59. SPECTATOR : SPORT ::

   (A) jury : trial

   (B) witness : crime

   (C) soloist : music

   (D) player : team

   (E) fan : grandstand

Ⓐ Ⓑ Ⓒ Ⓓ Ⓔ

60. WALK : AMBLE ::

   (A) work : tinker

   (B) play : rest

   (C) run : jump

   (D) jog : trot

   (E) go : come

Ⓐ Ⓑ Ⓒ Ⓓ Ⓔ

61. HILT : BLADE ::

   (A) holster : gun

   (B) sheath : knife

   (C) leash : dog

   (D) stem : leaf

   (E) petal : branch

Ⓐ Ⓑ Ⓒ Ⓓ Ⓔ

62. RULER : DISTANCE ::

   (A) king : country

   (B) yardstick : dimension

   (C) barometer : weather

   (D) microscope : size

   (E) thermometer : temperature

Ⓐ Ⓑ Ⓒ Ⓓ Ⓔ

63. HAMMER : TOOL ::

   (A) tire : wheel

   (B) wagon : vehicle

   (C) nail : screw

   (D) stick : drum

   (E) saw : wood

Ⓐ Ⓑ Ⓒ Ⓓ Ⓔ

SPT/HSPA, FCAT, MEAP HST, MCAS, GEE21, Regents Exams, SOL, NCCT, AHSGE, GHSGT, B
, NCCT, AHSGE, GHSGT, BST, BSAP, WASL, CAHSEE, TAAS, OGT, HSPA, FCAT, MEAP
GT, HSPT/HSPA, FCAT, MEAP HST, MCAS, GEE21, Regents Exams, NCCT, AHSGE, GHS
GHSGT, BST, BSAP, WASL, CAHSEE, TAAS, OGT, HSPA, FCAT, MEAP HST, MCAS

CHAPTER
9

READING

64. FLIPPERS : DIVER ::

   (A) baton : runner

   (B) cap : ballplayer

   (C) gloves : skater

   (D) tights : dancer

   (E) spikes : golfer

Ⓐ Ⓑ Ⓒ Ⓓ Ⓔ

65. BRAGGART : DIFFIDENCE ::

   (A) benefactor : generosity

   (B) pariah : esteem

   (C) partisan : partiality

   (D) savant : wisdom

   (E) sycophant : flattery

Ⓐ Ⓑ Ⓒ Ⓓ Ⓔ

66. DIATRIBE : BITTERNESS ::

   (A) dictum : injury

   (B) critique : even-handedness

   (C) polemic : consonance

   (D) encomium : praise

   (E) concordance : disagreement

Ⓐ Ⓑ Ⓒ Ⓓ Ⓔ

67. TRAVESTY : RIDICULE ::

   (A) reproduction : provoke

   (B) forgery : deceive

   (C) imitation : feign

   (D) treachery : reprieve

   (E) poetry : comprehend

Ⓐ Ⓑ Ⓒ Ⓓ Ⓔ

68. AUTHOR : NOVEL ::

   (A) composer : piano

   (B) artist : easel

   (C) sculptor : statue

   (D) painter : color

   (E) mechanic : oil

Ⓐ Ⓑ Ⓒ Ⓓ Ⓔ

69. MAGNANIMOUS : PETTY ::

(A) arrogant : insolent

(B) valiant : belligerent

(C) passionate : blase

(D) munificent : generous

(E) circumspect : prudent

Ⓐ Ⓑ Ⓒ Ⓓ Ⓔ

SOLUTIONS FOR ANALOGY VERSUS DIGITAL

Do you think you got all of those correct? Then you must have some vocabulary, because there are some words in there that I didn't know until I looked them up. Check out these solutions.

57. **The correct answer is (C).** To *smash* something is to do much greater damage than merely *crack* it. To *scream* is to make a much greater noise than to *whisper*.

58. **The correct answer is (D).** A *surgeon* is necessarily *dexterous* (skillful in using his or her hands), and an *acrobat* is necessarily *agile*.

59. **The correct answer is (B).** A *sport* is viewed by a *spectator*, and a *crime* is viewed by a *witness* (if the police are lucky).

60. **The correct answer is (B).** To *amble* is to *walk* unhurriedly without a predetermined destination. To *tinker* is to *work* aimlessly without a pre-determined direction.

61. **The correct answer is (D).** A *hilt* (handle) is the part of a sword to which the *blade* is attached. Similarly, the *stem* is part of a plant to which a *leaf* is attached. If you're not happy about this one, consider each of the other pairs. You'll see why none of them works.

62. **The correct answer is (E).** A *ruler* is used to measure *distance*, and a *thermometer* is used to measure *temperature*.

63. **The correct answer is (B).** A *hammer* is a *tool*, and a *wagon* is a *vehicle*.

64. **The correct answer is (E).** *Flippers* and *spikes* are each footgear for a sport: *flippers* for the *diver* and *spikes* for the *golfer*.

65. **The correct answer is (B).** A *braggart* (offensively boastful person) lacks *diffidence* (modesty), just as a *pariah* (outcast) lacks *esteem* (regard).

66. **The correct answer is (D).** A *diatribe* is a speech full of *bitterness*. An *encomium* is speech full of *praise*.

67. **The correct answer is (B).** A *travesty* is an imitation intended to *ridicule*. A *forgery* is an imitation intended to *deceive*.

68. **The correct answer is (C).** An *author* produces a *novel* while a *sculptor* makes a *statue*.

69. **The correct answer is (C).** One who is *magnanimous* (generous) is not *petty* (mean-spirited), just as one who is *passionate* (ardent) is not *blasé* (bored).

Anytime you hear or read a word you don't recognize, write it down. When you get home, or to the library, look it up. That's why the good lord created the dictionary!

I sure hope you're eager to analyze some reading passages, because I see some coming up.

Now Analyze This, Part 2

Questions 70–81 are based on the following passage.

Alexander Wilson was a poet and a naturalist. Born in Scotland in 1766, he emigrated to Pennsylvania in 1794 and soon became a full-time naturalist. This excerpt on hummingbird nests is from a nine-volume work titled American Ornithology, *published in 1808–1814.*

Line About the twenty-fifth of April the Hummingbird usually arrives in Pennsylvania; and about the tenth of May begins to build its nest. This is generally fixed on upper side of a horizontal branch, not among the twigs, but on the body of the branch itself. Yet I have known instances where it was attached by the side
5 to an old moss-grown trunk; and others where it was fastened on a strong rank stalk, or weed, in the garden; but these cases are rare. In the woods it very often chooses a white oak sapling to build on; and in the orchard, or garden, selects a pear tree for that purpose. The branch is seldom more than ten feet from the ground. The nest is about an inch in diameter, and as much in depth. A very
10 complete one is now lying before me, and the materials of which it is composed are as follows: The outward coat is formed of small pieces of bluish grey lichen that vegetates on old trees and fences, thickly glued on with the saliva of the

bird, giving firmness and consistency to the whole, as well as keeping out mois-
ture. Within this are thick matted layers of the fine wings of certain flying
15 seeds, closely laid together; and lastly, the downy substance from the great mullein, and from the stalks of the common fern, lines the whole.

The base of the nest is continued round the stem of the branch, to which it
closely adheres; and, when viewed from below, appears a mere mossy knot or
accidental protuberance. The eggs are two, pure white, and of equal thickness
20 at both ends. . . . On a person's approaching their nest, the little proprietors
dart around with a humming sound, passing frequently within a few inches of
one's head; and should the young be newly hatched, the female will resume her
place on the nest even while you stand within a yard or two of the spot. The
precise period of incubation I am unable to give; but the young are in the habit,
25 a short time before they leave the nest, of thrusting their bills into the mouths
of their parents, and sucking what they have brought them. I never could perceive that they carried them any animal food; tho, from circumstances that will
presently be mentioned, I think it highly probable they do. As I have found
their nest with eggs so late as the twelfth of July, I do not doubt but that they
30 frequently, and perhaps usually, raise two broods in the same season.

70. In line 2, the word "fixed" most nearly means

   (A) changed

   (B) improved

   (C) found

   (D) understood

   (E) undermined

Ⓐ Ⓑ Ⓒ Ⓓ Ⓔ

71. According to the author, all of the following are places where
one could find a hummingbird EXCEPT

   (A) on the upper side of a branch

   (B) on a moss-grown trunk

   (C) on a white oak sapling

   (D) on a pear tree

   (E) in the meadow

Ⓐ Ⓑ Ⓒ Ⓓ Ⓔ

72. Why does Wilson mention the "old moss-grown trunk" and "strong rank stalk" (lines 5–6)?

    (A) To compare relative sizes of birds

    (B) To establish the birds' eating patterns

    (C) To illustrate non-typical nesting behaviors

    (D) To delineate plant life in Pennsylvania

    (E) To complete a list of related flora

    Ⓐ Ⓑ Ⓒ Ⓓ Ⓔ

73. When Wilson remarks that the birds' nests resemble an "accidental protuberance" (line 19), he implies that

    (A) the nests are messily constructed

    (B) nests may be destroyed accidentally

    (C) the nests are usually invisible

    (D) the nests are designed to blend into their surroundings

    (E) most nests resemble the beak of the bird itself

    Ⓐ Ⓑ Ⓒ Ⓓ Ⓔ

74. The phrase "little proprietors" (line 20) refers to

    (A) children in the orchard

    (B) eggs

    (C) naturalists

    (D) shop owners

    (E) nesting pairs of hummingbirds

    Ⓐ Ⓑ Ⓒ Ⓓ Ⓔ

75. When Wilson remarks that he "never could perceive" hummingbirds feeding their nestlings animal food (lines 26–27), he is suggesting

    (A) that his eyesight is failing

    (B) his limitations as an observer

    (C) that animal food may, in fact, be eaten

    (D) that no animal food is eaten

    (E) that hummingbirds eat only at night

    Ⓐ Ⓑ Ⓒ Ⓓ Ⓔ

76. The fact that Wilson has found nests with eggs "so late as the twelfth of July" indicates that

    (A) birds do not lay eggs before June

    (B) most eggs are found earlier than July 12

(C) the eggs are not likely to hatch

(D) the birds began nesting late in the season

(E) some birds abandon their nests

ⒶⒷⒸⒹⒺ

77. The hummingbirds' nest is composed of all of the following EXCEPT

(A) moss

(B) lichen

(C) the wings of flying seeds

(D) a downy substance from fern stalks

(E) hummingbird saliva

ⒶⒷⒸⒹⒺ

78. How does Wilson reconstruct the makeup of the nest?

(A) By taking apart a nest that hangs in the orchard

(B) By watching a hummingbird build a nest in the stable

(C) By reading a report by John Audubon

(D) By inspecting a nest that lies on his desk

(E) By making a copy of a nest he has observed

ⒶⒷⒸⒹⒺ

79. Which of the following can be inferred about the hummingbirds' habits?

(A) They flourish only in Pennsylvania.

(B) Their broods each consist of a single egg.

(C) They migrate in the spring.

(D) They always raise two broods in a season.

(E) They spend the winter in Pennsylvania.

ⒶⒷⒸⒹⒺ

80. The main purpose of this passage is to describe

(A) the nesting behavior of the hummingbird

(B) the mating behavior of the hummingbird

(C) the relative size of the hummingbird

(D) hummingbirds in Pennsylvania

(E) young hummingbird fledglings

ⒶⒷⒸⒹⒺ

SPT/HSPA, FCAT, MEAP HST, MCAS, GEE21, Regents Exams, SOL, NCCT, AHSGE, GHSG1, B
L, NCCT, AHSGE, GHSGT, BST, BSAP, WASL, CAHSEE, TAAS, OGT, 5T/HSPA, FCAT, MEAP
OGT, HSPT/HSPA, FCAT, MEAP HST, MCAS, GEE21, Regents Exams NCCT, AHSGE, GH

CHAPTER **9**

READING

81. If Wilson were to study crows, he would be likely to

   (A) stuff and mount them

   (B) observe them in the wild

   (C) read all about them

   (D) mate them in a laboratory

   (E) dissect them

Ⓐ Ⓑ Ⓒ Ⓓ Ⓔ

SOLUTIONS TO NOW ANALYZE THIS, PART 2

70. **The correct answer is (C).** In this context, the word *fixed* means situated or found, not its more common meanings—repaired, changed, or altered.

71. **The correct answer is (E).** All of the other choices are explicitly mentioned by the author as the resting places of the hummingbird.

72. **The correct answer is (C).** Wilson states that nests are sometimes attached to such objects, but "these cases are rare" (lines 5–6).

73. **The correct answer is (D).** The nest is not easily seen, but it is not invisible, as choice (C) suggests. Wilson describes seeing it from below (line 18).

74. **The correct answer is (E).** Wilson refers to the proprietors darting around to protect the nest (line 21).

75. **The correct answer is (C).** Wilson believes that hummingbirds feed their young such food, saying, "I think it highly probable they do" (line 28). However, he has not seen it.

76. **The correct answer is (B).** Since Wilson takes this to mean that hummingbirds may raise two broods (lines 26–27), the only possible answer here is choice (B).

77. **The correct answer is (A).** According to the passage (lines 10–11), the nest is composed of bluish-gray lichen glued on with hummingbird saliva, the wings of flying seeds, and downy substances from fern stalks and from the great mullein (another kind of plant).

78. **The correct answer is (D).** Line 10 shows that Wilson is looking at something that "is now lying before me."

79. **The correct answer is (C).** It can inferred from the sentence that the hummingbirds migrate into Pennsylvania (presumably from the south) "about the twenty-fifth of April." None of the other choices is supported by the passage.

80. **The correct answer is (A).** Although other details about the hummingbird are included, the passage focuses on hummingbirds' nesting.

81. **The correct answer is (B).** Most of Wilson's observations in this piece happen in the wild; it is safe to assume that he would study crows the same way.

Superman, Spiderman, and the X-Men are modern-day superheroes. But long before them were older, regional superheroes. Read on and see.

Mythical Heroes of Yore

(If you don't know where *yore* is, look it up. You just may be surprised by its location.)

Questions 82–86 are based on the following passage.

Achilles, the Greek hero, and Cuchulain, the Champion of Ireland, achieved mythical status because of their acts of courage. The following passages compare the two heroes and their heroic feats.

Passage 1—Achilles, Defender of Honor

Line When Achilles heard that his friend Patroclus had been killed in battle, he became so despondent that his friends feared he might end his own life. When word of his complete and agonizing distress reached his mother, Thetis, in the depths of the ocean where she resided, she raced to his side. She found him in a
5 highly distraught state, feeling guilty that he, in some way, might have been responsible for his friend's demise. His only consolation were thoughts of revenge for which he needed the help of Hector. However, his mother reminded him that he was without armor, having lost his recently in battle. His mother, however, promised him that she would procure for him a suit of armor from
10 Vulcan far superior to the one he had lost. Achilles agreed and Thetis immediately repaired to Vulcan's palace. Thetis found Vulcan busy at his forge making magical tripods that moved forward when they were wanted, and retreated when

CHAPTER
9

dismissed. Vulcan immediately honored Thetis's request for a set of armor for her son, and ceasing his own work, hastened to meet her demands. Vulcan
15 created a magnificent suit of armor for Achilles. The shield was adorned with elaborate ornaments. The helmet had a gold crest, and the body of the armor was perfectly suited to his body and of the very finest workmanship. The armor was completed in one night. When Thetis received it, she descended to Earth, and laid it down at Achilles' feet at the first dawn of day.

20 Seeing the armor brought the first signs of life to Achilles that he had felt since the death of his friend Patroclus. The armor was so splendid that Achilles was stunned at the sight of it. Achilles went into battle with his new armor, consumed with rage and thirst for vengeance that made him an unbeatable foe. The bravest warriors fled from him or were killed by his lance.

Questions 87–93 are based on the following passage.

Passage 2—Cuchulain, Champion of Ireland

Line In days of yore, the men of Ulster sought to choose a champion. They enlisted the help of Curoi of Kerry, a wise man, to help them reach their decision. Three brave men, Laegire, Connall Ceamach, and Cuchulain indicated that they wished to be considered. Each was told that he would have to meet the challenge of a
5 terrible stranger. When the stranger arrived, all were in awe of him. "Behold my axe," the stranger said. "My challenge is this. Whoever will take the axe today may cut my head off with it, provided that I may, in like manner, cut off his head tomorrow. If you have no champions who dare face me, I will say that the men of Ulster have lost their courage and should be ashamed."

10 Laegire was the first to accept the challenge. The giant laid his head on a block. With one blow the hero severed it from the body. Thereupon the giant arose, took the head and the axe, and headless, walked slowly from the hall. The following night the giant returned, sound as ever, to claim the fulfillment of Laegires' promise. However, Laegire did not come forward. The stranger scoffed at the
15 men of Ulster because their great champion showed no courage. He could not face the blow he should receive in return for the one he gave.

The men from Ulster were sorely ashamed, but Conall Ceamach, the second aspiring champion, made another pact with the stranger. He, too, gave a blow

which beheaded the giant. But again, when the giant returned whole and sound
20 on the following evening, the champion was not there.

Now it was the turn of Cuchulain, who as the others had done, cut off the
giant's head at one stroke. The next day everyone watched Cuchulain to see
what he would do. They would not have been surprised if he had not appeared.
This champion, however, was there. He was not going to disgrace Ulster. In-
25 stead, he sat with great sadness in his place. "Do not leave this place till all is
over," he said to his king. "Death is coming to me soon, but I must honor my
promise, for I would rather die than break my word."

At the end of the day the giant appeared.

"Where is Cuchulain?' he cried.

30 "Here I am," answered Cuchulain.

"Cuchulain, your speech is morose, and the fear of death is obviously foremost
in your thoughts, but at least you have honored your promise."

Cuchulain went toward the giant, as he stood with his great axe ready, and knelt
to receive the blow.

35 The would-be champion of Ulster laid his head on the block.

When the giant did not immediately use his axe, Cuchulain said, "Slay me now
with haste, for I did not keep you waiting last night."

The stranger raised his axe so high that it crashed upward through the rafters of
the hall, like the crash of trees falling in a storm. When the axe came down with
40 a sound that shook the room, all men looked fearfully at Cuchulain. But to the
surprise of all, the descending axe had not even touched him; it had come down
with the blunt side on the ground, and Cuchulain knelt there unharmed. Smiling at him and leaning on his axe, stood no terrible and hideous stranger, but
Curoi of Kerry, who had taken on the form of the giant to test the champions.
45 He was now there to give his decision.

"Rise up, Cuchulain," said Curoi. "There is none among all the heroes of Ulster
to equal you in courage and loyalty and truth. The Championship is yours."

Thereupon Curoi vanished, the assembled warriors gathered around Cuchulain, and all with one voice acclaimed him the champion.

82. The word "despondent" in Passage 1 (line 2) means

(A) very depressed

(B) in need of food

(C) angry

(D) embarrassed

(E) belligerent

Ⓐ Ⓑ Ⓒ Ⓓ Ⓔ

83. Achilles' feelings of guilt were related to

(A) the loss of his armor

(B) the loss of his last battle

(C) his estrangement from his mother

(D) the death of his friend

(E) his relationship with Vulcan

Ⓐ Ⓑ Ⓒ Ⓓ Ⓔ

84. In line 11, the word "repaired" means

(A) glazed

(B) retired

(C) replenished

(D) returned

(E) untouched

Ⓐ Ⓑ Ⓒ Ⓓ Ⓔ

85. Although not stated directly in the passage, it is obvious that Vulcan

(A) blames Achilles for his friend's death

(B) is a lower-level god

(C) is extremely powerful

(D) loves Thetis

(E) does not wish to help Achilles

Ⓐ Ⓑ Ⓒ Ⓓ Ⓔ

86. Achilles' feeling as he went into battle can best be described as
    (A) guilty
    (B) nervous
    (C) confident
    (D) depressed
    (E) arrogant

    Ⓐ Ⓑ Ⓒ Ⓓ Ⓔ

87. According to Passage 2, when the men of Ulster wished to select a champion they enlisted the help of
    (A) Curoi
    (B) the king
    (C) Laegire
    (D) Connall
    (E) Ceamach

    Ⓐ Ⓑ Ⓒ Ⓓ Ⓔ

88. The challenge that the would-be champion had to meet involved
    (A) fighting a giant with an axe
    (B) beheading a giant
    (C) competing against other men of Ulster
    (D) winning a match with the king
    (E) fighting Curoi of Kerry

    Ⓐ Ⓑ Ⓒ Ⓓ Ⓔ

89. According to the passage, the giant was unusual because
    (A) he was so tall
    (B) he was so huge
    (C) he defeated all his opponents
    (D) he remained alive while headless
    (E) he had three eyes

    Ⓐ Ⓑ Ⓒ Ⓓ Ⓔ

90. The word "sorely" (line 17) means
    (A) feverishly
    (B) utterly
    (C) angrily

(D) bitterly

(E) pitifully

ⒶⒷⒸⒹⒺ

91. Cuchulain appeared as promised to meet the giant because

(A) he was afraid

(B) he knew the giant would not kill him

(C) he knew the giant was Curoi

(D) he did not wish to fail his king

(E) he had given his word

ⒶⒷⒸⒹⒺ

92. In line 31, the word "morose" most nearly means

(A) serious and somber

(B) riotous and humorous

(C) indifferent and detached

(D) informed and knowledgeable

(E) satisfied

ⒶⒷⒸⒹⒺ

93. Cuchulain is sometimes called the "Irish Achilles," probably because of his

(A) honesty

(B) bravery

(C) strength

(D) wisdom

(E) intelligence

ⒶⒷⒸⒹⒺ

And so, on to the heroic solutions.

PRACTICE TOO (OR TWO)

SOLUTIONS FOR MYSTICAL HEROES OF YORE

82. **The correct answer is (A).** The context of the sentence, with its reference to taking his own life, supports this choice.

83. **The correct answer is (D).** Sentence 3 specifically cites the cause of Achilles' feelings of guilt.

84. **The correct answer is (D).** In this context, Thetis is traveling or returning to Vulcan.

85. **The correct answer is (C).** The passage refers to Vulcan's palace and his ability to create magical tripods, indicating that he is quite powerful.

86. **The correct answer is (C).** With his new armor and his feelings of righteousness, Achilles is confident as he goes into battle.

87. **The correct answer is (A).** Sentence 2 in passage 2 states that they enlisted the help of Curoi of Kerry.

88. **The correct answer is (B).** The champion did not have to fight the giant; the champion had to behead the giant, although there was an additional "catch."

89. **The correct answer is (D).** Although choices (A) and (B) might be appealing, the fact that giant remained alive while headless was what made him so unusual.

90. **The correct answer is (B).** The context of the sentence supports the definition in choice (B), as the men of Ulster were completely or utterly ashamed.

91. **The correct answer is (E).** Cuchulain is a man to whom his word is his bond; he had to meet the giant because he had given his word.

92. **The correct answer is (A).** His speech is serious and somber (sad) because he is afraid of imminent death.

93. **The correct answer is (B).** The quality that Achilles and Cuchulain share is courage.

Almost the Home Stretch

Don't worry ... we're *almost* there. These particular sets of exercises comprise what is probably the most difficult type for most students, and so we have chosen this type as the concluding practice passage in the book. Keep your wits about you, and listen carefully to the voice inside your head, and you should have a really positive experience.

Directions: This exercise consists of a passage in which particular words or phrases are underlined and numbered. Following the passage, you will see alternative words and phrases that could be substituted for the underlined part. You must select the alternative that expresses the idea most clearly and correctly or that best fits the style and tone of the entire passage. If the original version is best, select "NO CHANGE." The exercises also include questions about entire paragraphs and the passage as a whole. These questions are identified by a number in a box, like 1, 2, etc.

After you select the correct answer for each question, mark the oval representing the correct answer either in the book or on a separate sheet of scrap paper.

The Girls Choir of Harlem

It is rare to hear of choirs composed <u>of just girls</u>. In fact, for every girls' choir in
94

the United States, there are four boys' and mixed choirs. But the Girls Choir of Harlem <u>in 1977 was founded</u>, to complement the already existing and
95

<u>justly renowned</u> Boys Choir.
96

<u>To this day,</u> the Boys Choir of Harlem overshadows the Girls Choir. They have
97

been around longer <u>(1968 was when they were founded),</u> and have received the
98

attention needed to gain funding and performance opportunities. The boys have appeared in some of the world's <u>most prestigious</u> musical settings. They have sung
99

a sunrise concert for the Pope on the Great Lawn in New York's Central Park; <u>they have traveled to Washington, D.C., and seen the Lincoln Memorial.</u> Such
100

glorious moments have eluded their female counterparts. During the 1980s, when funds dried up, the Girls Choir temporarily disbanded. However, in 1989, <u>the choir were</u> reassembled, and in November of 1997, they made their debut at

     101

Alice Tully Hall at Lincoln Center, performing music by Schumann and Pergolesi before an audience of dignitaries (including <u>the mayors wife</u>) and thousands of

               102

music lovers. [1] The choir members speak confidently of someday becoming lawyers, doctors, and politicians—jobs that once appeared out of reach to them. [2] Both the Girls Choir and the Boys Choir of Harlem act as havens for inner-city children, <u>giving</u> kids from broken families and poverty-stricken homes new

     103

confidence and hope for their future. [3] The boys and girls in the choirs attend the Choir Academy, a 500-student public school with a strong emphasis on singing. [4] <u>It's</u> a fine learning environment that has given the girls ambitions

     104

most of them never before considered. [105]

Now that the Girls Choir of Harlem is beginning to receive some of the recognition that the boys have long enjoyed, perhaps corporations and wealthy individuals will be motivated <u>for giving generously</u> to support the choir and ensure it will

          106

never again have to shut down <u>for lack of money.</u>

       107

94. (A) NO CHANGE

  (B) just of girls'.

  (C) only of girls.

  (D) of girls, alone.

Ⓐ Ⓑ Ⓒ Ⓓ

95. (A) NO CHANGE

  (B) (Place after *But*)

  (C) (Place after *was*)

  (D) OMIT the underlined portion

Ⓐ Ⓑ Ⓒ Ⓓ

96. (A) NO CHANGE

  (B) famous (justly so)

(C) renowned, justly,

(D) just renowned

Ⓐ Ⓑ Ⓒ Ⓓ

97. (A) NO CHANGE

(B) As of today,

(C) On this day,

(D) At the moment,

Ⓐ Ⓑ Ⓒ Ⓓ

98. (A) NO CHANGE

(B) (having been founded in 1968)

(C) (their founding dates to 1968)

(D) (since 1968)

Ⓐ Ⓑ Ⓒ Ⓓ

99. (A) NO CHANGE

(B) more prestigious

(C) very prestigious

(D) prestige-filled

Ⓐ Ⓑ Ⓒ Ⓓ

100. Which of the alternative clauses would most effectively support the assertion made in the previous sentence about the musical appearances of the Boys Choir?

(A) NO CHANGE

(B) they have produced recordings enjoyed by listeners around the world.

(C) they have sung on the same bill as Luciano Pavarotti, the great Italian tenor.

(D) they sing a wide variety of music, both classical and popular.

Ⓐ Ⓑ Ⓒ Ⓓ

101. (A) NO CHANGE

(B) it were

(C) the choir was

(D) the girls

Ⓐ Ⓑ Ⓒ Ⓓ

102. (A) NO CHANGE

(B) the mayor's wife

   (C) the mayors' wife

   (D) a wife of the mayor

Ⓐ Ⓑ Ⓒ Ⓓ

103. (A) NO CHANGE

   (B) they give

   (C) thus giving

   (D) and it gives

Ⓐ Ⓑ Ⓒ Ⓓ

104. (A) NO CHANGE

   (B) Its

   (C) They offer

   (D) That is

Ⓐ Ⓑ Ⓒ Ⓓ

105. Which of the following sequences of sentences will make
the paragraph most logical?

   (A) 1, 4, 3, 2

   (B) 2, 1, 4, 3

   (C) 2, 3, 4, 1

   (D) 3, 4, 1, 2

Ⓐ Ⓑ Ⓒ Ⓓ

106. (A) NO CHANGE

   (B) generously for giving

   (C) to give generously

   (D) for generosity in giving

Ⓐ Ⓑ Ⓒ Ⓓ

107. (A) NO CHANGE

   (B) because they are lacking money.

   (C) as a result of money being lacking.

   (D) without money.

Ⓐ Ⓑ Ⓒ Ⓓ

Item 108 poses a question about the essay as a whole.

108. Suppose the writer had been assigned to write an essay describing the musical achievements of the Girls Choir of Harlem. Would this essay successfully fulfill the assignment? Why or why not?

SOLUTIONS AND EXPLANATIONS FOR THE GIRLS CHOIR OF HARLEM

94. **The correct answer is (C).** It's more graceful, idiomatic, and clear to leave the prepositional phrase "of girls" intact, putting the modifying adverb "only" in front of the phrase rather than in the middle of it.

95. **The correct answer is (B).** In most sentences, a modifying phrase like "In 1977" that tells when the event described in the sentence takes place fits best at the beginning. In this case, it would slip in nicely after the introductory conjunction *But*.

96. **The correct answer is (A).** The idiomatic phrase "justly renowned" is perfectly clear and correct as used in the original sentence.

97. **The correct answer is (A).** The other answer choices change the meaning of the phrase in a way that isn't logical, given the context. The sentence is explaining how and why the Boys Choir overshadows the Girls Choir, given the history of the two organizations. Thus, it makes sense to introduce the sentence with the phrase "To this day," which says that the Boys Choir still overshadows the younger Girls Choir, even twenty years after the Girls Choir was founded.

98. **The correct answer is (D).** All of the answer choices say the same thing; choice (D) does it most concisely.

99. **The correct answer is (A).** Since all of the world's musical settings are being compared (at least implicitly), the superlative adjective "most

prestigious" is needed, rather than the comparative "more prestigious" or some other form.

100. **The correct answer is (C).** The writer is trying to suggest that the Boys Choir has performed on many "prestigious" occasions. The concert for the Pope is an example; so is performing on the same bill as Pavarotti. The other statements, while interesting, don't describe prestigious occasions for musical performances.

101. **The correct answer is (C).** The collective noun *choir* is normally treated, for grammatical purposes, as a singular word; therefore, it should be paired with the singular verb *was reassembled* rather than the plural *were*.

102. **The correct answer is (B).** The correct form of the possessive here would be "the mayor's wife."

103. **The correct answer is (A).** The original wording is grammatically correct and clear. Choice (B) would turn the sentence into a run-on; choice (C) needlessly adds the word "thus"; and choice (D) uses the pronoun "it," whose antecedent and meaning aren't clear in the context.

104. **The correct answer is (A).** The original "It's" is perfectly correct. In this context, "it's" means "it is," so the form of the word that includes an apostrophe is right.

105. **The correct answer is (C).** Sentence 1 draws a conclusion based on the rest of the paragraph, so it logically belongs last. Sentence 2 introduces the paragraph's overall topic, so it makes sense to put that one first. And sentences 3 and 4 clearly belong together, in that order.

106. **The correct answer is (C).** The idiomatic expression is "motivated to do something" rather than "motivated for doing something."

107. **The correct answer is (A).** The phrase "for lack of money" is an idiomatic and familiar one. Choices (B) and (C) are verbose and awkward by comparison; choice (D) is vague and hard to understand.

108. **The correct answer is No.** Read the explanation of the assignment carefully: the writer has been asked to "describe the musical achievements" of the choir. The essay we've read explains a bit about the choir's history and its importance in the lives of its inner-city members, but it really doesn't describe their musical achievements.

SPT/HSPA, FCAT, MEAP HST, MCAS, GEE21, Regents Exams, SOL, NCCT, AHSGE, GHSGT, BS
, NCCT, AHSGE, GHSGT, BST, BSAP, WASL, CAHSEE, TAAS, OGT, ST/HSPA, FCAT, MEAP
OGT, HSPT/HSPA, FCAT, MEAP HST, MCAS, GEE21, Regents Exams, NCCT, AHSGE, GHS

CHAPTER
9

The Home Stretch

Well, the last set of exercises you did were almost the home stretch; now, you are in the home stretch—just a few more passages to go.

Remember when we said that some questions might have only *four* options? Well, in this section, you'll find practice with these types of problems as well as with more open-ended questions.

Does This Compute?

In the 1960s and 1970s, available jobs in the computer industry were relatively scarce. As computers became more affordable and more practical in the 1980s, more computer technicians and programmers were needed. During the 1990s, computers moved into nearly every facet of life. Individuals and businesses became more dependent on computers in the 1990s than ever before.

109. If this trend continues, it is safe to predict which of the following will occur in the next decade?

(A) computers will take over many jobs once performed by humans

(B) there will be an increased need for workers in the computer industry

(C) computers will become more reliable and fewer workers will be needed in the computer industry

(D) nine out of every ten individuals will go to work in the computer industry

Ⓐ Ⓑ Ⓒ Ⓓ

SOLUTIONS FOR DOES THIS COMPUTE?

> 109. **The correct answer is (B).** By making an evaluation of the trend in the passage, you can predict that the number of computer industry jobs will increase as the number of computers increases.

Renaissance Masters

Renaissance Masters at the Hammond Museum
by Nathan Barber

Line The traveling art exhibition "Italian Renaissance Masters" recently made a stop at the Hammond and gave local art enthusiasts an opportunity to witness some of the masterpieces of the Italian Renaissance without having to travel abroad. While many of the works of art took my breath away, the one work that stood
5 out was the "David" by Michelangelo. The polished marble hero stood glistening in the lights of the museum hall as passersby stopped in awe. The colossal athletic figure spoke to all who stared in amazement. The gentle slopes and curves of his body, the incredible detail on his hands and feet and the perfectly proportioned torso told a story of a craftsman who toiled for countless hours in
10 search of perfection. The master had created a work of art that looked like it might step down from the pedestal at any moment. The figure looked like a Roman god. Every detail had been artfully considered. The hero's hair, cloak, and facial features all looked lightly delicate though they were made of solid marble.

15 I enjoyed all of the art and highly recommend the exhibit to everyone. However, I must suggest that you save the "David" for last as all other works of art simply pale in comparison.

PT/HSPA, FCAT, MEAP HST, MCAS, GEE21, Regents Exams, SOL, NCCT, AHSGE, GHSGT, BS
NCCT, AHSGE, GHSGT, BST, BSAP, WASL, CAHSEE, TAAS, OGT, /HSPA, FCAT, MEAP
GT, HSPT/HSPA, FCAT, MEAP HST, MCAS, GEE21, Regents Exams, NCCT, AHSGE, GHS

CHAPTER
9

READING

110. Which of the following lines from the passage exemplifies the use of personification?

   (A) "the works of art took my breath away"

   (B) "The colossal athletic figure spoke to all"

   (C) "other works of art simply pale in comparison"

   (D) "The polished marble hero stood glistening"

Ⓐ Ⓑ Ⓒ Ⓓ

111. The passage is most likely which of the following?

   (A) a work of fiction

   (B) an excerpt from a play

   (C) a magazine review

   (D) an inter-office memo

Ⓐ Ⓑ Ⓒ Ⓓ

112. The figure referred to in the passage is most likely a

   (A) model

   (B) character in a movie

   (C) sculptor

   (D) sculpture

Ⓐ Ⓑ Ⓒ Ⓓ

113. The line "The figure looked like a Roman god" is an example of

   (A) alliteration

   (B) simile

   (C) metaphor

   (D) personification

Ⓐ Ⓑ Ⓒ Ⓓ

114. The overall mood or tone of the passage could best be described as

   (A) apprehensive

   (B) reserved and stoic

   (C) negative and condescending

   (D) positive and laudatory

Ⓐ Ⓑ Ⓒ Ⓓ

115. Describe in one sentence the writer's feelings about what he saw at the exhibition.

SOLUTIONS FOR RENAISSANCE MASTERS

110. **The correct answer is (B).** By saying that the figure, a sculpture, spoke to all, the writer is using a literary technique called personification. In other words, the writer gave human qualities to an inanimate object.

111. **The correct answer is (C).** The passage is a review or critique of an art exhibition and of a specific work of art in the exhibition.

112. **The correct answer is (D).** The figure described by the writer is a very famous sculpture by the Renaissance artist Michelangelo. The sculpture is called "David."

113. **The correct answer is (B).** By saying the figure "looked like" a Roman god, the writer is using a literary tool called a simile. A simile makes a comparison using *like* or *as*.

114. **The correct answer is (D).** The writer uses language that gives much praise throughout the passage.

115. **Sample answer:** The writer expresses his wonder and amazement, especially about the statue, "David."

Democracy Gumbo

The following was written for the Op/Ed page of a high-school newspaper.

DEMOCRACY GUMBO
by E. V. Hammond

Line What do you think was the "stepping stone" of the government that was formed
by the founding fathers? Do you think that the ideas came to them "out of thin
air"? The idea of democracy first came from the people of ancient Athens,
Greece. In fact, the word democracy is from a Greek word that means "rule of
5 the people." This means that in a democratic government, the people share in
running the government. The founding fathers used the Greek ideas to help
them form the Constitution. Our forefathers also used other ideas of democracy, such as civic virtue, representative democracy, and an idea that the Iroquois
Indians used—a confederacy. The two ideas or elements that I think were most
10 important when the founding fathers were trying to form our government were
Roman democracy and the ideas of John Locke.

The ancient Romans had a senate, which was really a group of about 300 men.
In the beginning, they also had officials who were elected. Even though they
were elected, the Romans were really run by a small group of rich people. This
15 democracy was called representative because the people who were elected were
supposed to represent the people. All of the people could vote, but only the
people who owned small farms or sold and traded goods could be elected to
offices in the government. Later, around 287 BCE, all Romans were equal, but
not really. The government wasn't a democracy. It was a republic. I think that
20 the United States is a republic in certain ways. The idea that all people were
equal was important to the founding fathers when they formed the Constitution, but I think that today the idea that all people are created equal is more and
more important. The United States is strong because there are so many different kinds of people. If some people are treated better than others, it's very
25 unfair and that goes against the ideas that the founding fathers had. We have to
remember, though, that the founding fathers' concept of who was "equal" dif-
fered from our ideas today.

John Locke was from England. He wrote about politics and also about how
governments were run. He wrote about natural rights. He said that the gov-
30 ernment should be run for the people. The government shouldn't be for the
rulers. Democracy is about natural rights, or basic rights. I believe that there

are certain rights that we should all have. One of them is justice. Everyone should be treated fairly. Another natural right is liberty. People died so we could be free. John Locke believed that people had "certain inalienable natural
35   rights to life, liberty, and property." The founding fathers believed when they wrote the Constitution that they had to make sure that people's rights were protected. The founding fathers even used similar words.

The Iroquois Confederacy was a good example of what the "new" government should be like. The Confederacy was made up of five, and later, six, tribes in
40   New York. The tribes stood together in battle and that made them strong enough to have a council. The council had 50 sachems and each tribe had one vote. The people in the colonies knew that most of the Indians lived a democratic life, since their tribes had their own governments. They had councils similar to our local, state, and national courts. The colonists could see that this was some-
45   thing they could do.

There were other ideas or elements that we learned this year that are important when you form a government for the people. For example, the Magna Carta said that the people and the ruler had to abide by the same rules. The ruler couldn't just set rules and not follow them. Also, Jean Jacques Rousseau wrote
50   a "social contract." He believed that rulers did not have a divine right to rule (theocracy). The idea of civic virtue was important because it means that you have to put the good of the country before your own interests. Hammurabi's Code was important because the laws were written down so every body could see them.

55   All of these ideas were important to the founding fathers and to me. They had a chance to come up with a government that was not like what they were used to and thought was wrong. They started a new type of government so everyone would be treated fairly and equally.

116. The word "democracy" comes from a Greek word that means

(A) all for one

(B) run the government

(C) rule of the people

(D) right to rule

Ⓐ Ⓑ Ⓒ Ⓓ

117. Which of the following is an OPINION in this passage?

   (A) The people share in running the government..

   (B) John Locke was from England.

   (C) The Iroquois Confederacy was made up of five, and later, six tribes in New York.

   (D) The United States is strong because there are so many different kinds of people.

          Ⓐ Ⓑ Ⓒ Ⓓ

118. According to the passage, the "inalienable rights" mentioned are all EXCEPT

   (A) life

   (B) liberty

   (C) happiness

   (D) property

          Ⓐ Ⓑ Ⓒ Ⓓ

119. The writer probably wrote this editorial to be

   (A) informative

   (B) entertaining

   (C) contradictory

   (D) indifferent

          Ⓐ Ⓑ Ⓒ Ⓓ

120. In the editorial, the expression "out of thin air" means_____

   (A) falling from the sky

   (B) without thought

   (C) unreachable

   (D) out of this world

          Ⓐ Ⓑ Ⓒ Ⓓ

121. The writer's editor believes that he needs one more sentence that ties together his concluding paragraph. Revise the paragraph to reflect the writer's beliefs by adding a sentence or two.

SOLUTIONS FOR DEMOCRACY GUMBO

116. **The correct answer is (C).** In the first paragraph, the author provides the English translation, "rule of the people."

117. **The correct answer is (D).** Answer choices (A), (B), and (C) are rooted in fact. In answer choice, (D), the statement, "The United States is strong" might be interpreted as fact, but the addition of the statement, "..because there are so many different kinds of people" is clearly an opinion of the author.

118. **The correct answer is (C).** The passage does not mention happiness as an inalienable right.

119. **The correct answer is (A).** The author's purpose is to inform the reader.

120. **The correct answer is (B).** The author explains that the founding fathers used the idea of democracy from various sources and not "without thought," as "out of thin air" means.

121. **Sample answer:**

However, we need to make sure that what the founding fathers and the other early citizens did to make this country what it is today are not erased.

Miniature Golf

The following is an advertisement for a miniature golf course.

CRANBURY BOG MINIATURE GOLF

Cranbury Bog offers four spacious 18-hole miniature golf courses over acres and acres of countryside.

It's challenging…and fun! Cranbury Bog is like no other miniature golf course in the world!

After your games, you can relax in the state-of-the art clubhouse or out on the deck.

We guarantee you'll enjoy yourself. Check us out.

Two-for-one on Fridays. Bring the kids. Available for parties.

FEES:	
Adults (18+)	$15.00
Students (12–17)	$10.00
Children (3–11)	$ 5.00
Seniors (55+)	$ 2.50

Children under 3 years are not permitted in the clubhouse.

122. According to the advertisement, why is Cranbury Bog unlike any other miniature golf course?

(A) Cranbury Bog does not allow children.

(B) Cranbury Bog is available for parties.

(C) Cranbury Bog sits on more acreage than any other golf course.

(D) The advertisement does specify the reason.

(A) (B) (C) (D)

123. It can be inferred that "two-for-one-Fridays" means

(A) Two people can play for the price of one only on Fridays.

(B) It only costs $1.00 to play on Fridays.

(C) Friday is the only day that two people can play.

(D) Kids can only play on Fridays.

Ⓐ Ⓑ Ⓒ Ⓓ

124. According to the fee chart, how much does it cost for someone who is 54 years old?

(A) $15.00

(B) $10.00

(C) $2.50

(D) There is no charge.

Ⓐ Ⓑ Ⓒ Ⓓ

Solutions for Miniature Golf

122. The correct answer is (D). The advertisement makes the claim that Cranbury Bog is not like any other miniature golf course, but it doesn't offer the reasons why.

123. The correct answer is (A). Of the answer choices given, there is only one possible correct answer. The advertisement does not mention that there are limits to how many people or how many times a person can play. It also does mention that the fees change on particular days.

124. The correct answer is (A). According to the fee chart, a senior citizen is one who is 55 years old or older. The $15.00 fee applies to an adult who is not yet 55 years old.

A Wormery

The following is a list of ingredients and directions for creating a wormery.

WORMERY

What You'll Need

❏ A quart-sized glass jar

❏ Sand

❏ Dark garden soil

❏ A trowel

❏ Worms

❏ Rotted leaves or compost

❏ A spray bottle of water

❏ **Black** construction paper big enough to wrap around the jar

❏ Tape

❏ Scissors

❏ Paint

How to Make

1. Put a layer of sand about 1 1/2 inches deep in the glass jar

2. Put a layer of soil about the same depth on top of the sand.

3. Keep alternating the layers of sand and soil. Make sure you smooth each layer as you go.

4. Place 4 worms to the top layer of soil.

5. Cover the top layer with a layer of rotted leaves or the compost.

6. Spray the leaves or the compost with water.

7. Cut the black construction paper so it fits around the jar.

8. Place a strip of tape down one edge of the paper.

9. You can decorate the paper with the paint, if you'd like.

10. Wrap the paper around the jar.

11. After a few days remove the paper to see what the worms have done to the layers.

125. How deep is each layer of sand?

126. Why do you need to use a glass jar for the wormery?

127. Why do you need a trowel?

128. Which one of the directions is optional?

129. Why is it necessary to use black construction paper?

130. How can you best demonstrate what the worms have done to the layers of sand and soil after a few days?

Solutions for a Wormery

125. Each layer of sand should be as deep as each layer of soil: 1 1/2 inches deep.

126. You need a glass jar so you can see what the worms have done to the layers of sand and soil.

127. You need a trowel to dig the sand and the soil and place them in the jar.

128. It's not necessary to paint the black construction paper. The directions state, "…only if you want to."

129. The most likely reason to use black construction paper would be to keep light out. The directions don't present a reason.

130. There could be various answers to the question. One way to demonstrate the worms' activity is to draw a picture—another way would be to make a graph.

SPT/HSPA, FCAT, MEAP HST, MCAS, GEE21, Regents Exams, SOL, NCCT, AHSGE, GHSGT, BS
, NCCT, AHSGE, GHSGT, BST, BSAP, WASL, CAHSEE, TAAS, OGT, HSPA, FCAT, MEAP
DGT, HSPT/HSPA, FCAT, MEAP HST, MCAS, GEE21, Regents Exams, NCCT, AHSGE, GHS

CHAPTER
9

The Last Word(s)

We have covered every type of question that is likely to be asked on a high-stakes exit exam. Covered them? No, we've smothered them. If you've done well on this final practice chapter, then congratulations. You're ready to knock 'em dead. If you have done any less than splendid, then maybe it's time to figure out which type of question is giving you trouble, and go back over that type until you feel thoroughly comfortable with it. Don't hesitate to go back over the grammar review in Chapter 6. Good luck on test day.

Notes

Notes

Notes

Notes

Notes

Notes

Notes

Notes

Notes

Notes

Your everything education destination...
the *all-new* Petersons.com

When education is the question, **Petersons.com** is the answer. Log on today and discover what the *all-new* Petersons.com can do for you. Find the ideal college or grad school, take an online practice admission test, or explore financial aid options—all from a name you know and trust, Peterson's.

www.petersons.com

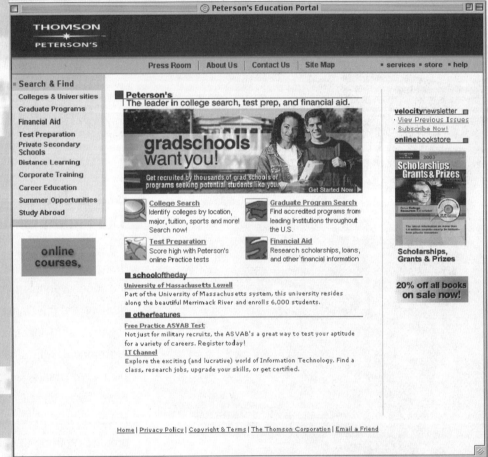

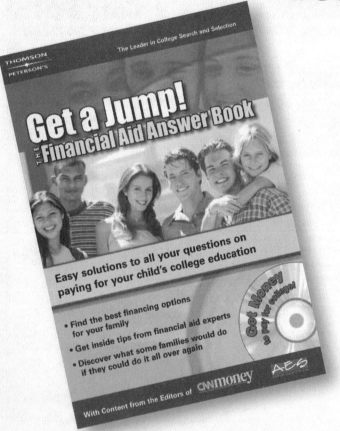